The Governance of
Norman and
Angevin England
1086–1272

The Governance of Norman and Angevin England 1086-1272

W.L. Warren

Professor of Modern History
The Queen's University of Belfast

Stanford University Press
Stanford, California
1987

The Governance of England

1 The Governance of Anglo-Saxon England 500–1087
   H.R. Loyn
2 The Governance of Norman and Angevin England 1086–1272
   W.L. Warren
3 The Governance of Late Medieval England 1272–1461
   A.L. Brown*

*to be published in 1988

Stanford University Press
Stanford, California
©1987 W. L. Warren
Originating publisher: Edward Arnold Ltd
First published in the U.S.A. by Stanford University Press, 1987
Printed in the United States of America
ISBN 0-8047-1307-3
LC 85-61473

Contents

Map 1: The shires in 1086
(adapted from J.R. Lander, *Ancient and Medieval England: Beginnings to 1509*, The Harbrace History of England, ed. J.B. Blum, Harcourt-Brace-Jovanovich, New York).

Map 2: Royal forests in the thirteenth century (from W.L. Warren, *Henry II*, Eyre Methuen).

Kings of England and dukes of Normandy 1066-1272

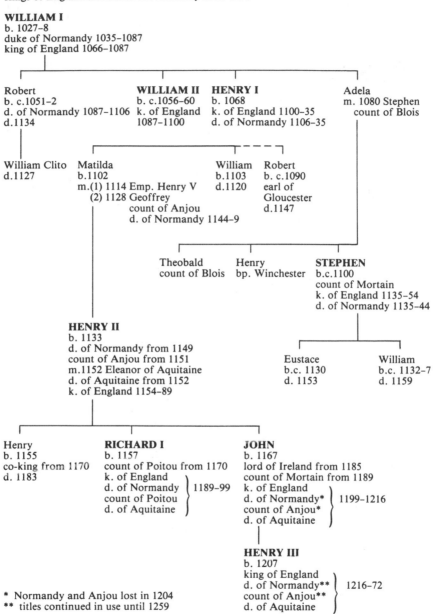

WILLIAM I
b. 1027-8
duke of Normandy 1035-1087
king of England 1066-1087

Robert
b. c.1051-2
d. of Normandy 1087-1106
d.1134

WILLIAM II
b. c.1056-60
k. of England
1087-1100

HENRY I
b. 1068
k. of England 1100-35
d. of Normandy 1106-35

Adela
m. 1080 Stephen
count of Blois

William Clito
d.1127

Matilda
b.1102
m.(1) 1114 Emp. Henry V
(2) 1128 Geoffrey
count of Anjou
d. of Normandy 1144-9

William
b.1103
d.1120

Robert
b. c.1090
earl of
Gloucester
d.1147

Theobald
count of Blois

Henry
bp. Winchester

STEPHEN
b.c.1100
count of Mortain
k. of England 1135-54
d. of Normandy 1135-44

HENRY II
b. 1133
d. of Normandy from 1149
count of Anjou from 1151
m.1152 Eleanor of Aquitaine
d. of Aquitaine from 1152
k. of England 1154-89

Eustace
b.c. 1130
d. 1153

William
b.c. 1132-7
d. 1159

Henry
b. 1155
co-king from 1170
d. 1183

RICHARD I
b. 1157
count of Poitou from 1170
k. of England
d. of Normandy } 1189-99
count of Poitou
d. of Aquitaine

JOHN
b. 1167
lord of Ireland from 1185
count of Mortain from 1189
k. of England
d. of Normandy* } 1199-1216
count of Anjou*
d. of Aquitaine

HENRY III
b. 1207
king of England
d. of Normandy** } 1216-72
count of Anjou**
d. of Aquitaine

* Normandy and Anjou lost in 1204
** titles continued in use until 1259

Abbreviations

Annales Monastici	*Annales Monastici*, ed. H.R. Luard (5 vols, Rolls Series, 1864–9).
BIHR	*Bulletin of the Institute of Historical Research.*
Bracton	Henry de Bracton, *De Legibus et Consuetudinibus Regni Angliae*, ed. G.E. Woodbine, translated with revisions and notes by S.E. Thorne (4 vols, Cambridge, Mass., 1968–77).
Close Rolls	*Close Rolls of the Reign of Henry III* (15 vols, London, 1902–75).
DB	Domesday Book, cited from the Record Commission edition, ed. A. Farley and H. Ellis (4 vols, London, 1783–1816, reprinted Southampton, 1861–4).
Dialogus	*De Necessariis Observantiis Scaccarii Dialogus qui vulgo dicitur Dialogus de Scaccario*, ed. and translated by C. Johnson (London, 1950).
Documents 1258–67	*Documents of the Baronial Movement of Reform and Rebellion, 1258–1267*, selected by R.F. Treharne, ed. I.J. Sanders (Oxford, 1973).
Econ. HR	*Economic History Review.*
EHD	*English Historical Documents*: vol. i, *c.*500–1042, ed. D. Whitelock (London, 1955, 2nd ed., 1979); vol. ii, 1042–1189, ed. D.C. Douglas and G.W. Greenaway (London, 1953); vol. iii, 1189–1327, ed. H. Rothwell (London, 1975).
EHR	*English Historical Review.*
Gesetze	F. Liebermann, *Die Gesetze der Angelsachsen* (3 vols, Halle, 1903–16).
Glanvill	*Tractatus de Legibus et Consuetudinibus Anglie qui Glanvilla Vocatur*, ed. G.D.G. Hall (London, 1965).

Howden	*Chronica Rogeri de Houedene*, ed. W. Stubbs (4 vols, Rolls Series, 1868–71).
Leges Henrici	*Leges Henrici Primi*, ed. L.J. Downer (Oxford, 1972).
Paris	Matthew Paris, *Chronica Majora*, ed. H.R. Luard (7 vols, Rolls Series, 1872–83).
Pipe Roll	The Great Roll of the Pipe; cited by the regnal year of the king as reckoned by the exchequer; for editions see E.B. Graves, *A Bibliography of English History to 1485* (Oxford, 1975), p. 474.
P & M	F. Pollock and F.W. Maitland, *The History of English Law before the time of Edward I* (2 vols, 2nd ed., Cambridge, 1898, reprinted with an introduction by S.F.C. Milsom, Cambridge, 1968).
Regesta	*Regesta Regum Anglo-Normannorum*, vol. i, 1066–1100, ed. H.W.C. Davis (Oxford, 1913), vol. ii, 1100–1135, ed. C. Johnson and H.A. Cronne (Oxford, 1956), vol. iii, 1135–54, ed. H.A. Cronne and R.H.C. Davis (Oxford, 1968).
Rolls Series	*Rerum Britannicarum Medii Aevi Scriptores, or Chronicles and Memorials of Great Britain and Ireland in the Middle Ages*, published under the authority of the Master of the Rolls.
Rot. Lit. Claus.	*Rotuli Litterarum Clausarum*, ed. T.D. Hardy (2 vols, Record Commission, 1833–44).
Rot. Lit. Pat.	*Rotuli Litterarum Patentium, 1201–1216*, ed. T.D. Hardy (Record Commission, 1835).
Rot. de Ob. et Fin.	*Rotuli de Oblatis et Finibus, temp. Regis Johannis*, ed. T.D. Hardy (Record Commission, 1835).
Select Charters	*Select Charters and Other Illustrations of English Constitutional History*, ed. W. Stubbs (9th ed., revised by H.W.C. Davis, Oxford, 1913).
TRHS	*Transactions of the Royal Historical Society*; the 5th series is cited unless otherwise specified.
VCH	*Victoria History of the Counties of England.*

Preface

In writing this book my intention has been to explore the workings of
government rather than to describe the mechanisms of administration. In practice it proved easier to conceive of how it should be
written than actually to write it, and I am grateful for the patient
indulgence of the editor and publisher. To Professor A.L. Brown I am
indebted not only for the helpful advice and pertinent criticism one
might expect of an editor, but also for enjoyably hospitable weekends
in Glasgow, warmed by the finest Scotch whiskey, during which with
the skills of an experienced tutor he prompted me to explain and
justify and confront questions which I would sooner have ducked. It is
fitting that I should also acknowledge the contribution of former
students, now established as solicitors, civil servants, politicians, and
teachers, who bravely undertook an optional course on Angevin
government and obliged me to reflect more deeply upon the sources.
To my colleague, Dr Judith Green, I am grateful for unravelling the
mysteries of the Pipe Roll of 1130, for allowing me to see the type-
script of her recently published book on the government of Henry I,
and for volunteering for the chore of proof-reading. She cannot, however, be held responsible for the interpretations I have put upon the
evidence, nor can those whose publications are cited herein. I should
explain that the Bibliographical Notes are intended to indicate to the
reader who would wish to inquire further the principal publications on
the topics of each section; and they are put at the beginning of chapters
to facilitate abbreviated references in the footnotes. They have grown
rather longer than the editor expected, but should not be regarded as
comprehensive. I would never have finished this book without the
devoted and efficient services of my secretary, Mrs Yvonne Smyth.
She has seen it through numerous versions and revisions, kept me
gently afloat on the sea of paperwork which afflicts every head of a
university department nowadays, and shielded me from the world
when in the throes of composition.

W.L.W.
Belfast
February 1987

Introduction

By 1066 the notion that there was such a thing as 'the kingdom of the English' already had a century of consolidation behind it. It was not, however, an ethnic and cultural unity. The kingdom was a conglomerate of Anglian, Saxon, 'Jutish' and Danish elements, with in the north-west an admixture of Norse, and in some regions a marked Celtic substratum. The territorial bounds of the kingdom where it confronted the Welsh and the Scots were in 1066 still undefined, and even among those who acknowledged allegiance to the 'king of the English', regional identities predominated. There must have been wide variations in the sense of 'belonging' to a united kingdom between the descendants of those who formed part of the West-Saxon nucleus of the kingdom, those who had thrown in their lot with the rising fortunes of the ruling house of Wessex, and those who had bowed to its military superiority. In the far north which had only lately and imperfectly been brought into the united kingdom there was still a tendency in the reign of Edward the Confessor to speak of 'the kingdom of the English and of the Northumbrians', and it is significant that resistance to Norman rule in the decade after the battle of Hastings had a markedly regional rather than national character.

What gave the kingdom cohesion, and established it as something more than a political artifact, was that it had the three fundamental elements which identify a governed society: it had a central authority, an administrative structure and judicial institutions. It would be a mistake to assume that the administrative structure was uniform across the realm, or that judicial institutions operated in the same way everywhere; but the essential point is that there were administrative and judicial mechanisms which answered to the requirements of a central authority. The success of the English kingdom rested upon the appropriateness and acceptability of its governmental apparatus; and its appropriateness is a major reason for the high degree of continuity between Anglo-Saxon government and Norman government. Hence this book, though chiefly concerned with the period after 1066 must take account of the Anglo-Saxon inheritance.

In the two centuries following the Norman Conquest crucial changes occurred in the functioning of the central authority, in the range of its administrative activities, and in its penetration into all parts of the realm. Anglo-Saxon government was highly compartmentalized; government was chiefly local government, and its operations were most clearly defined and most frequently performed at the lower levels of the administrative structure. Essentially, local communities were expected to govern themselves, and they did so as much to protect their own interests as to service the royal interests. Royal representatives could if necessary invoke royal authority to apply the sanction of force; but royal representatives did not administer local communities. There was no hierarchy of royal officials and there were no formally constituted offices of state. The necessity for the intervention of the central authority in the government of the realm was reduced to a minimum. In contrast, by the middle of the thirteenth century royal authority was constantly exercised through an elaborate, bureaucratic, administrative system which reached out regularly into local communities and could deal directly with individuals. The pattern of local government was still basically what it had been in Anglo-Saxon times, but the intervention of royal administration drastically altered the way government in the localities functioned. In short, central authority had become central government, and the way it operated and the way it was controlled had become political issues. How and why this change came about are the principal themes of this book.

Our knowledge of the operations of central administration is patchy before the development of systematic record-keeping in the later twelfth century. Thereafter the record is increasingly voluminous. Our knowledge of the operations of local government remains fragmentary for it was largely without record, and we encounter it only in so far as, for one reason or another, it entered the purview of royal officers. We must be careful not to allow our greater knowledge of central administration to lead us to exaggerate its importance in government as a whole or to presume its effectiveness. Its development was a slow, fitful and sometimes contentious process. For much of the period with which this book is concerned royal government was an occasional not a regular feature in the lives of most people, and the means for the direct exercise of royal authority were restricted in scope. The essence of the matter is that early medieval societies were in practice fashioned and controlled more by social, economic and religious factors than by institutionalized government and the will of rulers, more by immemorial custom than by law defined by authority, more by the influence of those who dispensed local patronage than by the power of the state. That is not to say that before the development of royal government kings were of little more than symbolic account; on the contrary, the king made the state; but custom made society, and the function of the state was to safeguard the customs by which society was regulated and to ensure to each of its members the peaceful enjoyment of legitimate rights. To this end kings were held to be divinely endowed with a monopoly of the legitimate use of force; some ecclesiastical writers called it a 'ministry of terror'. But this awesome power was seen more as the ultimate deterrent to those who would disrupt the social order, from within or without, rather than as the mainspring of government. It was not expected that an eleventh-century king would undertake the management of the realm. His duty was to see that others did it in accordance with requirements of custom and the dictates of the Church.

We should not, however, suppose that before the development of royal government there was less government or no government at all; there was instead a different kind of government – government by the mechanisms of social control. A man who in practice was constrained to fear the wrath of God and abide by the dictates of the Church, who was required to bow to the will of his lord, and who found it necessary to hold the good opinion of his neighbours and heed the counsel of his kinsfolk, was no less obliged to conform than one who is directed by royal officials, watched over by a police force, and disciplined by a magistracy. Central authority had to make use of the traditional social bonds and sanctions in the government of the realm; the degree of its dependence lessens with the development of royal administration; but it could never in medieval times do without them. We must therefore begin by considering the bonds which held together the society over which kings attempted to rule.

Bibliographical Note

The Bonds of Society

J.E.A. Jolliffe's unconventional and misleadingly entitled book *The Constitutional History of Medieval England from the English Settlement to 1485* (first published London, 1937, 4th ed., 1961) is a stimulating study of 'the underlying currents behind government' with penetrating observations on the bonds of society. The work of social anthropologists can illuminate the workings of medieval society; see for example, the introductory chapter to *African Political Systems* by the editors, M. Fortes and E.E. Evans-Pritchard (Oxford, 1940), M. Gluckman, *Politics, Law, and Ritual in Tribal Society* (Oxford, 1965), and 'Civil war and theories of power in Barotse-land: African and medieval analogies', *Yale Law Journal*, 72 (1963), 1515–46; L. Mair, *An Introduction to Social Anthropology* (Oxford, 1965), chapter 7, and G. Lienhardt, *Social Anthropology* (Oxford, 1964), chapter 3, discuss 'politics without the state'; E. Gellner, *Saints of the Atlas* (London, 1969), explains 'oath-helping' as a method of peace-keeping. For the characteristic features of European society in the period of this book the best introduction is still M. Bloch, *La Société Féodale*, translated as *Feudal Society* (London, 1961), even though some of his views have to be modified in the light of research which he stimulated. There is a useful though miscellaneous collection of articles in *Lordship and Community in Medieval Europe*, ed. F.L. Cheyette (New York, 1968).

Kindred

For the role of kindred in early medieval society see Jolliffe, *Constitutional History*, pp. 2, 9–10, 57–9; H.R. Loyn, *Anglo-Saxon England and the Norman Conquest* (London, 1962), pp. 292–7, and 'Kinship in Anglo-Saxon England' in *Anglo-Saxon England* 3, ed. P. Clemoes (Cambridge, 1974), pp. 107–209; B. Phillpotts, *Kindred and Clan in the Middle Ages* (Cambridge, 1913), abridged in *Early Medieval Society*, ed. S.L. Thrupp (New York, 1967), pp. 3–16.

Community

Fundamental is S. Reynolds, *Kingdoms and Communities in Western Europe 900–1300* (Oxford, 1984); see also her 'Law and communities in western Christendom c. 900–1140', *American Journal of Legal History*, 25 (1981), 205–24. For the historical geography of human settlement see R.A. Dodgshon, 'The early Middle Ages 1066–1350' in *An Historical Geography of England and Wales*, ed. R.A. Butlin (London, 1978), pp. 81–118. On the development of urban communities there is an extensive literature best approached via S. Reynolds, *An Introduction to the History of English Medieval Towns* (Oxford, 1977). On rural communities see especially H.M. Cam 'The community of the vill', first published in *Medieval Studies presented to Rose Graham*, ed. V. Ruffer and A.J. Taylor (Oxford, 1950), pp. 1–14, reprinted in H.M. Cam, *Law-Finders and Law-Makers in Medieval England* (London, 1962), pp. 71–84, and in *Lordship and Community in Medieval Europe*, ed. F.L. Cheyette (New York, 1968), pp. 256–67. There is much illuminating information in G.C. Homans, *English Villagers of the Thirteenth Century* (Cambridge, Mass, 1941).

Lordship

This important topic has not yet been thoroughly explored except in its economic aspects; it may be approached through M. Bloch 'The rise of dependent cultivation and seignorial institutions', in *The Cambridge Economic History of Europe*, i (2nd ed. Cambridge, 1966), chapter vi. See

1

The Bonds of Society

Nowadays we tend to think that the kind of society any state has is determined by the type of government it has. In the Middle Ages the type of government it was possible to have was largely determined by the kind of society over which it was trying to rule. Government was more about controlling and managing society than about changing it. It is true that government developed at the will of enterprising rulers; but a successful ruler was like a gardener training an apple tree: he might prune and cut back, select and encourage, but he could work only with what was already there. It is proper to begin not with the structure of government but with the structure of society.

In the Middle Ages every man, unless he were a hermit, a leper, or

---

also: G. Duby, *The Early Growth of the European Economy* (French ed. 1973, English translation London, 1974), especially chapters 6 and 8; J. Critchley, *Feudalism* (London, 1978); Jolliffe, *Constitutional History*, chapter III, part i; F.M. Stenton, *The First Century of English Feudalism* (2nd ed. Oxford, 1961), especially chapters ii-iv; and the long introduction by D.C. Douglas to his edition of *Feudal Documents from the Abbey of Bury St Edmunds* (London, 1932).

Kingship

On the ideology of Christian kingship see especially: K.F. Morrison, *The Two Kingdoms* (Princeton,1964); W. Ullmann, *The Carolingian Renaissance and the Idea of Kingship;* J.M. Wallace-Hadrill 'The *via regia* of the Carolingian age', in *Trends in Medieval Political Thought*, ed. B. Smalley (Oxford, 1965), pp. 22-41, reprinted in J.M. Wallace-Hadrill, *Early Medieval History* (Oxford, 1975), pp. 181-200; F. Kern, *Kingship and Law in the Middle Ages* (English translation, Oxford, 1939); J. Boussard, 'La notion de royauté sous Guillaume le Conquérant', *Annali della fondazione italiana per la storia amministriva*, 4 (1967), 47-77; P.H. Sawyer, *From Roman Britain to Norman England* (London, 1978), p. 184ff. On coronation ceremonies see: P.E. Schramm, *History of the English Coronation* (Oxford, 1937); H.G. Richardson, 'The coronation oath in medieval England; the evolution of the office and the oath', *Traditio* 16 (1960), 111-202; H.G. Richardson and G.O. Sayles, *The Governance of Mediaeval England* (Edinburgh, 1963), chapter VII and Appendix I. For some pregnant observations on pre-Conquest English kingship see J.L. Nelson, 'Inauguration rituals', in *Early Medieval Kingship*, ed. P.H. Sawyer and I.N. Wood (Leeds, 1977), pp. 50-71. On post-Conquest kingship see J.E.A. Jolliffe, *Angevin Kingship* (London, 1955), especially the Introduction and chapters I and II. There is much of interest in H.A. Myers, 'The concept of kingship in the Book of the Emperors ('Kaiserchronik')', *Traditio* 27 (1971), 205-30.

an outlaw, had relationships with other men which shaped the pattern of his life. For most men there were three distinct but overlapping sets of such relationships: with his kinsmen, with his lord and with his neighbours. These sets of relationships provided the bone structure and sinews out of which society and the body politic were fashioned. Early-medieval government did not have the means to deal directly with individuals except at the highest level: it could normally approach the majority of its subjects only as members of a kindred, a lordship, or a community of village or town.

These three kinds of social groupings were of course prevalent throughout western Europe, but in differing proportions and degrees of importance. Often one of the elements predominated, lending a particular character to the structure of society, and hence to the government which could be conveniently erected upon it. In regions where kindreds were dominant – in Ireland, for example, or the lands around the Baltic sea – lordship long retained the form of clan chieftainship, towns were few and exotic, and institutional government developed, if at all, only with faltering steps. There is, indeed, an inverse relationship between the strength of kindred groups and the effectiveness of state governments. In striking contrast there were parts of Europe, notably in northern Italy and Provence, where towns survived from Roman times to become the prime focus of social as well as economic life, drawing the surrounding countryside into their orbits, and acknowledging only fitfully and distantly any external authority. Elsewhere in western Europe in the eleventh century rural and urban communities came to be dominated by the castles of powerful warlords who owed little to clan loyalties and whose ambition was the formation of territorial principalities.

In eleventh-century England the royal laws barely acknowledged that the king's subject were members of kindred groups, and only incidentally recognized that his humbler subjects were dependents of lords. The basic unit of social and administrative organization, assumed to be universal, was the 'neighbourhood' – a settlement of people living close enough together to be in virtual daily contact and identifiable as a community inhabiting a place with a name. In practice it might be a small town, a nucleated village, a more dispersed village with a scattering of homesteads, or a group of hamlets. Such groupings of neighbours were known to Anglo-Saxon rulers as 'tuns' and to their Norman successors as 'vills'. For judicial and fiscal purposes neighbourhoods were grouped into districts known officially as 'hundreds', and the hundreds were administrative subdivisions of larger entities known to the Anglo-Saxons as 'shires' and to the Normans as 'counties'. Shires were virtually self-contained units for all administrative purposes, answerable separately and directly to the king. The organization of the realm for purposes of government was then conceived of as a set of communities, rather than as a set of clans, or a mosaic of landlords' estates. Nevertheless, in the life of the component communities, and often in their functioning as units of government, kindreds and lords had a role to play. The former had a diminishing function, the latter an increasingly important one. To appreciate what was involved let us look more closely at the three sets of relationships.

Kindred

The kindred group in not easy to identify in eleventh-century England and harder to describe. In comparison with the kindreds whose rights are entrenched and particularized in Welsh or Irish law, English kindred groups appear half-formed and never achieving the cohesion, identity and status of clans. One sign is the paucity in the English language of words to describe kin relationships beyond the nuclear family of two or three generations, failing to distinguish clearly between patrilineal and matrilineal relationships, and lapsing into an undifferentiated 'cousinage' and 'kin'. A major part of the reason is that the kings who united England set their faces against kindred organisation. Their re-ordering of the realm into shires gradually effaced the memory of earlier tribal confederacies. They undermined the main props of kindred solidarity, the notion of the family ownership of land and the blood-feud. They assigned lordship over land to individuals and conveyed by charter the right to alienate and bequeath. They made laws to limit feud and eventually outlawed it. In both the laws and in later Anglo-Saxon literature loyalty to a lord was extolled above loyalty to a kin, and loyalty to a king above all. But why kings of England succeeded when other rulers had to compromise with kindred groups is a mystery, and to what extent they succeeded in practice is uncertain. It is more than likely that there were medieval equivalents of Blackmore's Doones of Exmoor, particularly in remoter areas. The important point, however, is that the laws did not accord kindreds protection and privileges.

On the other hand, we should hesitate before relegating kindreds to the sidelines of English history. They did not lose all *raison d'etre* because they were denied a formal place in the organisation of society. They retained important social functions which government has assumed only in recent times in caring for the sick, the infirm, the elderly, the fatherless and widows. Moreover, there survived probably well into the twelfth century disguised functions of the kindred in disciplining erring members. The practice of requiring kinsmen to support with solemn oaths an accused man protesting his innocence did not necessarily secure justice but obliged the kindred to consider how far it was prepared to fly in the face of public opinion, and to restrain persistent troublemakers. Similarly the heavy monetary penalties levied on the guilty by way of fines and compensation were usually beyond the capacity of an individual to pay, forcing him to apply to his kinsmen for help, and prompting them to lay down the conditions on which they would render it. Such methods could be effective, but not reliably so, and the trend in later Anglo-Saxon laws was to seek alternatives to the kindred in the matter of peace-keeping: requiring a lord to be among the oath-helpers, and requiring men to find pledges among their neighbours for their appearance to answer charges, and to discharge financial penalties. While, therefore, kinship remained one of the important bonds of society, it was no longer one which by the time of the Norman Conquest had an explicit function in English governance.

Community

It has been said that 'England was, on the eve of the Norman Conquest, one of the most highly urbanized parts of Europe';[1] but this is a comparative judgement, and while market towns and trade were undoubtedly of major importance economically, not more than 10 per cent of the population lived in towns, and they were of little consequence in the ordering of society and in administrative organization. The way that the realm was managed made no provision for towns apart from the special case of 'boroughs'. Each shire had at least one, and usually only one borough which developed into the 'county town'. The borough was a royal institution and its inhabitants paid dues to the crown. It was the headquarters of the king's agent in the shire, the shire-reeve or 'sheriff', and frequently also the seat of the bishop. The borough was principally an administrative centre, though developing also as a major trading centre for the shire.

There was no generic term in Old English for the urban community – the 'town' in the modern sense of the term. The same word 'tun' was used of all local communities, covering both settlements exclusively of agrarian cultivators, and those which embraced a wider range of occupations. Those which we might recognize as urban communities were treated like all tuns as constituent elements of the hundred, or, if large enough, as hundreds in themselves. There were some large towns which might be dignified as 'cities'; but of these there were not more than half a dozen; and

[1.] P.H. Sawyer, *From Roman Britain to Norman England* (London, 1978), p. 204.

after London, York and Winchester, it is not easy to say which others deserved to be distinguished. The one clear example of a city which can bear comparison with continental cities was London. Significantly it had a distinct place in the Anglo-Saxon polity, it was treated warily by both English and Norman rulers, and it was left largely to govern itself. Commonly it was treated as if it were a separate shire.

Boroughs were important in the organization of the realm, whether or not they were also important as trading centres and the seat of a bishop. The borough came nearest to providing an urban underpinning to English society, but rarely until the thirteenth century anything more than an underpinning. Many of the inhabitants were dependents of lords who had estates in the shire, their tenements sometimes treated as detached portions of lords' manors. Their function was to maintain a town-house and depot where their lord's men could deal with merchants, the king's officers, and the bishop's servants. Lords themselves would temporarily reside in the borough while attending the shire court which met there. Earlier kings had tried to confine trading transactions to the boroughs where they could be properly supervised; and although the development of trade had overwhelmed such restrictions, the boroughs alone had special courts meeting frequently to attend to the special needs of merchants. Until the Norman Conquest the boroughs were the usual muster places for the shires' military forces. Many of them were also places where coin was minted by moneyers licensed by the crown and supervised by royal officers. The distinctive features of boroughs doubtless gave the regular inhabitants a sense of corporate identity; but there were not as yet municipal corporations with powers of self-government, nor would there be until at least the later twelfth century.

The overwhelming majority of the population in eleventh-century England were country dwellers deriving their livelihood more or less directly from agriculture. For the most part those who worked the land were not dispersed over the countryside in scattered farmsteads, but congregated into tightly-knit village settlements. This is a generalization to which many exceptions can be found. The nature of the terrain, the form of husbandry which could be conveniently practised on the prevailing soil type, and sometimes simply social habit dictated other patterns, and there were regions and more localized districts where scattered farmsteads or hamlets were more usual than villages. The nucleated village, however, was typical of arable farming, and arable farming was typical of the greater part of eleventh-century England: the royal commissioners who made the Domesday Survey assessed the productive resources of manors principally in terms of 'ploughlands' and plough-teams. It was in terms of close-knit rural settlements that the three authorities of the time – royal, ecclesiastical and seigneurial – organized themselves. From the point of view of royal government the basic administrative unit was the 'tun-ship' (in post-Conquest terminology, the 'vill'); from the point of view of the Church organizing the basic provision of ecclesiastical services it was the 'parish'; from the point of view of landlords organizing their estates it was what the Normans called a 'manor'.

The importance of the vills as the basic units in which royal government conceived of the realm is illustrated by the fact that some Domesday vills were artificial administrative constructs. Although the vill is commonly to be identified with a single village, there were vills which embraced both a main village and smaller settlements, and some vills without a village core at all, consisting of a group of hamlets and homesteads. The point is that government only operated in terms of vills.

The fact that some vills were undoubtedly artificial casts doubt on whether vills in general can be conceived of as genuine communities capable of undertaking communal responsibilities. It may be argued that in so far as villagers constituted a community it was as dependents of a landlord, and that the effective unit was the manor. It is certainly true that many villages were the creation of landlords. The process of forcing homesteaders to transfer themselves to villages for the landlord's convenience in obtaining labour probably began in tenth-century Wessex, and was still proceeding after the Norman Conquest particularly in the North and in East Anglia. It is equally true, however, that not all villages were landlords' creations, and that as Domesday Book clearly shows the identity of village and manor was far from normal. In the areas of Danish settlement especially, large villages were common, embracing sustantial numbers of freemen, and under a divided lordship which could exact dues and services but not effectively control the life of the community. In contrast there were many villages, particularly in the Midlands and in Wessex, comprising a majority of serfs under strict manorial control. In short, there was much variety in practice and it would be rash to generalize.

Nevertheless there are good reasons for regarding vills as something more than artificial administrative concepts, and even manorialized villages as having a community life independent of their landlord. They were more often than not communities in the sense of being self-conscious neighbourhoods differentiating themselves from neighbouring vills; and in the sense also of being united by common customs and of joining together for the feasts and festivals of the agrarian year. Many also, though perhaps not all, were communities in the formal sense that the villagers might band themselves together to regulate the life of the village, to assume common burdens, and to bear joint responsibilities.

It is in the more formal sense that village communities appear in thirteenth-century records as 'the community of the vill', which could sue and be sued at law, and might even have a corporate seal. Villagers then appear as an organized community both *vis-à-vis* the lord of the manor and in dealings with the king's government. By the middle of the thirteenth century the management of manors and village affairs was passing from oral tradition to written record, and thenceforward there is a surviving mass of court rolls, custumals, and accounts testifying to the ways by which manor and village were regulated. Naturally such records have much to say about the rights of the lord of the manor, the exaction of services and rents due to him and the imposition of penalties upon those who defaulted in due service. They speak of the power of landlords over the lives and livelihood of their bondsmen and their families, in the levying of death duties, and of payments for permission to leave the village even for a limited period, or for permission to marry off a daughter. The grip of the manor on the bondsmen could be so tight, the rights of the lord so pervasive, that it might readily be assumed that the law of the land stated a simple fact when it declared that those in bondage in the manor (the 'villeins' as the law called them) were entirely at the will of their lords.[2]

The records, however, contradict this ruthless principle of the law in several ways. The economical management of a lord's estate depended largely on the performance of unpaid services by the villagers as a condition of their tenancies. Theoretically a lord could enforce the services he required; but it was a rash lord who bore too heavily upon his villeins. Individually they might be at his mercy, but collectively they could make difficulties for a wilful lord. There is plenty of evidence for passive resistance, the go-slow, the strike, and sabotage, any of which could disrupt the economy of the manor. The formula for peace was a tacit agreement to co-operate, the villeins largely taking on the running of the landlord's estate, and the lord allowing them a measure of self-government. The manor court, though nominally the vehicle for the enforcement of the lord's rights, assumed in practice the character of a tribunal for the reconciliation of conflicting interests and the satisfaction of grievances. The lord's rights and the villeins' duties were defined in detail in the 'custom of the manor', which by defining, set limits to what the lord could reasonably exact. The villeins themselves as suitors of the court were the guardians of the custom and applied it on the juries and inquests by which the manor court operated. Furthermore the villeins commonly appointed officers from among themselves who would treat with the lord's bailiff about the daily workings of the estate and see to the performance of due services.

2. Bracton, iii. 131.

It would of course be rash to assume that what can be read in the manorial records of the later thirteenth century applied also to the late eleventh. Estate management had in the meantime become something of a conscious art, professionalized by lords' stewards. It seems likely that the procedures employed in thirteenth-century manor courts, such as juries and inquests, were an imitation of the developing practices of the common law in the royal courts. It is possible that the duties required of vills by the royal government, few in number and occasional in the early twelfth century but numerous and frequent in the thirteenth, fostered a self-conscious corporate spirit among villagers, which lords allowed as an alternative to having to take on the king's business themselves. It could be that vills were attempting to emulate the newly incorporated towns – a feature of the thirteenth century notably absent from an earlier period. In short, it might be argued that the community of the vill was still a fledgling in the thirteenth century, a cuckoo in the nest of the manorial economy, fostered upon reluctant landlords by the demands of developing royal government and the example of the towns.

Such evidence as there is of earlier practice, sparse though it is, however, decisively contradicts such a conclusion. It suggests that close-knit rural communities, if not precisely with the kind of organization to be seen in thirteenth-century records, were of considerable antiquity, that relations between the tillers of the soil and their landlords were rarely one-sided, and that the self-government of thirteenth-century towns was simply a more advanced and articulated form of that prevalent in the villages, and that the royal government in laying burdens upon the vills confidently rested itself on well-established habits of communal action.

In support of this argument may be cited the manorial surveys and custumals which survive from an earlier period, reaching back at least to the early twelfth century, which, though not numerous, all testify to a well-defined custom of the manor.[3] But there is also, and more decisively, some administrative and legal evidence. Working backwards from thirteenth-century evidence we may first observe that a royal writ of 1255 declared that 'by the law and custom of our realm it is well established that villagers and the communities of the vills of our realm may prosecute pleas and plaints in the royal courts and in the courts of others'.[4] Next, we may observe that when after the loss of Normandy in 1204 King John sequestered the estates in England of those who sided with the king of France, he called upon the reeve and four men from the relevant villages to testify to the lands in question,

3. E.g. *EHD* ii. 821–35.
4. *Close Rolls 1254–56*, p. 173.

and entrusted the custody of the estates to the same villagers.[5] The use by the crown of representatives of the vill to testify to the property of a manor without reference to the lord reaches back of course to 1086, for it was the main method by which information was collected and tested for the Domesday Survey. Even more significant, however, is a passage in the *Leges Henrici Primi*, a handbook to legal practice of the early twelfth century, which tells that at meetings of the shire court a lord could answer for all the estates which he held in the county, or his steward could deputize for him, but that if both were absent 'the reeve, the priest, and four of the most substantial men of the vill shall attend on behalf of all'.[6] We should, however, note that in this passage lordship and community are alternatives: we must not overlook either.

Lordship

Lordship is one of the most salient features of medieval society. Manorial lordship – the control exercised by landlords over the peasants who worked their estates – is only one aspect of it. Lordship extended to freemen as well as serfs. For the Normans it was axiomatic that every man should have a lord. They expected that lordship would be hierarchical: that the lords of manors would themselves have lords. Even the greatest barons would have a lord in the king. In all the documents of this period the king is not simply king: he is the 'lord king' (*dominus rex*). The king was distinctive in being the only person in the realm who did not have an earthly lord; but even he had a superior in the Lord God. For members of the ruling class as well as ordinary freemen and serfs to be tied in to networks of lordship is a distinctive and characteristic feature of the Middle Ages. If the communal organizations of vill, hundred and shire were the bone-structure of medieval English society, the ties of lordship were the sinews which articulated it. The few exceptions which did not naturally fall into lordship's embrace, such as merchants and Jews, could barely be encompassed by society at all; special provision had to be made for them by taking them under the protection of the crown.

The pervasiveness of the notion of lordship is reflected in metaphorical usage. 'Lord' is a word which a Christian will use of his God, any subject of his king, a clergyman of his bishop, a monk of his abbot and a wife of her husband. Even in the stricter use by a dependant of a superior, lordship covered a variety of relationships which we might seek to distinguish but which for them were subsumed under a

[5.] *Rotuli Normanniae*, ed. T.D. Hardy (Record Commission, 1835), i.122–43, especially pp. 131, 135.
[6.] *Leges Henrici*, 7.7.

common idea: the relationship, for example, of a warlord and his followers, of a nobleman and his retainers, of a patron and his clients, of the master of a household and his servants, of a landlord and tenants. The common notion behind all these usages is that of *dominion*, for the lord is more than a superior in rank: he is a *dominus* exercising authority over those who acknowledge his lordship. Lordship, in short, was authority personified. It was a more immediate and accessible kind of authority than that of Church and State. The authority residing in lordship was a potent factor in the control of people and in the disciplining of society, all the more compelling when it disposed of the land from which everyone's livelihood was ultimately derived. It might be harnessed to the government of the realm; it could interpose itself between king and subjects as a more directly accessible source of protection and patronage; and it might, if not restrained, presume to demand a prior loyalty.

Kingship and lordship were akin. Kingship was an exalted lordship which had no superior under God; lordship was a kind of petty kingship. Part of the ancestry of medieval lordship lay in the Dark-Age chieftains who had wielded a quasi-regalian authority over their people. Developing kingship siphoned off regalian rights from the chieftains whom it subordinated, but rarely drained it completely from the great lords who replaced them. In some of the dues paid to medieval lords there are relics of ancient tribute; in some of the courtesies paid to medieval lords there is more than a token deference; to some of the jurisdiction exercised by lords there clung a notion of an inherent right to share in the jurisdiction belonging to the crown, which long resisted attempts by kings to qualify it as delegated right. Where kingship was generally strong, as in medieval England, there was a tendency in the long term for kingship and lordship to draw apart – kings acquiring or assuming not merely a superior but a distinctive authority, and lords moving towards their later status of landowners whose prestige and influence lay in abundant wealth, and whose power was largely economic. But the two were never quite sundered in the Middle Ages; kings did not remove themselves into the uniqueness of absolute monarchy, nor lords shed that authority over others which sprang not from office or commission but simply from the fact of lordship.

The readiness with which medieval man accepted subjection to the will of another and regarded it not merely as natural but as an indispensable part of the social order is the broadest of gulfs separating the medieval mind from our own. Modern society has not merely dissolved the bonds of lordship: it has repudiated them as indefensible constraints upon the liberty of the individual. The liberty of the individual, however, is as nothing without a state able and willing to protect it; and in medieval circumstances a powerful patron was frequently the only available substitute for the protection of the state. In submitting to a lord a man traded part of the freedom he himself could ill defend. He gained security, for a lord's primary duty was to maintain his man, to protect him in his tenure, to defend him in his status and livelihood, against the depredations of others, against the hazards of misfortune, and perhaps also against the burdens of taxation and military service.

The security afforded by lordship put stability into medieval society. That was its indispensable function. It did not always put stability into the state – but that is another matter. Creating a stable society was not of course lordship's only social function. It was also a mechanism for gaining, controlling and distributing wealth. This was far from being merely a matter of extracting it from a dependent peasantry and accumulating it in the hands of a ruling class. The mere accumulation of wealth had less attraction in medieval than in modern society, for there were few ways in which to spend it, and even fewer ways in which to invest it profitably. Hence the wealthy were rarely satisfied with wealth itself: their ambitions were more likely to fasten upon prestige and influence. The means to both was gift-giving. Generosity was generally held to be the mark of good lord, and a lord's prestige was reckoned by the size of his following. The principal beneficiaries were the monks who interceded continually with God on society's behalf, and the men who served the lord in peace and war. The largesse of a lord was not in the form of 'free gifts', for gift-giving in primitive societies the world over is part of a social mechanism: the gift lays an obligation upon the recipient, which can only be discharged by a reciprocal gift of equal value. Unless and until it is discharged the recipient remains not simply indebted but also duty-bound. Gift-giving took the place of contracts of service: a lord, for example, will retain his household servants not simply by feeding and rewarding them but also by regular gifts, commonly of robes.

The most prized gift a lord could make was the gift of an estate – that is to say not simply land but land with peasants to work it and produce revenue from it. Such gifts were only for the most deserving and useful of recipients: to those of the lord's trusted retainers whom he wished to keep in his service beyond the point at which they wished to marry and settle down, or to those who could extend the lord's influence and power by being drawn into his entourage. The gift of land with dependent peasantry upon it made the recipient a lord in his own right, though of course a lesser lord than the lord from whom it was received and to whom he remained obliged. Such a gift established a peculiar obligation in the recipient for it was one which could never finally be discharged. There was no reciprocal gift the recipient could make of equal value, except by surrendering the estate back into the giver's hands. While he held it the recipient was under a perpetual obligation, of which his homage and his loyalty and his service were the tokens but not the discharge. He remained the donor's 'man'. Vassalage was the social order of the ruling class and the distinctive characteristic of medieval lordship.

Vassalage was a personal bond consecrated by a solemn oath, and sustained by social attitudes which ranked faith-keeping (fidelity) as a moral imperative. The Latin word *fidelis* was commonly used in the eleventh century to describe a vassal. In the vernacular the common word was *baro* (baron) meaning originally simply a 'sworn man'. Personal bonds, however, could weaken, as one generation succeeded another, or as property passed to collateral branches of a family, or if an alternative lord became a greater power in the neighbourhood and proffered a preferable patronage. A gift of land in the form of a transfer of property could not then cement a personal bond of fidelity into a permanent relationship. There were alternatives to grants of full ownership: a lease for a fixed term, or an arrangement by which the recipient had the benefit of the revenues accruing from an estate without being given the ownership of it. Both these forms of tenure – 'loan-land' and the 'benefice' – were familiar in Anglo-Saxon England, and the latter became the normal way of endowing the parish priest, the 'beneficed' clergyman. But such forms of tenure did not recommend themselves as appropriate to the honourable relationship between lord and vassal, particularly at the higher levels. So in pre-Conquest times vassalage relationship remained very personal, and lordships were constantly dissolving and reforming.

After the Norman Conquest, however, great lordships achieved a remarkable stability and longevity. The reason is that the Normans brought with them a form of tenure developed on the continent and recently adopted in Normandy: an estate granted not in full ownership but as a 'fee' or 'fief' – the *feudum*, from which the word 'feudal' properly derives. Fief-holding as a form of land-tenure solved two problems: it enabled lords to reward their followers by making gifts of land without thereby impoverishing themselves, and created between lords and vassals a bond so strong that it could endure from generation to generation.

There were three distinctive features of fief-holding. First, the lord who granted lands as a fief was not making a gift of the land itself, but was granting the use of the land and of those who dwelt on it. The recipient is said in charters to 'have and to hold' the land 'from' the grantor and his heirs. The recipient does not become the owner of the land, but the tenant of it (from the Latin word *teneo*, meaning to hold). The grant of a fief therefore does not convey property: the tenant is given possession of it but it still belongs to the grantor. The tenant could not give it away, sell it, or partition it, at least not without the permission of the lord from whom he held it. Secondly, although this form of tenure conveyed rights, very substantial rights over the peasants who worked the land, the grantor himself continued to enjoy rights over the fief even when the tenant was in possession. Although the tenant had been given possession of the revenues, the lord could draw upon them in ways which came to be regularized in custom. The feudal tenant was as a condition of holding his fief required to render an honourable form of service to his lord. The most honourable form was military service, and the most typical was knight service. The amount of knight service required came to be specified precisely, and the vassal had to provide it out of the resources of the fief. Furthermore the lord could call upon his vassals to aid him from the resources of the fief for special needs, extraordinary expenses, or emergencies. Some of the aids were regarded as obligations (such as helping to pay the ransom of a captured lord), others as voluntary contributions. What then is involved in fief-holding is a sharing of rights over the land between lord and vassal. The third distinctive feature of fief-holding was that the sharing of rights between lord and vassal could be extended to further sharings. Although the holder of a fief could not dispose of it or give part of it away, he could provide for his own followers and dependants by sub-letting parts of his fief on similar conditions to those by which he held from his lord. He himself would remain answerable for the whole to his lord, but he would now have vassals of his own who were answerable to him for the parts. In this way were created hierarchies of fief-holding. The relationships would be solemnly entered into and publicly advertised by oath-takings; but there was now an effective sanction against oath breaking, for the grant of a fief was conditional upon the vassal's continued fidelity and service. If he broke faith the fief was forfeited and reverted to the lord.

Important consequences followed from the principles of fief-holding. The sharing of rights gave a lord and his vassals a joint and continuing interest in the lands which they shared. If the lord is to continue to receive due service, he will be concerned about the integrity of the fief which he has granted to a vassal. He will not wish to see it fragmented by being partitioned among co-heirs. Hence he will wish to retain control over the succession to fiefs. Fiefs were normally granted to a vassal and his heirs, but it fell to the lord to decide who the heir should be, and the heir could not enter upon the fief until he had sworn to be the lord's man, and agreed the payment of a form of inheritance known as a 'relief'. The acceptance of the oath of homage and of the relief was the mechanism by which lords controlled succession. If the heir were under age and could not undertake the obligations of fief-holding, such as military service, then the fief reverted temporarily to the lord and he had wardship of the heir until he was old enough to take the oath. A lord had of necessity to concern himself with the family life of fief-holding vassals. For example, his interests could be affected by the marriages of his vassals and their children, for marriage could form an alliance with another and possibly hostile vassalage group. It was reasonable then for the lord to expect to be consulted and to insist on a power of veto. In practice he might wish to arrange convenient marriages for his vassals and their children, and his help could be vital for younger sons who had no expectation of succeeding to their father's fief.

A lord and his vassals thus constituted a kind of artificial kindred group, substituting the tie of fidelity for the tie of blood. And just as a kindred would expect to settle matters of common concern in a family conclave, so too did the vassalage group. Part of the customary service expected of a vassal was that he should attend his lord when summoned to render him honest counsel. This might be held to be duty; but in fact the taking and giving of counsel was essential to the stability and hence the strength of a great lordship. If, for example, a lord were contemplating defiance of his own superior he would need to know how far his vassals would support him, for he was powerless without their armed service. On the other hand he needed their advice in the settlement of disputes within the vassalage group, either between his vassals, or between himself and his vassals. It was the duty of a good lord to 'do right' in matters such as claims to inheritance, the proper provision for wives and widows, the administration of fiefs in wardship, the exaction of obligations and the punishment of defaulters and faith-breakers. But more than a duty it was necessary that he do right if he were to retain the fidelity of his vassals and preserve the integrity of his lordship. So what happened in practice was that before making a decision or judgement the lord took counsel with his vassals as to what he should do, and a body of custom developed about what was right and proper in the relations of lords and vassals. Although therefore a lord had power of jurisdiction over all that pertained to his lordship and held a court to which all his sworn men were bound, he did not make the law nor determine the judgement: it was the suitors of the court, the vassals themselves, who decided what the custom was, or what it ought to be, and advised the lord on how it should be applied, and gave a verdict which the lord could then enforce. So the lord's authority did not give him an absolute or autocratic power. Vassals might in practice defer to their lord's wishes, but he could not override their reluctance without endangering the loyalty upon which his power rested. An element of consent, or at least assent, was therefore built into the fief-holding (or 'feudal') relationship.

Fief-holding achieved a particular importance in England after 1066 because it was the only way that William the Conqueror would make grants to his barons. They in turn provided for their dependants and followers by granting part of their lands as fiefs owing a portion of the military service which they themselves were required to render to the king. Estates which Anglo-Saxons had held in full ownership were handed over to Normans to be held as fiefs. Even though the Church retained its extensive pre-Conquest estates, the bishops and the abbots of the greater monasteries were required henceforward to hold their lands on condition of feudal tenure. In consequence the ruling class became totally feudalized. All the hierarchies of fief-holding culminated in the crown. The principles of fief-holding applied to the relations between the king and the leading men. The royal court was the court for the king's vassals, the tenants-in-chief, and therein the king as feudal overlord would be expected to observe the principles of good lordship and the practice of counsel and assent. In a sense lordship was tamed by being universally subjected to the obligations and implications of fief-holding. But at the same time it raised questions about the relationship of the vassalage structure to the communal organization of the realm, and about how kingship itself was to be perceived, whether as a lordship over vassals or as a sovereignty over all subjects.

Kingship

It is not easy to know how people in the late eleventh century conceived of kingship. There was no constitutional theory of monarchy. The voices we hear are those of the clergy, who speak for the most part not of the powers and functions of kingship but of the attributes of the ideal king. He should exercise prudence, courage and self-restraint; he should pursue justice and wisdom, display mercy, fear God. Whether there was a specifically English tradition of kingship is difficult to say because both its ideology and its symbolism were imported. Eleventh-century English writers on kingship drew almost exclusively on the concept of Christian kingship elaborated by late ninth-century Frankish ecclesiastics for the successors of Charlemagne. It consciously set Christian kingship apart from the traditions deriving from barbarian and pagan kingship and found a new basis for an unassailable royal authority. It was divine grace which conferred upon a Christian king the right to rule. It set him above and apart from other laymen. He was the Vicar of God on earth, into whose care and protection the people of his realm were committed, and who owed him a duty of obedience as to the Elect of

God. For the old rulership deriving a charisma and mystical authority from a blood relationship with an immemorial royal race was substituted a rulership consecrated by divine intervention and grace. But while seeking a powerful royal authority as the best protection for the Church against a predatory aristocracy, ecclesiastics also sought a monarchy they could control, and were concerned to avoid the kind of theocratic dictatorship which had prevailed in the later Roman empire, which Charlemagne himself had embodied, and which persisted at Constantinople. They insisted that unction made the ruler a special kind of layman not a priest-king with authority to dictate to the Church, and that divine grace was conferred to do God's will not his own. In the coronation liturgy which gave expression to such views the anointing of a king was made to appear conditional on his solemn oath to protect the Church and its ministers and to respect established laws. Royal authority was thus intended to be unassailable but something short of absolutism. How far such views penetrated the minds of the king's subjects is unknowable. We should be wary of assuming that a coronation ceremony was designed to proclaim a conception of kingship to the general public. Very few people witnessed a coronation ceremony in the early Middle Ages. Very little is known of most coronations because chroniclers had no first hand knowledge of them, and had to draw inferences from liturgical texts. The elaboration of coronation ceremonial into a public spectacle, with leaders of lay as well as ecclesiastical society performing ceremonial services in honour of a new king, did not develop before the thirteenth century. In the earlier period the coronation ceremony (described by contemporaries as the 'ordination' of a king) was a strictly ecclesiastical affair, the ceremonial affirmation of a pact between a king and the bishops for mutual assistance and protection. The one person the ceremony was intended to impress was the new king himself, putting him in awe of the tremendous responsibility he undertook in receiving the power to do God's will.

The overriding practical value of the coronation ritual was that it identified who was rightfully king in an age when there were no fixed rules of hereditary succession. In the whole period covered by this book no ruler succeeded to the throne by undisputed title with the sole exception of Richard I (1189–99). Successors to the throne emerged in a variety of ways. Designation before the end of the previous reign was the preferred method, consistently followed by the Capetian rulers of France; but in England it not infrequently had to yield to conquest or *coup d'état*. Once, however, an acceptable or irresistible successor had emerged, the coronation ceremony advertised and fixed the succession. However irregular or dubious the means of attaining the throne, coronation and unction made the fact of kingship irrefutable:

as the Bible declared, 'Who shall stretch forth his hand against the Lord's anointed and shall remain innocent?'

There were two other manifestations of regality which reached a wider public. One was the practice of formal crown-wearings. The Peterborough Chronicle relates of King William I: 'thrice he wore his crown every year, as often as he was in England; at Easter he wore it at Winchester, at Whitsuntide at Westminster, and at midwinter at Gloucester; and then there were with him all the rich men from all of England.'[7] It is usually assumed that this was a Norman innovation to buttress the Conqueror's kingship, but there is some evidence to suggest that it may have been a well-established English practice, unremarked because it was normal.[8] How regularly crown-wearings were held by the Conqueror's successors is similarly not well attested, but there can be no doubt of the continuity of the practice, until Henry III multiplied its frequency and elaborated its ceremonial. A feature of formal crown-wearings from the earliest times was the chanting of *laudes*, liturgical praises, in honour of the ruler in the image of Christ the king.[9] This was of Byzantine origin; and so too was the manifestation of regality on the royal seal which portrayed the king enthroned and bearing an orb and sceptre or sword in the manner of a Byzantine *basileus*. It is arguable that herein are signs of an alternative tradition of kingship embracing a marked element of ruler-worship which the western Church had tried to expunge from the ceremonies it controlled.

We should not, however, assume that royal propaganda was any more successful than clerical propaganda in imposing a particular conception of kingship. There are indeed grounds for suspecting that the period from 1066 to 1272 was one of unwonted uncertainty and hesitation about the precise nature of kingship and the respect to be paid to it. The Normans were accustomed to a powerless king of France, and to a duke who exercised royal functions within his duchy without benefit of unction. And while the achievement of a crown by their duke was no doubt a matter for congratulation, they may well have wondered what it meant, for the establishment of Norman rule in England coincided with an unprecedented argument in western Europe about the nature of royal authority. It started as a bitter dispute between Henry IV of Germany and Pope Gregory VII as to whether royal power could defy the bishop of Rome, and whether the

---

[7.] *The Anglo-Saxon Chronicle*, ed. D. Whitelock, D.C. Douglas, and S.I. Tucker (London, 1961), sub anno 1087, *Select Charters*, p. 95.
[8.] On crown-wearings and the evidence for earlier practice see Richardson and Sayles, *The Governance of Medieval England*, pp. 405ff., and, for a differing view, H.E.J. Cowdrey, 'The Anglo-Norman Laudes Regiae', *Viator* 12 (1981), p. 50.
[9.] On the *laudes* see Richardson and Sayles, pp. 406–9, Cowdrey, pp. 37–78, and E.H. Kantorowicz, *Laudes Regiae* (Berkeley, California, 1946).

pope could depose a ruler of whom he disapproved; but it provoked a pamphleteering debate which reverberated in France and England as well as in the Empire, disturbing previously unquestioned assumptions and casting doubt on the proper interpretation of precedents and texts on which it had been customary to rely. Views of royal authority were canvassed which ranged from divine right to the argument that a king deserved obedience only while he observed a contract with the people who elected him as king.[10] An anonymous Norman writer about 1100 collected several differing views and their supporting arguments without attempting to resolve the contradictions or reach a conclusion; and it would not be surprising if his noncommittal standpoint were common.[11] Moreover, we should observe that twelfth-century chroniclers showed no particular reverence for kings. William of Malmesbury wrote in the 1130s a comprehensive history of the *Deeds of the Kings of England* without alluding to or even implying an ideology of kingship. He thought royal authority necessary for maintaining good order, and he approved of strong kings as more likely to secure it. He thought a king had no right to intervene in ecclesiastical matters, but deplored excessive piety in a ruler as likely to weaken his resolve. Effectiveness was his basic criterion in judging kings: the exercise of power in a way that was profitable to the realm was of more concern that the source and nature of royal authority.[12] Furthermore, we should note that whatever traditional theory said of the sinfulness of raising a hand against the Lord's anointed, there were rebellions against royal authority in every reign between 1066 and 1272, and in least four of the eight reigns an intention to dethrone the existing king. Whatever else may be said about kingship in this period, awe of its majesty was not a notable feature.

Uncertainty about the survival of traditional notions of kingship after the Norman Conquest has led some historians, notably J.E.A. Jolliffe to argue that post-Conquest kingship was of a radically different type. The royal power which developed remarkably in post-Conquest England he sees as derived from the principles of feudal lordship, not from 'the Saxon crown or as a borrowing from the reviving study of Roman law, still less from anything to be derived from Christian kingship'; rather 'it is from the stem of feudal jurisdiction

10. I.S. Robinson, *Authority and Resistance in the Investiture Contest* (Manchester, 1978).

11. The 'Norman anonymous' is commonly assumed to have been an extreme royalist, but this is probably a mistaken view, cf. Robinson, pp. 144-5 and F. Barlow, *The English Church 1066-1154* (London, 1979), pp. 192-7. For the influence of ecclesiastical reformers on the English coronation see N.F. Cantor, *Church, Kingship, and Lay Investiture* (Princeton, 1958), pp. 137ff.

12. J.G. Haahr, 'The concept of kingship in William of Malmesbury's *Gesta Regum* and *Historia Novella*', *Medieval Studies* 38 (1976), 351-71.

that there grows up the full tree of English royal power.' In England, he argues, the power of the Norman kings and their successors 'was to be based not wholly or mainly on the *jura regalia* of their predecessors, though these were faithfully claimed and recorded. It was derived rather from something radically new, from a concept of jurisdiction inherent in all lordship. . . . Ultimately they were kings because they were already lords. . . . In its maturity feudalism achieved a peculiar sense of the justicial quality inherent in all who possessed *dominium* and the most eminent of all lords was the king.'[13]

This thesis has been cited in order to dispute it; but we must allow that a new element enters into the kingship of England after the Norman Conquest. It is most graphically illustrated on the royal seal. The royal seal was double-sided, and that of King Edward the Confessor bore on both sides a similar representation of the king enthroned and holding the symbols of majesty. The seal of William the Conqueror and his successors bore this image on one side only; on the other the ruler appears on horseback accoutred as a knight and identified with feudal lordship.[14] This dual image expresses the dual character of post-Conquest kings: they were royal sovereigns and feudal suzerains. This dual character is expressed also in a curious practice which persisted from the Conquest until 1272. Earlier rulers, as later, took the title of king from the moment of their accession; but in this period rulers entitled themselves kings only after the coronation ceremony. In the interval between accession and coronation a new ruler was styled 'Lord' (*dominus*), and after coronation as 'Lord King'. The most telling instance of this practice is the way King John styled himself. He held two kingdoms: England and Ireland, but he was never formally crowned as king of Ireland; the titles that he bore were 'King of England and Lord of Ireland.' We might then suppose that lordship was regarded as the prior, inherent quality in a ruler, and kingship a kind of traditional but largely symbolic top-dressing. Such a conclusion would be false.

King John may not technically, in current usage, have become 'king of Ireland' but he always behaved as if his authority there were no less royal than in England. What these examples illustrate is that the duality of kingship was recognized but not that the element of feudal lordship predominated. The practice of not using the royal title until after coronation and anointing suggests that post-Conquest rulers set a special value upon unction. It was a twelfth-century king, Henry II, who incorporated the phrase 'king by the grace of God' in the royal titles. Moreover, post-Conquest kings did not allow the obligations of vassals to their lords to obscure their allegiance as subjects of the

[13]. Jolliffe, *Angevin Kingship*, pp. 10, 31, 23, 24.
[14]. Illustrated in R.A. Brown, *The Norman Conquest* (London, 1984), p. 171.

crown. We are told that in August 1086 King William I summoned all his tenants-in-chief to attend him on Salisbury Plain with their knights, 'and when they came he required their knights to swear fealty to himself against all men'.[15] Thereafter anyone who entered upon a fief, whomsoever his lord, had to swear allegiance to the king in the presence of a royal officer. Records were kept of those who had sworn.[16] Moreover kings insisted that anyone, as a subject of the crown, was available for the royal service irrespective of his homage to a lord.[17]

Jolliffe's thesis involves him in a paradox. While arguing that post-Conquest kingship 'received its validity' from the jurisdiction inherent in feudal suzerainty, he finds it necessary to explain that it achieved 'its peculiar strength' by abusing the principles of feudal lordship: 'by arrogating to themselves a discretionary power which they denied to their vassals', twelfth-century kings attained 'an abuse and use of jurisdiction that was near to sovereignty.'[18] The discretionary power cannot be denied; but the duality of their role is sufficient explanation. They exploited to the full their power as feudal overlords, but did not allow it to replace their unique authority as kings.

Medieval thinkers were deeply conscious of the need for an overriding reliable authority in a society which lived by customary rules and an experience which usually reached no further than the memory of the oldest inhabitants. Hence they invested both pope and king with an indisputable authority which could be accepted as reliable because in both cases it was derived directly from God. The ideology of Christian kingship and the unquestioning acceptance in the western Church of papal primacy both reflect this fundamental need for authority. In the earlier Middle Ages it was not thought necessary to impose restraints upon the exercise of such authority apart from traditional reminders that authority should be exercised only with counsel, and that popes and kings were answerable to God. Formal restraints were not considered because it was expected that the exercise of overriding authority would be infrequent and indirect. It was assumed that ultimate authority would be exercised only when invoked to solve a problem, right a wrong, or correct an abuse. It was a different matter if pope or king translated authority into action, intervening on their own initiative to command, direct and control.

[15.] Florence of Worcester, *Chronicon ex Chronicis*, ed. B. Thorpe (London, 1848–9), ii. 19, *Select Charters*, p. 96.
[16.] *Red Book of the Exchequer*, ed. H. Hall (Rolls Series, 1897), p. 412, translated in *EHD* ii. 907, and the Assize of Northampton (1176), cl. 6, *EHD* ii. 412.
[17.] *Dialogus*, p. 84.
[18.] Jolliffe, *Angevin Kingship*, pp. 33, 34, 35.

When this started to happen in the early twelfth century it was generally resented, and it is from then that we begin to encounter first a defence of the legitimate authority of bishops and secular lords, and later arguments for formal restraints. Popes and kings were expected to make laws – that was the concrete expression of their reliable authority – but they were expected to operate by exhortation and arbitration, requiring local authorities to apply the laws, not intervening to enforce them unless local authorities failed in their duty. Government was expected to be, in the main and normally, local government. In England royal government was still in the early twelfth century narrowly conceived. A lawbook of the time states: 'the king is constituted to this end that he rule the kingdom and the people of our Lord and all the Holy Church and defend them from those who seek to injure them, and to destroy and extirpate wrongdoers.'[19] This was a traditional view which might already seem out of line with the reality of the exercise of royal power, yet it largely encompasses what William of Malmesbury seems to have expected of kings.

In point of fact English kings had already before the Norman Conquest expanded the scope of the acceptable exercise of royal authority by an astute use of the problem-solving function of that authority. The kingdom of England was made by kings. It was put together by military power, and it held together by the acceptance of one ruler. A common allegiance was the basis of peace between former provincial kingdoms, diverse peoples and regional identities. The crown was more than merely a symbol of unity, it was its active principle. Only the transcendent authority of the crown could reconcile divergent traditions and if necessary make new laws for the realm as a whole. A Norman commentator on English law, speaking of the diversity of regions and their customs, drew attention to the special value of 'the tremendous authority of the royal majesty in its continual and beneficial pre-eminence over the laws.'[20] A striking instance of the value of overriding royal authority was its intervention in the economic life of the realm. Political union opened up the country to easier trade, both between the regions and from overseas; but trade needed to be serviced by an authority which transcended local interests. It was the crown which provided protection for travellers and merchants, which offered the royal boroughs as safe havens for traders, which made laws to safeguard legitimate transactions and to warrant the transfer of ownership of goods, which licensed markets and fairs, which limited the restrictive effects of local tolls, and ensured an acceptable medium of exchange by providing a

[19.] Leges Edwardi Confessoris, cl. 17, *Gesetze*, i. 642.
[20.] *Leges Henrici*, 6.2a.

uniform coinage of reliable quality.[21] On the other hand it did not attempt to control, direct and supervise the government of the realm from the centre but contented itself with organizing government in the localities to service local needs with a high degree of local autonomy. It could not have succeeded in holding the realm together without enlisting the co-operation of great lords; but although it allowed lords to be effective instruments for the exercise of royal authority in the localities, it did not allow them to appropriate royal authority to themselves. The confusion and conflation of royal authority with lordly power, so common on the continent, was avoided by organizing the realm not upon lordships but upon communities. The utility of a transcendent, undivided royal authority was crucial to the development of government after 1066, but so too was the communal structure through which it was made effective. It is to the way the realm was organized that we must turn next.

[21.] On the economic aspects of English kingship see Sawyer, *From Roman Britain to Norman England*, pp. 225–31, and his 'Kings and merchants' in *Early Medieval Kingship*, ed. P.H. Sawyer and I.N. Wood (Leeds, 1977), pp. 139ff.

Bibliographical Note

The Anglo-Saxon Legacy

Fundamental to any study of the period is F.M. Stenton, *Anglo-Saxon England* (Oxford, 1943, 3rd ed. 1970). For more recent research and views see P.H. Sawyer, *From Roman Britain to Norman England* (London, 1978). Particularly helpful on society is H.R. Loyn, *Anglo-Saxon England and the Norman Conquest* (London, 1962); and for government see especially his *The Governance of Anglo-Saxon England 500–1087* (London, 1984), 'The king and the structure of society in late Anglo-Saxon England', *History* 42 (1957), 87–100, and 'Anglo-Saxon England: reflections and insights', *History* 64 (1979), 171–81. There is a survey of royal government on the eve of the Norman Conquest in F. Barlow, *Edward the Confessor* (London, 1970). Any attempt to understand the period will profit from F.W. Maitland, *Domesday Book and Beyond* (Cambridge, 1897; Fontana edition, with an introduction by E. Miller, London, 1960, which is here cited), and J. Campbell, 'Observations on English government from the tenth to the twelfth century', *TRHS* 25 (1975), 39–54. F.E. Harmer, *Anglo-Saxon Writs* (Manchester, 1952) is indispensable not only for its documents but also for its long introduction and extensive annotation.

The Normanization Of England

For society and government in Normandy D. Bates, *Normandy Before 1066* (London, 1982) is indispensable. For the social consequences of the Conquest, F.M. Stenton, *The First Century of English Feudalism* (Oxford, 1932, 2nd ed. 1961) is still fundamental, and the introduction by D.C. Douglas to his edition of *Feudal Documents from the Abbey of Bury St Edmunds* (London, 1932) is particularly valuable. On the Conquest and its consequences see D.C. Douglas, *William the Conqueror* (London, 1964), H.R. Loyn, *The Norman Conquest* (London, 1965, 3rd ed. 1982), R.A. Brown, *The Normans and the Norman Conquest* (London, 1969), F. Barlow, *William I and the Norman Conquest* (London, 1965), T. Rowley, *The Norman Heritage* (London, 1983). Recent work is reviewed in M. Chibnall, *Anglo-Norman England, 1066–1166* (Oxford, 1986). On some of the less well appreciated aspects of the Norman settlement G.W.S. Barrow, 'The pattern of lordship and settlement in Cumbria', *Journal of Medieval History* 1 (1975), 117–38, and W.E. Kapelle, *The Norman Conquest of the North* (London, 1979) are illuminating. I have avoided the term 'feudalism' in this book while recognizing the importance of feudal institutions; for contrasting views see R.A. Brown, *Origins of English Feudalism* (London, 1973) and E.A.R. Brown, 'The tyranny of a construct: feudalism and historians of medieval Europe', *American Historical Review* 79 (1974), 1063–88. For the Domesday survey see H.R. Loyn, *The Governance of Anglo-Saxon England 500–1087*, (London, 1984) and R.W. Finn, *The Domesday Inquest and the Making of Domesday Book* (London, 1961). On the vexed question of the purpose of Domesday Book see V.H. Galbraith, *Domesday Book. Its Place in Administrative History* (Oxford, 1974) and S. Harvey, 'Domesday Book and Anglo-Norman governance', *TRHS* 25 (1975), 175–93. See also E.M. Hallam, *Domesday Book through Nine Centuries* (London, 1986). Translations of Domesday entries and detailed discussions of them appear in volumes of the *VCH*.

2
The Governance of England
c.1086

The Anglo-Saxon Legacy

The shires

Domesday Book shows an England organized into shires. The Normans called them 'counties' in line with continental practice, but they made no changes to the English structure. The word 'shire' signifies a portion cut off from a larger entity. We should hesitate to describe them as 'administrative subdivisions' of the realm; this is what they became in time, for the shire organization proved to be a convenient framework into which administrative functions could be fitted; but in the eleventh century each shire operated independently as a kind of miniature version of the realm as a whole. The main purpose in forming shires was to organize in managable units the levying of royal rights – of what was owed to the king in duties, dues and services – not directly to administer and only indirectly to govern the realm. Shires had not been created all at once in accordance with an administrative masterplan, but piecemeal as a united kingdom was put together; and frequently shiring involved simply superimposing a form of organization on what was there already.

Beneath the superstructure of shires England remained a patchwork of regional societies. Superficially it might seem that a united kingdom had been forged by the expansion of Wessex in the aftermath of the Danish invasions, first absorbing those parts of England rescued from Danish rule, and then subjugating the Danish dominions themselves; but to think in terms of 'absorption' and 'subjugation' is to mistake the nature of the unification. The combination of English England and Danish England was more akin to the Anglo-Scottish Union of 1707 than to a process of conquest; and in the eleventh century it made little difference whether the union was ruled over by an Englishman or a Dane.

Neither portion of this political union was homogeneous. On the English side, it is true, much that had once distinguished the old kingdom of Mercia from Wessex had become blurred as Saxons and Angles had merged in resistance to the Danes, but the process of merger had not extended equally to all parts of greater Wessex. The Londoners, the men of Kent and the South Saxons had joined as allies, adjusting themselves to the rule of Wessex but never fully absorbed. London at the time of the Norman Conquest showed many signs of developing as a semi-autonomous city-state. Kent and Sussex were treated as shires, but their internal structures and ways of working owed more to traditions deriving from the days when they were independent kingdoms than to West-Saxon models. On the borderlands of Wales the shires carved out of the former tribal districts of the Magonsaetan and the Wreconsaetan were not quite like the neighbouring shires of midland England, and were doggedly to retain distinctive features of local government throughout the Middle Ages – in the case of Cheshire indeed becoming wholly distinctive. North of Cheshire there lay an indeterminate district, a kind of appendage to old Mercia, not quite English and not quite Danish, which no one knew what to call and which Domesday Book labels 'Between the Ribble and the Mersey' (*Inter Ripam et Mersham*).[1] Cornwall, similarly, was still a kind of appendage to Wessex, more like a colony than an integral part of the kingdom, where English lords had simply superseded Celtic lords with very little change in the infrastructure of Cornish society.

On the Danish side of the union there were marked differences between, on the one hand, the region where Danish settlement was heavy – the district of the 'Five Boroughs' of Derby, Lincoln, Nottingham, Leicester and Stamford – and, on the other hand what might be called the dependent provinces of East Anglia and Northumbria. East Anglia was probably second only to Kent in the degree to which it preserved the lineaments of an ancient kingdom long after the extinction of its native dynasty; Danish overlordship had given it no more than a light colouring of foreign influence. Danish overlordship of the far north also lacked deep roots; and although the collapse of the far-flung kingdom of York in 954 had brought the lands north of the Humber into the union, Northumbria still seemed even a century later to be merely tacked on rather than incorporated into the united kingdom.[2]

The way that the kingdom was put together had a marked and lasting influence upon the way it was organized and upon administrative structures. There was what might reasonably be called a 'standard

---

[1.] *DB* i. 269b, *VCH Lancashire*, i. 269ff., ii. 175–80.
[2.] J.M. Kemble, *Codex Diplomaticus Aevi Saxonici* (London, 1839–48), nos. 770, 811, cf. 787, 993, Barlow, *Edward the Confessor*, p. 136, D. Whitelock, 'The dealings of the kings of England with Northumbria', in *The Anglo-Saxons*, ed. P. Clemoes (London, 1959), pp.70–88.

scheme' for local government derived from West-Saxon practice which, though it was not consistently applied over the kingdom as a whole, nevertheless provided the conceptual framework within which central government approached matters of local government. The 'standard scheme' may most clearly be seen in the Midland shires formed in the tenth century. Shiring involved essentially two elements: an organizing structure and the assessment of liability to public burdens in units of assessment known as *hides*. In origin the shire was a military district with a focal point in a well-defended place (the shire *burgh* or 'borough' from which the shire itself usually derived its name) which served both as a defensive bastion and as the mustering centre for the shire's military forces. For the purpose of levying public duties the shire was subdivided into rural districts known as *hundreds*, each bearing an assessment of approximately 100 hides. The hundred's assessment was distributed over its townships and rural settlements in blocks of five or a multiple of five hides. Into this structure were fitted the mechanisms for public order, justice and policing, and for these functions there were regular assemblies (known to the English as *gemots* and to the Normans as *courts*) meeting in each hundred every three or four weeks, and for the shire as a whole at least twice a year. The burgh stood apart from the hundred organization and had its own court meeting at least three times a year; but other towns formed part of a hundred even if a major and sometimes dominant part of it. The management of the king's estates was organized shire by shire, each estate managed by a *reeve* under the supervision of a 'shire-reeve' or *sheriff* with headquarters in the shire burgh. The sheriff was responsible for all dues which might fall to the king within the shire, so it was also his duty to see that the courts of hundred, burgh and shire functioned properly. For some purposes, such as policing, a hundred might be subdivided into 'tenths' or *tithings*; but the way a hundred functioned was much influenced by local circumstances and customs, and although the sheriff would be concerned with how effectively it operated, central government did not generally try to penetrate below the hundred level. Hundreds might be grouped for special purposes, for example into 'shipsokes' bearing liability for the construction, provisioning and manning of ships for the royal fleet; local circumstances and practical considerations might dictate permanently pairing hundreds or truncating them; but the persistence of such terms as 'double-hundred' and 'half-hundred' itself testifies to the hundred as the basic unit of organization delimited by the assessment system.

Shiring was a characteristic feature of the spread of West-Saxon rule; but for reasons which may in part be political and in part the practical difficulty of forcing existing alternative arrangements into a

Procrustean bed, uniformity yielded to compromises and accommodations. In the northern Danelaw the existing Danish military districts were not inappropriately treated as shires; but Yorkshire and Lincolnshire were and remained large and anomalous 'triple shires', Yorkshire divided into 'thirds' or *ridings*, and Lincolnshire into the *parts* of Kesteven, Holland and Lindsey. These and the neighbouring Danish-dominated shires of Derby, Nottingham and Leicester were subdivided not into hundreds but into *wapentakes*. In later administrative practice hundreds and wapentakes were regarded, or at least treated, as equivalents; but there are many indications that, not only in their origins but also in the way they functioned, Danish wapentakes differed markedly from English hundreds.[3] East Anglia does not appear to have been effectively shired before the Conquest: Norfolk and Suffolk took shape as shires only after a long and rather notional division into the 'North folk' and 'South folk'. In Kent the hundreds were unusually small and numerous, and were partitions (mainly, it seems, for fiscal purposes) of intermediate units of local government, the *lathes* (or 'leets' as Domesday Book calls them) surviving from a time before the ancient kingdom passed under West-Saxon rule.[4]

All these regions were assessed to public burdens and taxes by some other system than the West-Saxon hide. In the shires divided into wapentakes the assessments were reckoned in *carrucates*, or 'ploughlands', arranged by a duodecimal method of counting in groups of six. Carrucating seems however to have been principally for purposes of taxation and military service, for there are traces of a persistent underlying alternative system of assessment for other public burdens which may even antedate the Danish invasions.[5] In Kent the assessment was by *sulungs* or *yokes*, terms which also imply a reckoning by the ploughteam. Characteristically East Anglia also had its own system: the numerous settlements there were not each assigned a rateable value as part of the hundred: instead there were taxation districts known as *leets*, and each component settlement contributed in a fixed proportion to burdens laid upon the leet as a whole. In unshired Northumbria there was no formal assessment system at all: dues were rendered to the king but in the form and incidence of tributes and services anciently rendered to local chieftains.

Even in the rest of England where shires were reckoned by hundreds and hides, the standard scheme did not always mean uniformity in practice. An extreme case is Worcestershire. Superficially it seems a

[3.] O.S. Anderson, *The English Hundred Names*, Part 1 (Lund, 1934), pp. xxiff.
[4.] *VCH Kent*, iii. 179ff.
[5.] F.M. Stenton, *Types of Manorial Structure in the Northern Danelaw* (Oxford, 1910), pp. 87–9, and *Anglo-Saxon England*, pp. 639–40.

shire of particularly regular form. In Domesday Book it bears assessment of 1200 hides, and was partitioned into 12 hundreds. But the sheriff had untrammelled jurisdiction in only five of them: seven were entirely in the lordship of the Church – the triple-hundred of Oswaldslaw belonging to the bishop of Worcester, two hundreds belonging to the distant abbey of Westminster, and one each to the local abbeys of Evesham and Pershore. These ecclesiastical hundreds were not however compact territorial units: they were artificial constructions put together from scattered parcels of church land. For example Evesham's hundred, reckoned at precisely 100 hides, had a detached portion of 15 hides lying in the city of Worcester. The triple-hundred belonging to 'the church of Worcester' (that is to say to the bishop and cathedral chapter) had numerous scattered portions which not only confused the administrative geography of Worcestershire but also absurdly confused the boundaries of the shire itself. The river Avon constituted a natural boundary between the shires of Worcester and Gloucester, but in fact because of the lands belonging to the church of Worcester, 'Worcester-shire' spilled across the river and cast forth outliers – six detached enclaves scattered across northern Gloucestershire, another large one within the bounds of Warwick-shire, and a tiny one nestling on the border between Gloucestershire and Oxfordshire.[6] But although exceptional, Worcestershire was not unique. Artificial hundreds and 'private' hundreds were quite widespread. There were in some shires enclaves of 'special jurisdic-tion' where lordship and local government ran together, where the sheriff had restricted jurisdiction, and where dues normally owed to the king were diverted to the local lord, and which constituted therefore little regalities known as 'sokes' or later as 'liberties'. There were several large ones in the east Midlands and East Anglia: the soke of Peterborough, for example, and the liberties of Ely, Bury St Edmunds and Ramsey. There are signs that several, perhaps the majority of the major enclaves, derived from an ancient *regio* or chieftainry which had survived to nestle within the shire constructed around it; and it seems likely that putting them into trustworthy hands had been a means of ensuring their loyalty at a time when royal autho-rity ran feebly in the region. Some, most notably the Soke of Peter-borough, survived until modern times as 'local authorities' with powers analogous to those of a county.[7]

The shire structures of pre-Conquest England were the product of

---

6. *VCH Worcestershire*, i. 235ff., Maitland, *Domesday Book and Beyond*, pp. 451–8, C.S. Taylor, 'The origins of the Mercian shires', in *Gloucestershire Studies*, ed. H.P. Finberg (Leicester, 1957), map p. 36, D. Hill, *An Atlas of Anglo-Saxon England* (Oxford, 1981), map 178, p. 99.

7. H.M. Cam, 'The king's government as administered by the greater abbots of East Anglia', *Liberties and Communities* (Cambridge, 1944), pp. 183–204. The soke of Peterborough originally comprised the eight hundreds of Oundle but in modern times became reduced to two.

diverse circumstances, and of varying traditions reshaped but not standardized by the intervention of royal authority. They were not sacrosanct: shire boundaries were sometimes redrawn, hundreds thrówn together or truncated, assessments revised. There had once been a shire of Winchcombe, but it was merged with Gloucestershire in the reign of Ethelred II.[8] The assessment of Northamptonshire was changed at least three times before the Conquest.[9] The carrucating of the northern Danelaw overlaid an older system of assessment and may have been intended as the first stage of an uncompleted project for carrucating the whole kingdom.[10] It might have been expected that the Normans would continue the process – overhauling, reshaping and smoothing out the inconsistencies and anomalies which history had written into the English system. But nothing of the kind happened. One of the curious consequences of the Conquest was virtually to freeze the shire pattern and the diverse assessment systems as they existed in the days of Edward the Confessor.[11] Only the hundred boundaries tended to shift, and more often, it seems, by local tampering than by considered decision.[12]

For the simple purposes of shire organization in the eleventh century the diversity of shires was of no consequence. It did not matter, for example, what kind of customary law was applied locally, provided it *was* applied, and that there *was* a structure of courts in which to apply it. There was no point in disturbing alternative systems which worked satisfactorily, as in Kent, or East Anglia or the Danelaw; and it was impracticable to insist on uniformity in border areas where the needs of constant local defence and the traditional social structure made close-knit lordships the only convenient organizing principle; or to expect that standard structures would work in standard ways where the underlying patterns were non-standard, as in Cornwall or between the Ribble and the Mersey. The point is, however, that what was sensible and practicable in the eleventh century came, as a consequence of the Norman Conquest, to fix the structure for succeeding centuries, and developments in government which could barely have been envisaged in the eleventh century had to fit themselves to what the eleventh century left behind. This consolidation at an early stage of a non-standardized structure of shires had several important consequences for the history of English government. It meant that when a more active central government wished to

---

8. Taylor, 'The origin of the Mercian shires', pp. 25–6.
9. C. Hart, *The Hidation of Northamptonshire* (Leicester, 1970), p. 45.
10. Sawyer, *From Roman Britain to Norman England*, p. 196.
11. W.L. Warren, 'The myth of Norman administrative efficiency', *TRHS* 34 (1984), 121–8.
12. An exception may be the hundreds of Shropshire which seem to have been reorganized after the Domesday survey, *VCH Shropshire*, i. 285.

penetrate into the shires it could not readily do so without the active co-operation of those in the shires who were knowledgeable about the complexities and peculiarities of its workings. It meant that measures intended for the realm as a whole were liable to metamorphose when they encountered the custom of the shire. It meant that royal government had to be translated into shire government. This itself promoted self-conscious self-government in the shires, which was in turn to determine the distinctive composition of the English parliament and of the Commons as a conference of shire representatives, and to lead eventually to the 'county commonwealths', as Namier called them, of the eighteenth century; but although there was a long period of evolution involved in these developments, the distinctive character of many of the English shires which fostered a sense of identity and a loyalty to shire custom was there from the beginning.[13]

The internal organization of the shire, whether by hundreds or wapentakes, was essentially a mechanism for exacting the king's rights; and it is significant that the Latin term frequently applied to the king's officers in the shire is *exactores*. On to this basic function were grafted two others for the preservation of the peace and what was termed 'the redress of wrongs.' These three functions of course overlapped and usually found a common focus in the hundred court. Nevertheless they do not merge: they are, for example, identified as three distinct functions in a royal writ of 1234 which elucidated the implications of Magna Carta for the holding of the courts of hundred and wapentake.[14] Moreover it has to be recognized that in practice the three functions did not always run together in the court of the hundred, and even when they had once been brought together could subsequently be separated out. Peace-keeping in the borderlands of Wales and in much of the north was, as it can be seen in the twelfth century, a prerogative of lordship (and anciently no doubt of local chieftains).[15] In some shires the imposition of a hundred structure did not absorb traditional arrangements but shared its functions with them: the numerous small hundreds of Kent, for example, operated as sub-units, mainly for fiscal purposes, of the half dozen *lathes* into which the old kingdom had traditionally been divided. Hundreds frequently, and increasingly so, shared some of their peace-keeping and judicial functions with those estate-holders who had the 'liberty' or 'franchise' of exercising some aspects of government over men who lay within their 'soke' or jurisdiction. It is appropriate then to look at

13. Cf. A. Everitt, 'Country, county and town: patterns of regional evolution', *TRHS* 29 (1979), 79–108.
14. *Close Rolls 1231–34*, pp. 588–9, *EDH* iii. 350–1.
15. R. Stewart-Brown, *The Serjeants of the Peace in Medieval England and Wales* (Manchester, 1936), W. Rees, 'Survivals of Celtic custom is medieval England', in *Angles and Britons*, ed. H. Lewis (Cardiff, 1963), pp. 148–68.

each of these aspects of local government rather than to the structures through which they were administered.

The king's rights

There is a sense in which the king of the English was the heir separately of each of the several provincial and numerous petty rulerships into which England had once been divided, and entitled to the rights enjoyed by each and every one of his predecessors. This did not in practice, however, lead to a vast and unmanageable accumulation of varied rights in royal hands, partly because there were common features in the ancient rights of rulership, and partly because the dues and services owed to local rulers of old were in the united kingdom partitioned between the king and those who shared with him in the exercise of authority – principally his earls, bishops and sheriffs, but also his *thegns*, those of his subjects who owed him a special allegiance and received his patronage. The agglomeration of old rulerships did, however, leave behind a kind of dialect of local custom and some regional variations which could be wholly distinctive, as, for instance, the 'noutegeld', a levy on cattle, in Northumbria. To the multifariousness of English custom Domesday Book bears frequent testimony. Nevertheless, if we look to the stems instead of the branches it is possible to categorize in general terms the rights which accrued to the crown.

First were what we may call *domainal rights* – the rents and services owed to the king by tenants on the royal estates, extensively but unevenly scattered over the shires, and the customary dues of boroughs and royal towns. Within a generation of the Conquest, if not before, it became the normal practice for the sheriff to render to the king's exchequer a fixed composite sum, known as the *ferm* or 'farm of the shire' in respect of all domainal rights in his charge.

Secondly there were dues and services which had their origin in *the obligation of subjects to provide for the upkeep of the king's Household and servants*. Some of these were frequent and regular such as food renders and the provision of labour and materials for the maintenance of the king's dwellings; some were occasional such as hospitality for the king's agents, fodder for their horses, carrying and carting services, or turning-out to help when the king went hunting. Though such services were the most basic of royal rights and integral to the organization of the old petty kingdoms, they are by the time of the Conquest the hardest of all to identify, though still having a very real existence to those who had to render them. They are hard to identify because they had usually become submerged in more general renders or had ceased to be royal. Some were commuted for money payments and are disguised under general terms such as 'hundred pennies', or miscellaneous 'scots' and 'dues', or simply as 'customs' (that is to say, customary payments). If they reached the crown it was not as identifiable payments but as part of the *ferm* of the shire. Many of the petty dues and services passed with the land and its inhabitants when the king granted an estate and would henceforth be levied by the landlord as part of his manorial rights. Some became attached to the offices of the king's servants in the shire, who could then, for example, levy hospitality, fodder and carrying services on their own authority. Some became absorbed into more general perquisites of office, such as 'sheriff's aid'. Though they pass from view as explicit royal rights, they nevertheless remained in their mediatized form a regular part of local administration, surfacing from time to time in the records of inquiries into local government, such as the thirteenth-century *Hundred Rolls* and *Quo Warranto* proceedings.[16]

Thirdly, there were *the obligations of all subjects for the maintenance of the realm* – what we might call 'public sevices'. They were threefold: military service, borough service – the erection, upkeep and manning of borough fortifications – and bridge service, the construction and repair of bridges. Whatever other rights to services kings might grant away, they were careful to reserve these public duties. Liability was by the time of the Conquest reckoned by the assessments in hides or carrucates. Domesday Book, for example, records as a custom of Berkshire: 'If the king was sending forth an army anywhere, one armed man went from each five hides, and for his provision or pay four shillings for two months was given him from each hide'.[17] The formation after the Conquest of feudal tenures owing specified military service tended to obscure the more general obligation resting on all the king's free subjects, but it surfaced from time to time as a shire militia called out in time of crisis, and was reorganized in 1181 by Henry II's Assize of Arms. The general obligation to maintain and man the walls of boroughs tended to fade after the Conquest for privately held castles were substituted for communal fortifications as the principal defensive system. The upkeep of town walls tended then to fall on the burgesses themselves, though in Lincolnshire in the thirteenth century *murage* – a payment for 'wall work' – was still levied on the wapentakes.[18] Bridgework did not cease

16. N. Neilson, *Customary Rents* (Oxford, 1910), especially chapter VI and the table on pp. 201–2 of 'rents from geldable land', E.B. Demarest, 'The hundred pennies', *EHR* 33 (1918), 62–72, and ' "Consuetudo regis" in Essex, Norfolk and Suffolk', *EHR* 42 (1927), 161–79, R.H.C. Davis, *The Kalendar of Abbot Sampson* (London, 1954), pp. xxxff. That sheriffs kept rolls of regalian rights is indicated in *Liber Memorandum Ecclesie de Bernewell*, ed. J.W. Clark (Cambridge, 1907), p. 238.
17. *DB* i. 56, *EHD* ii. 866.
18. Neilson, *Customary Rents*, p. 141.

to be a prime obligation resting upon the taxable population of the shire though the hidage assessment. Usually it was commuted to a money payment known as *pontage*, levied by the sheriff as often as necessary, though sometimes the obligation devolved upon specified estate-holders. In Hertfordshire in the thirteenth century lists were kept of those who owed pontage services, either in being wholly responsible for small bridges or for a specified footage of larger ones, with three persons who had the duty of inspecting all bridges in the shire and of riding over them before the king came to cross, to ensure that they were safe. At Rochester the obligation was distributed pier by pier: the bishop being responsible for the first and third, and a consortium of small freeholders for the sixth.[19]

Fourthly, there were *the king's rights to judicial penalties and forfeitures*. At meetings of the shire court the first item of business was 'the due rights of the Christian faith', that is to say the enforcement of the Church's law; and the second item on the agenda was 'the king's pleas' (*regis placita*).[20] These royal pleas, to judge from the lawbooks produced for the guidance of the Normans, were legal actions in which the crown was a party directly or indirectly. Among them we may distinguish first the enforcement of obligations owed to the crown: the exaction of penalties for neglect of the public services, for example, or of the duty of joining in the pursuit of criminal suspects (the 'hue and cry').[21] Secondly there were what might be called offences against the discipline of the courts: failure to answer the summons of a judicial officer, contempt of the judgement of a court, bearing false witness, delivering an unjust judgement, harbouring fugitives from justice.[22] Thirdly there was a wide range of offences which might be classed as contempt of the king's majesty: breach of the peace which he had personally conferred on a place or an occasion, violation of the protection he had extended to individuals, assaults upon his servants, contempt of his writs or commands, obstruction of his officials, encroachments upon his property, concealment of his chattels, trespassing upon his hunting rights, damage to his highways or counterfeiting his coinage.[23] Fourthly, there were crimes which though not committed against the king himself seem to have been regarded as a serious affront to the peace of his realm, which could not be adjudged by any court except a court acting under direct royal authority. According to an early twelfth-century lawbook they included arson, secret slaying, killing a man in a fight, premedit-

19. *Ibid.*, pp. 137–41.
20. *Leges Henrici*, 7.3.
21. *Ibid.*, 13.9, 65.2, 66.6.
22. *Ibid.*, 53.1, 34.3, 11.7, 13.4 and 34.1.
23. *Ibid.*, 10.1, 10.2, 13.1, 12.2, 35.

ated assault, attacks on dwellings, robbery, ambush and rape.[24] Administering these royal rights was not straightforward. There seems to have been some regional variation both in what constituted the 'king's pleas' and in the penalties exacted for similar offences: in Oxfordshire, for example, the penalty for neglect of military service was 100 shillings, but in neighbouring Berkshire it was forfeiture of all land.[25] Moreover not all the penalties levied in the courts in the king's name actually reached him: some were absorbed into the *ferm* of the shire or went directly to the sheriff and other royal reeves – a useful incentive for the pursuit of offenders. The profits of some pleas, however, were said by the lawbook known as the *Leges Henrici Primi* to 'belong peculiarly and exclusively to the royal treasury' and are described as 'royal pleas' (*dominica placita regis*) or as 'reserved rights' (*iura retenta*).[26] Even of these, however, some lords were privileged to receive the penalties and the forfeitures levied upon their men; and some few with 'special jurisdiction' might even have 'reserved' cases assigned to their courts and retain the profits.

Fifthly, and of major importance in the development of administrative processes, was *the king's right to draw upon the resources of his subjects* in the form of a tax which the Anglo-Saxons called 'geld'.[27] The origins of geld are obscure, though a main root of it probably lies in the levy of tribute from subject peoples as a mark of an overlord's ascendancy. The geld of the West-Saxon rulers was, however, more systematic and sophisticated than the exaction of tribute by the Bretwaldas of old. It was levied throughout the shires on the units of assessment in money payments. Gelds might be 'general' or for special purposes. The entry in Domesday Book for Berkshire, which is unusually informative about established practice, records that 'when in the time of King Edward a general geld was given, each hide throughout the whole of Berkshire used to give three pence before Christmas and as much again at Pentecost.'[28] Special gelds, probably at higher rates, might be levied for a standing army (*heregeld*), for shipbuilding (*shipgeld*), or to buy off Danish invaders (the notoriously heavy *Danegeld* first raised in 991).[29] After the Conquest 'geld' and 'danegeld' became interchangeable terms, perhaps because the Conqueror levied it at rates higher than anyone could remember since the years of emergency. The normal rate in the twelfth century was two shillings on the hide.[30]

24. *Ibid.*, 10.1.
25. *DB* i. 154b, 56b.
26. *Leges Henrici*, 9.11, 10, 19.1, 35.2.
27. On pre-Conquest geld see Stenton, *Anglo-Saxon England*, pp. 636–41, Loyn, *Anglo-Saxon England and the Norman Conquest*, pp. 305–14.
28. *DB* i. 56b; cf. 30a: 'the common geld which no one escapes'.
29. The three gelds are distinguished in *DB* i. 336b, cf. Harmer, *Anglo-Saxon Writs*, p. 514.

Remarkable though it was, and indeed unique in the Europe of the time, the geld system was a rough and ready means of taxing the resources of the realm. The assessment in terms of hides and carrucates was artificial and arbitrary. Only accidents of history and political considerations prevailing at the time when a shire was given a rating in assessment units can explain why Wiltshire had by far the highest rating of all the shires, well ahead of much more populous Norfolk or Lincolnshire, or why wealthy Kent should have a modest rating, or Cornwall one so low as to be no more than symbolic, or account for the disparities within Lincolnshire of the rating of its several parts of Kesteven, Lindsey and Holland.[31] In the first flush of the reconquest of territory from the Danes Northamptonshire and Cambridgeshire were given punitive assessments; but later the policy changed, the Danes had to be placated, the Cambridgeshire hidation was halved, and that of Northamptonshire reduced by varying amounts across its hundreds, roughly proportional to the intensity of Danish settlement.[32] There was clearly a political advantage in being able to vary assessments according to circumstances, but equally clearly the burden of taxation was not closely or consistently related to the ability to pay.

Geld is commonly described as a 'land tax', but this is misleading. The fixing of geld liability did not begin by assigning a rateable value to individual holdings of land; on the contrary, it derived from a subdivision among the hundreds or wapentakes of the hidage assessment cast upon the shire as whole, and the determining factor in that was probably the number of armed men required for military service. The hundred's allocation of hides was at some time, it seems, distributed over its constituent communities in blocks of five hides: larger communities rated at five or a multiple of five hides, and smaller communities (including hamlets and isolated homesteads) grouped together to form a five-hide unit. Geld levy by this means would thus have been a communal responsibility giving some scope for adjusting the incidence of tax upon individuals.[33] The paying unit was the local community (the *tun* or *vill*), the hundred was the collecting unit, and the shire the accounting unit. By the time of the Conquest, however, the communal responsibility had for the most part dissolved: the

[30.] On post-Conquest geld see J.A. Green, 'The last century of danegeld', *EHR* 96 (1981), 241–58.

[31.] On inequalities and disparities see the tables in Maitland, *Domesday Book and Beyond*, pp. 29, 464–5, and the discussion on pp. 530ff; see also J.H. Round, *Feudal England* (London, 1895, cited from the reset edition of 1964), pp. 84–6.

[32.] C. Hart, *The Hidation of Cambridgeshire* (Leicester, 1974), and *The Hidation of Northamptonshire* (Leicester, 1970).

[33.] Round, *Feudal England*, pp. 83ff.

hidage for which the hundred had to answer had, at least for gelding purposes, become broken up into numerous small lots (reckoned if necessary in fractions of hides or carrucates) and permanently attached to parcels of land; and those responsible for collecting and paying the geld due were the holders of estates (which the Normans termed 'manors'). At the time of the Domesday Survey there were still many individual freemen and 'sokemen' who themselves answered for geld on their holdings, but the bulk of the geld was rendered to the collectors by greater landlords answering for the hidage on their manors and of course recouping themselves from their tenants. Geld can thus be said to have become a 'land tax' in the sense that payment had become attached to landholdings; but it has to be remembered that assessments in terms of hides or carrucates or fractions thereof were not valuations of land in terms of measurement or value but simply indications of liability to tax and public services. Domesday Book reveals wide disparities in the reckonings of land by units of assessment and by other kinds of valuation. It may be noted too that Domesday Book, which rarely wastes words, speaks frequently of 'hides for the geld' which may imply that assessments for fiscal purposes had frequently parted company with assessments for other purposes. Moreover it has to be remembered that not all land gelded. Untilled land (the 'waste' or the 'forest') was not hidated, and land brought into cultivation after the local hidation became fixed might escape geld liability. Some of the king's manors were not hidated, and some were hidated but did not geld: presumably the reason originally was that they rendered other heavy services directly to the king, but they could carry their anomalous status with them even when they passed to other hands.

The gelding system had a certain flexibility: the burden of tax could, for example, be temporarily reduced on a province devastated by invaders by the application of a simple formula such as reckoning every three hides as two. It could be used to supplement the endowment of churches by decreeing an arbitrarily low hidation, or more subtly by remitting geld payment and allowing the holders to collect it for themselves. For example, the huge manor of Chilcomb which was assigned to the support of the monks of Winchester cathedral and had land for 68 ploughs was rated at only one hide, though it originally answered for 100.[34] Domesday Book records of the manor of Maugersbury belonging to the abbot of Evesham that there were eight hides liable to the geld 'and the ninth hide belongs to the church of St Edward; King Ethelred gave it quit of geld'.[35] The king might by his writ reduce or permanently remit or temporarily pardon the payment

[34.] *DB* i. 41, *VCH Hampshire*, i. 463ff., Harmer, *Anglo-Saxon Writs*, pp. 373–4.
[35.] *DB* i. 175b.

of geld by individuals. Domesday Book notes, for example, that of a manor of 20 hides at Wenlock in Shropshire four hides were absolved from geld in the time of Cnut; and of the land of a certain Aluui at Rockbourne in Hampshire that the hundred declared that in the time of Edward the Confessor it was quit of geld and in warrant 'he has the seal of King Edward'.[36] The collectors of geld at the hundred of Albretesberge in Dorset in 1084 reported that 'from one hide which a certain widow holds at farm of Humphrey the chamberlain the king does not have geld because it is said that the queen remitted it for the soul of her son Richard'.[37] More generally the king might remit geld to his servants, or, as William I did on the occasion of a levy of a triple-geld of six shillings on the hide, remit payment on his barons' demesne lands (that is to say the 'home farm', the portion of their lands worked by labour services and not let out to tenants). Scope for the exercise of patronage by the crown was thus conveniently enhanced; but flexibility such as this emphasized the arbitrary character of the system. What it lacked, at least in the form inherited and continued by Norman rulers, was flexibility to adjust to real values or to the spread of cultivation. For the purpose of symbolic tribute the old communal levy had much to recommend it; as an emergency measure for raising large sums of money swiftly the assessment upon estate holders had a drastic efficiency which other rulers might justly envy; but as a method for regular tax-gathering, into which the Normans converted it, the geld was far from satisfactory, not least because a burgeoning population, an expanding agriculture and a rising prosperity passed it by.

Geld nevertheless did have the merit, from the government's point of view, of being cheap and easy to gather in. At the local level, however, it demanded careful record keeping, up-to-date information, and not a little expertise. The collectors in the hundred had to know to a precise fraction the hundred's gelding liability, they had to know who was responsible for paying and the exact allotment of hidage to each, they had to have details of exemptions and had to test claims of remission by the king's writ or the witness of the hundred court. Moreover they had to keep a careful check on who paid where, for estates, particularly large estates, overflowed hundred boundaries, and influential landlords might insist on discharging a geld liability which lay in one hundred at a manorial centre in another hundred.[38] The shire then had to audit the collectors' accounts, harry defaulters and if necessary punish them, and arrange for the transport of the money collected to the king's treasury at Winchester. The king's

---

36. *DB* i. 252b, 50, Harmer, p. 243 and n. 8.
37. *VCH Dorset*, iii. 128.
38. On geld collection see Maitland, *Domesday Book and Beyond*, pp. 154–63.

officers had then merely to satisfy themselves by scrutiny of the accounts that the shire had discharged its task properly and thoroughly.

Peace-keeping and the redress of wrongs

The problem of peace-keeping sorely troubled kings of the tenth century and was still a cause of serious anxiety in the eleventh. It was a problem exacerbated not only by the disruptive and demoralizing effects of warfare in the prolonged struggles with Danish invaders, but also by the enlargement of the kingdom itself, for the personal supervision of the peace possible for rulers of petty kingdoms was beyond the reach of rulers of all England. Yet it is very striking how frequently in their laws for the whole realm these kings busied themselves about the problems of theft and cattle-rustling and vagabonds, for which they felt themselves responsible but over which they had no means of exercising direct control. It must have been tempting to rely on traditional but haphazard methods for persuading kindreds to discipline their members, or to hand over the whole problem to local lords; yet kings set their faces against both the kindreds who terrorized their neighbourhoods and from whom no justice could be got, and against lords who protected their men whether in the right or in the wrong.[39] Instead they persisted in trying to develop communal methods of peace-keeping which ignored the kindred and which while enlisting the co-operation of lords did not become wholly dependent upon them. The peace was never as well kept as kings would have wished, and as befitted their dignity; but their efforts are historically important: they so well implanted communal responsibility that it became an enduring element of English practice, and they took the first steps in transforming the royal reeves in the shires from being merely exactors of the king's rights into officers of local government.[40]

Peace-keeping involved two related but distinct elements which we may differentiate as policing and pledging. The arrangements for policing in the eleventh century barely surface in the scanty surviving evidence, but there can be little doubt of the essential continuity in the principles, if less so in the detailed arrangements for giving effect to them, between the so-called Ordinance of the Hundred of the late tenth century and the royal edicts on peace-keeping of 1195 and 1242. Not until the Statute of Winchester in 1285 were the arrangements comprehensively overhauled, and even then much of the old

39. Loyn, 'The king and the structure of society in late Anglo-Saxon England', pp. 99–100.
40. W.A. Morris, *The Medieval English Sheriff to 1300* (Manchester, 1927), p. 20.

remained.[41] The basic principle was the fundamental duty of assisting the king in keeping the peace. The symbol of coming of age, of entering allegiance, and of acquiring personally the protection of the law in the public courts was a formal reception into the king's peace before the hundred court at the age of 12. Those received took an oath that they would keep the king's peace to the best of their ability, that they would not themselves be thieves, accessories to thieves or harbourers of them, and that they would attempt to arrest malefactors or at least report them to the peace-officers. The implication of the oath was the obligation to bear arms in the king's service at the command of his officers, and to join in the hue and cry in pursuit of suspected malefactors under pain of being treated as a suspect. It probably also involved from the beginning, as it certainly did later, the obligation to participate in 'watch and ward' – taking a turn at guarding the gates of walled towns or patrolling the highways of the hundred from sunset to sunrise and arresting strangers.[42] The supervision of policing was a function of the hundred, but implementing it had to rest on smaller and more localized units usually called *tithings*. Historians have commonly assumed that a 'tithing' was a group of ten men, but this interpretation rests on what seems to have been a confusion in the minds of early Norman writers of lawbooks between the Anglo-Saxon policing and pledging systems. The alternative explanation of the term, inherently more probable, and demonstrably true of many parts of the country is that a tithing was a policing district, notionally a tenth part of a hundred.[43] Originally it may have been conceived of as the policing service required from 10 hides, a unit which would have covered a substantial village or group of hamlets. In practice arrangements probably varied according to custom and circumstances, but the fundamental point is that the hundred had to arrange for policing in subdivisions, to one of which each freeman of the age of 12 had to be assigned for keeping the watch and arresting suspects. From the earliest mentions of the policing system it is the king's reeves who received the oaths and took charge of the hue and cry; and it is probable too that as soon as the office of sheriff became more clearly organized in the eleventh century he had to assume res-

41. The Hundred Ordinance, *EHD* i. 430, Proclamation for the preservation of the peace, 1195, *Select Charters*, p. 257, Form for the keeping of the peace, 1242, *EHD* iii. 357–9, Statute of Winchester, 1285, *EHD* iii. 460–2.
42. Cf. Leis Willelmi (*Gesetze*, i.492–520), cap.28: 'The guarding of roads: every ten hides of the hundred shall supply a man between Michaelmas and Martinmas'. The early history of watch and ward, before the edict of 1242, is obsure; but the antiquity of the obligation is reflected in local customs and payments such as 'wardpennies' collected in Neilson, *Customary Rents*, pp. 131–5.
43. The evidence and the arguments are reviewed in W.A. Morris, *The Frankpledge System* (New York, 1910), chapter 1. The confusion is manifest in *Leges Henrici*, 6.lb, in which the administrative arrangements and surety duties are run together.

ponsibility for ensuring that the tithings were properly organized in a twice-yearly visitation of the hundreds.[44]

This policing system was probably a better ordering of old obligations; but a unique feature in late Anglo-Saxon peace-keeping arrangements was that besides being a member of a local policing group every male over the age of 12 had also to be in 'borh', that is to say that he had to have designated sureties for good behaviour. A lord would normally go surety for his servants and serfs, but every other man had to demonstrate to the satisfaction of the hundred that he had sufficient pledges (probably 12) who would be answerable for his appearance in court in response to accusations, and who would themselves discharge any financial penalty laid upon him if he defaulted in the redress of a wrong he had committed. Here was an effective substitute for the kindred as a man's support group at law. Failure to find pledges deprived a man of 'law-worthiness' and robbed his oath of any value in resisting an accusation. He might then be forced to seek the protection of a lord, no doubt on onerous terms, who would vouch for him if he fell into suspicion. A man for whom no surety could be found might, if he incurred 'suspicion by all people', be summarily executed and buried in unconsecrated ground.[45] The primary and ostensible purpose of group pledging was to hold men to the judgements of the courts; but its effect and deeper purpose was to oblige men to hold the good opinion of their neighbours.

The practice of collective *borh* was colloquially known among the Anglo-Saxons as *friborg* or 'free-pleage'; the Normans who knew it not, and having no word for it, Gallicized the English term as *francpledge*; and it was as 'frankpledge' that the practice long survived as part of the peace-keeping arrangements of local government.[46] The post-Conquest practice of 'frankpledge', however, differed significantly from pre-Conquest 'friborg'. The Anglo-Saxon practice has been aptly termed 'the free engagement of neighbour for neighbour', and though pledging groups had to be formed to the satisfaction of the hundred court there was an element of choice involved.[47] Just as an insurance company might decline to insure a 'bad risk', so a pledging group might refuse to admit anyone notoriously untrustworthy, or decline further responsibility for a member convicted of crime. Indeed the element of choice was essential to the social sanction of the system. There was no such choice in post-Conquest frankpledge: groups were designated in the hundred and members

[44.] Morris, *Medieval English Sheriff*, pp. 20, 26, 27, 28. On the organization of the hue and cry by hundred and tithing see the Hundred Ordinance, *EHD* i. 430.

[45.] II Cnut 33, *EHD* i. 460.

[46.] Morris, *Frankpledge System*, chapter 1.

[47.] J.R. Green, quoted *ibid*, p. 3.

were obliged to become each others keepers. Moreover the exemption
of nobles from the collective *borh* of Anglo-Saxon times, together
with their families, servants and retainers held under their personal
surety (their *mainpast*) was extended after the Conquest to the clergy,
to knights and their families, and to other of the more substantial freeholders who had sufficient property to be pledged as security, and
upon which the sheriff could distrain as means of law enforcement. In
consequence, whereas the Anglo-Saxon collective 'borh' was a substitute for the kindred in matters of law enforcement, the Norman
'frankpledge' served the rather different purpose of disciplining the
peasantry. Some historians have seen in the transformation of *tithing*
and *borh* into frankpledge 'the pressure of a strong hand, the will of
an energetic legislator', and have identified William the Conqueror as
the man behind it.[48] But the one decree attributed to William I which
bears upon the matter speaks only of the old principles: 'every man
who wishes to be held as a freeman shall be in pledge (*in plegio*), so
that the surety shall hold him and deliver him to justice if he should
offend in any way. And if any such shall evade justice let his sureties
see to it that they pay forthwith what is charged against him, and clear
themselves of any complicity in his escape.'[49] Whether there was ever a
'legislative act' behind frankpledge must be extremely doubtful: it
seems rather to emerge as a consequence of a fading understanding of
Anglo-Saxon practice and a confusion between the police tithing
group and the collective surety group. In some shires the pledging
group seems to merge with the tithing, and in others the tithing seems
to have merged with the pledging group, for as soon as there are
records to cast light on the practice of frankpledge it is to be found
either as a territorial unit identified by the name of a place, or as a
group of 10 or a dozen or more men identified by the name of the
headman (or 'chief-pledge'). Nor was there any consistency in post-
Conquest terminology: the frankpledge appears as *francplegium* or
fridborg, as *decanna*, *tedinga* or *thethinga*, or in the south-east,
especially in Kent, as *borg* or *borgha*.

Securing justice for all men was a necessary aspect of peace-keeping
and a primary function of kingship. The king's duty towards most
men was, however, discharged not in doing justice but in seeing that it
was done. The method adopted was to draw into the organization of
shires and hundreds the ancient customary procedures by which men
in primitive society arbitrated disputes, recognized rights and
arranged settlements for injuries and wrongs, that peace might be
restored between kindreds and neighbours. The earliest mentions of
hundred courts and borough courts and shire courts in the Laws of

[48]. H.W.C. Davis in a review of Morris's book, *EHR* 26 (1911), 367.
[49]. *EHD* ii. 400, cl. 8.

Anglo-Saxon kings are in stipulations for regular meetings 'that every man might have his right and justice be done'.[50] But although these courts met at the behest of royal authority and were answerable to the king for defaults of justice, they cannot in any meaningful sense be described as 'royal' courts. They did not administer a body of royal law under the direction of judges appointed by the crown: they operated by customary procedures in applying customary law. Legal writers of the early twelfth century identified three distinct traditions of customary law: West-Saxon, Mercian and the law of the Danes; but we cannot get beyond instances of particular differences to defining the characteristics or even the territorial boundaries of these alleged categories. Nor do there seem to have been in England professional custodians of the customary law, as there were for example in Ireland and Scandinavia: the usages of the law were what the elders of the community assembled in a court said they were. There were of course some laws defined by the crown of generally universal application embodied in 'law codes', but these were supplements to custom or modifications of custom not codifications of custom; they were not numerous and were principally concerned with establishing the Church's rights and the king's rights and with improving the methods of peace-keeping. The judges of a plea were drawn from the 'suitors' of the court (that is to say, those who were duty-bound to attend) and selected by customary practices, subject to general rules such as that 'each person is to be judged by men who are of equal status and from the same district', or that 'No man may sit in judgement on his lord'.[51]

There were, of course, pleas in which the crown was involved directly or indirectly. The 'king's pleas' were broadly of two kinds: cases in which the king was an aggrieved party, and cases involving serious crime which by royal decree were reserved to the king's mercy. The most serious crimes were 'unemendable': they could not be settled by the payment of compensation but incurred a penalty of loss of life or limb and the forfeiture of property. Such 'reserved cases' could only be tried in the presence of someone to whom the king had assigned due authority, and the proceeds of forfeiture went directly to the royal treasury.[52] It might in consequence be necessary to hold a case over or transfer it from a local court to the shire; but the court which tried the king's pleas was the same court which tried other pleas. In a similar way the communal courts in Anglo-Saxon England adjudicated offences against 'God's law' as expounded to them by the

50. Ordinance of the Hundred, cl. 1, *EHD* i. 430, cf. *Leges Henrici*, 15.2. See also H.R. Loyn, 'The hundred in the tenth and early eleventh centuries' in *British Government and Administration*, ed. H. Hearder and H.R. Loyn (Cardiff, 1974), pp. 1–15.
51. *Leges Henrici*, 31.7,32.
52. *Ibid*, 19.1.

bishop or the archdeacon. In short, there might be distinctions of pleas but there were no distinctions of courts.

Royal authority commanded the convening of the communal courts but only the will of those who constituted the courts could make them effective. There was no other way. The pursuit and prosecution of offenders could be stimulated by financial inducements, diverting part of the profits of executing justice, for example, to the king's reeves.[53] Even the unholding of the Church's law was sustained by sharing out the proceeds of penalties on offenders: 'If a married man commits adultery the king or lord shall have the man and the bishop the woman for the purpose of exacting a penalty.' If a man withheld tithe all his tithable goods were seized, a tenth taken for the church to which he owed tithe, a tenth only was left for the offender himself, and the rest was partitioned between the bishop and the lord of the estate.[54] The involvement of lords is significant. They had the coercive power. Without their co-operation it is doubtful if the courts, particularly the hundred courts, could have functioned; without their sanction it is doubtful if the judgements of the courts could have been enforced.

Landlords and government in the localities

All landlords were drawn into local government, but in varying degrees and in a variety of ways. They could not escape involvement because every aspect of local government affected men who were in some way or other their dependents. Whether it was a matter of levying the king's rights, the composing of disputes, the settlement of compensation for injuries or the disciplining of troublemakers, landlords had interests to protect and a reputation to uphold. In practice the operation of shire and hundred must have rested heavily upon power-brokering between men who carried weight by reason of status, wealth and clientage. But the second and more fundamental reason why lords were drawn into local government was that the king expected them to assume responsibility for helping to manage the realm. This was not a privilege, it was a duty incumbent upon the office-bearers of the realm – the bishops who carried with them the authority of God, and the earls who carried with them the authority of the king – and also of those on whom the king bestowed his patronage in return for service, and who were known as the king's thegns.[55]

We hear of the thegns' work in upholding the king's government in

[53]. *Ibid*, eg., 9.11.
[54]. *Ibid*, eg., 11.2, 11.5, and for the tithe II Cnut 8.2.
[55]. On the king's thegns see H.R. Loyn, 'The king and the structure of society in late Anglo-Saxon England', pp. 96ff, and Harmer, *Anglo-Saxon Writs*, pp. 52–4.

the shires before we hear of the existence of sheriffs. The thegn was bound by his oath 'to be faithful and true, loving all that his lord loves and shunning all this his lord shuns'. Royal decrees gave the thegns acting together a decisive influence in judicial proceedings. The oaths of 12 leading thegns could put on trial suspected wrongdoers whom individuals might fear to accuse of crime. In the deliberations of a court the unanimous view of the thegns determined the matter; and if they disagreed a majority which eight thegns supported would carry the day. A lord who was accused of conniving at the escape of an accused man whom he should have led to justice, had to find five thegns to support him before he could clear himself by oath. A thegn who gave a false verdict through bribery or hatred, or who lent himself to an abuse of the law, was at the king's mercy and might lose his thegnly status.[56] Such were the requirements of the royal laws; but there can be little doubt that they only hint at the crucial importance which kings attached to the influence of their thegns.

The king's thegns were authorized, indeed perhaps required, to exercise some powers of local government directly over the dependent peasants on the estates which they received from the king. It was a mark of the status at least of a greater thegn to exercise the powers comprehended in a mnemonic formula known from the eleventh century as 'sac and soc, toll and team, and infangthief'. Of these terms *sac and soc* is the hardest to define, probably because its implications shifted and contracted with the development of alternative means of exercising royal authority. At the very least, however, it implied the extension to the lord's peasants on his estates of the kind of jurisdiction he would expect to have over members of his household: the power, that is, to pacify their quarrels, arbitrate their disputes, and punish petty thieving, brawling and wounding. *Toll and team* authorized a lord to oversee commercial transactions on his estates, particularly the buying and selling of cattle, to warrant legitimate transactions, and to adjudicate claims of stolen property. *Infangthief* conveyed the right to execute summary justice on a manifest thief, caught on the estate with stolen property on him.[57] These were useful rather than exalted powers, they were profitable, they helped in the consolidation of estate discipline; but above all they were valued as status symbols for they marked off the possessor as a *'potestas'*, as 'one in authority'.[58] It is difficult to believe, however, that estate-holders did not in fact exercise such powers over their dependents

56. III Edgar 3, IV Edgar 1.8, III Ethelred 3.1, 11, 13.2, II Cnut 15.1, 3.1, *EHD* i. 432, 433, 440, 441, 456, 459.
57. For discussion of these and other terms in this section see Harmer, *Anglo-Saxon Writs*, and N.D. Hurnard, 'The Anglo-Norman franchises', part 1, *EHR* 64 (1949), 289–327.
58. Cf. *Leges Henrici*, 20.2

before they were authorized to do so by royal charter and before there were hundred courts with jurisdiction. Indeed, we must assume that royal charters more often confirmed than granted and were part of a necessary process of delimiting the respective jurisdictions of landlords and the developing public courts.

The possession of the powers implied in 'sac and soc, toll and team, and infangthief' was as normal a mark of baronial status after the Conquest as of thegnage before the Conquest, and continued to be expressed in Anglo-Saxon terms. Its effect was to make the court in which the lord exercised his rights as landlord (the 'hallmoot' or, in post-Conquest terms, the 'manor court') also the vehicle for exercising a portion of the hundred's jurisdiction. Less normal but quite common was possession of a whole hundred and control of the hundred court by a lord. It is impossible to know how many hundreds were in the hands of lords at the time of the Conquest, though there is evidence to suggest that some 40 great lords may have between them held perhaps 130 hundreds or about a fifth of the whole. The overwhelming majority of these privileged holders of hundreds, some 30 of those that are known, were bishops or abbots; the few remaining were almost all earls or members of the royal family.[59] In many cases, perhaps most, putting a hundred into 'private' hands was a convenient way of assigning royal dues from a rural district to a favoured individual, church or monastery. The royal endowment of ancient bishoprics and abbeys took the form of grants not only of land (of which the founder might not have enough at his disposal) but also of royal dues and perquisites; so that instead of such royal dues becoming absorbed into the *ferm* of the shire for which the sheriff was responsible, they would survive as food renders, 'hundred pennies', 'hidage', and 'customs' payable to the lord who had the hundred. Many of the endowments were more ancient than the hundredal organization itself, so that it had not in fact been a matter of granting a hundred but of drawing the hundred boundaries around a privileged district. Hence the apparently anomalous hundreds: the scattered parcels of lands belonging to the church of Worcester which together constituted the 'triple-hundred' of Oswaldslaw, or the hundred of Damerham belonging to Glastonbury Abbey which consisted of two separate portions of abbey lands in the north and south of Wiltshire. Such privileges were primarily fiscal but since they included the king's share of penalties levied in the hundred, control of the hundred court came in practice to be part and parcel of the privileged status; and since there was little point in the king's reeves busying themselves in

---

[59.] H.M. Cam, 'The "private" hundred in England before the Norman Conquest', in *Law-Finders and Law-Makers* (London, 1962), pp. 67-70.

districts where there was little or nothing for them to collect for themselves or the king, the duty of managing the hundred would pass to the lord's officials instead of the king's.

Hundreds which were essentially landed estates over which the crown relinquished the royal hundredal dues and rights should be distinguished from hundreds which gave a controlling lord jurisdiction over men who were not his tenants, but freeholders or the tenants of other lords. There is no sign that these were anything but exceptional at the time of the Conquest. The most remarkable were in eastern England: the eight hundreds which centred upon Oundle and constituted the 'Soke' of the abbey of Peterborough, the block of five and half hundreds which the abbey of Ely controlled in south-east Suffolk together with the hundred of Ely itself and another hundred and a half in Norfolk, and the eight and a half hundreds which by gift of King Edward the Confessor made the abbot of St Edmund at Bury virtually the direct ruler of west Suffolk.[60] Within their hundreds these abbeys had extensive estates, but their hundred jurisdiction extended beyond their estates to embrace the men of other lords. There seems to be more involved here than the endowment with exceptional fiscal privileges of abbeys founded or refounded in a region reconquered from the Danes. Indeed the districts embraced by the monastic hundreds seem to have had an ancient identity, and we may see these 'special jurisdictions' as filling the shells of old chieftainries, and the purpose may have been to remedy a lack of effective royal influence in the region at the time, or perhaps to break the local dominance of less amenable lords.[61] The eight and a half hundreds conferred by the Confessor on Bury St Edmunds had previously been under direct royal control though assigned for fiscal purposes to the queen-dowager.

It is customary, and indeed convenient, to refer to hundreds controlled by lords as 'private' hundreds. It is indeed appropriate to distinguish them from 'public' hundreds in which royal officials moved more freely and had more to administer; but the term 'private' is misleading. It is not a term which the Middle Ages would have understood. Archbishops, bishops, abbots, earls and thegns (or barons) were not 'private citizens': they were as much an essential part of the king's service as his sheriffs and other ministers and all are commonly specifically addressed in royal writs to the shire. There was no difference in principle between a hundred managed by the king's reeve or a lord's reeve. We should guard against assuming that there was, in the

[60.] Cam, 'The king's government as administered by the greater abbots of East Anglia', pp. 183–204, E. Miller, *The Abbey and Bishopric of Ely* (Cambridge, 1951), chapter VII, H.W.C. Davis, 'The liberties of Bury St Edmunds', *EHR* 24 (1909), 417–31, R.H.C. Davis, introduction to *The Kalendar of Abbot Sampson*, pp. xivff.

[61.] Cf. W.T.W. Potts, 'The pre-Danish estate of Peterborough Abbey', *Proc. Cambridge Antiquarian Soc.*, 65 (1947), 13–27, and Cam, *Liberties and Communities*, p. 59.

early Middle Ages, anything special about a king's reeve: he was not a 'public servant' but the same kind of agent for his master as a lord's reeve. The difference in practice between 'private' and other hundreds lay mainly in the destination of the profits of hundredal jurisdiction. No law of the Anglo-Saxon kings ever found it necessary to distinguish between 'private' and other hundreds: the king's law was common to both. In the west country 'private' hundreds were more than usually common but it is impossible to identify them in the surviving accounts of the collectors of geld there in 1084.

The importance of the judicial powers conceded to 'private hands' has often been exaggerated and sometimes made the basis of an unwarranted conclusion that England offered numerous parallels to the continental 'immunity' which excluded royal officials from a priviledged district and left jurisdiction entirely in the hands of the 'immunist'. In point of fact what is really remarkable is the degree to which, at least by the middle of the eleventh century, the scope of private jurisdiction had been limited and its 'private' nature weakened if not undermined. There was no equivalent in Anglo-Saxon charters to continental grants of *'haute, moyenne et basse justice'*. The charters and writs of later Anglo-Saxon kings which granted or confirmed judicial powers did so not in general but in specific terms, and in specifying defined and by implication limited. What they specified was commonly 'low justice' and less frequently 'middling'.[62] By the time of the Conquest English kings had established a virtual monopoly of the 'bootless' or unemendable crimes – those which could not be settled by money payments but incurred loss of life or limb or outlawry. The sentence in such cases of serious crime could be pronounced only by the king himself or by the earl and bishop acting in his name in the shires. The only exception of a capital charge which was commonly granted to the jurisdiction of lords was the special case of *infangthief*. Many even of the more serious emendable crimes were also drawn with the *regis placita*; but favoured lords were sometimes allowed to share in these. The laws of Cnut identified six emendable pleas which though normally reserved to the crown might be the subject of grant. These were *mundbryce* (or *grithbryce*) – violating the protection granted by an official other than the king himself, *hamsocn* – an assault involving the invasion of a house or its courtyard, *forstal* – an assault involving waylaying or ambush on the king's highway, *fyrdwite* – the fine for neglect of military service, *flymenafyrmth* – the harbouring of outlaws, and *fihtwite* – the fine for fighting. Of these 'six royal forfeitures', as they were sometimes called, *mundbryce*, *hamsocn* and *forstal* seem to have been more

62. Hurnard, 'The Anglo-Norman franchises', pp. 289–327.

commonly granted, but even these not frequently. Cnut's laws prescribed heavy penalties for exceeding authorized jurisdiction.[63] The
twin processes of defining and reserving had the consequence of
limiting the ill-defined *sac and soc* to jurisdiction over the kind of
minor criminal offences which a later age would call misdemeanours.
Indeed, the limitation gave rise to the earliest known abuse of legal
procedure, for a legal writer of the early twelfth century criticizes the
tendency of complainants to exaggerate the offence done to them,
offering to prove that a simple assault was really *hamsocn* or involved
grithbryce and was thus beyond the jurisdiction of a lord's *sac and
soc*.[64] There would be little point in his criticism if even such cases of
aggravated assault were not commonly withdrawn from manor courts
to hundred or shire.

Moreover the reservation of all 'bootless' crimes and the more
serious emendable offences for trial and sentencing before a royal
official must have meant that such cases, though they may have begun
in hundred courts, had usually to reach a conclusion in the shire court.
The crucial factor was the presence of an authorized royal official
rather than, as yet, any formal definition of the competence of courts;
but the consequence must have been to emphasize the subjection of
'private' hundreds to the superior jurisdiction of the shire.

There were in England at the time of the Conquest some private
jurisdictions which amounted to 'immunities' totally exempt from the
supervision of the shire; but they were few in number, and with two or
three exceptions, were miniscule in size, for they were limited to the
precincts of ancient minsters and to the immediate vicinity of particularly favoured abbeys. Glastonbury Abbey could exclude all royal
officials and even, it claimed, the king himself from the town around
the abbey; Ramsey had an exclusion zone for a league around the
church of St Benedict; Ely had all royal rights in the Isle, but in its
hundreds in Norfolk and Suffolk had only the emendable royal forfeitures; St Edmunds had royal charters which conferred total
immunity on the town which came to be called Bury St Edmunds, but
more limited powers in the rest of its 'special jurisdiction'.[65] Bury St
Edmunds is, indeed, an illuminating case of the limitations on even
one of the greatest of the medieval English franchises. Its fiscal
privileges were of the highest order, for it had not only all the royal
dues from its hundreds but could even retain for itself any geld levied

63. II Cnut 15.2, *EHD* i. 456.
64. *Leges Henrici*, 22.1.
65. M.D. Lobel, 'The ecclesiastical banleuca in England', in *Oxford Essays in Medieval History presented to H.E. Salter* (Oxford, 1934), pp. 122–40, Hurnard, 'The Anglo-Norman franchises', pp. 316–21. On the claim of Glastonbury to exclude the king himself see *The Great Chartulary of Glastonbury*, ed. A. Watkin, i (Somerset Record Society, 1947), 220.

on the hidage of its lands. Its jurisdictional powers, however, may be thought of as a series of concentric circles of diminishing authority. In the restricted zone, the 'banleuca' of Bury St Edmunds itself, the abbot was supreme ruler. In the eight and a half hundreds of his 'special jurisdiction' he could hold a court which functioned like a shire court over all men of the hundreds not only the abbot's tenants. But this great 'liberty' never became a total immunity: in the twelfth century its hundreds still owed some suit to the shire court of Suffolk, the royal justices came to sit at the abbot's court at Cattershall for the hearing of the 'pleas of the crown', and the abbot significantly came to an arrangement with the sheriff of Suffolk to split between them the proceeds of 'sheriff's aid' levied on his hundreds.[66] Outside the eight and a half hundreds the abbey had numerous estates, but on these the abbot's jurisdiction reached no further than the six royal forfeitures. The abbey of Peterborough alone, south of the Humber, seems to have had greater jurisdictional powers than Bury St Edmunds: so far as the surviving evidence enables us to see, the Soke of Peterborough seems already to have been in the eleventh century as it was to remain until modern times, a shire within the shire, and its abbot was in effect the king's earl within the eight hundreds of the Soke.[67]

Apart from these rather special exceptions, it has to be said that there was only one real immunity comparable to the great continental immunities in England at the Conquest; and that, very significantly, was the earldom of Northumbria. The former kingdom of the Northumbrians was attached but not as yet integrated into the united kingdom of the English. It was governed by an earl whom the kings of the English appointed, but until 1055 they were careful to appoint him from leading local families. The earls owed allegiance to the kings of the English but the thegns of Northumbria owed allegiance to the earl. The king had no more than half a dozen small estates north of the Humber; all the rest of the former royal estates, all royal dues, and indeed all royal authority save for the appointment of bishops were in the hands of the earl. His authority, indeed, though marginally less than that of a duke of Normandy, was not unlike that of a count of Blois or a count of Anjou. There is no known Anglo-Saxon royal writ addressed to Northumbria. The organizing structure of shires and of hundreds or wapentakes reached no further than Yorkshire. The appointment by Edward the Confessor of an outsider, Tostig, brother

---

66. Hurnard, 'The Anglo-Norman franchises', pp. 324–7, Davis, *The Kalendar of Abbot Sampson*, p. xxxiii.
67. The soke of Peterborough has not been adequately studied, but see Cam, *Liberties and Communities*, pp. 184–204, and L.B. Gaches, *History of the Liberty of Peterborough* (Peterborough, 1905).

of Earl Harold of Wessex, to be earl of Northumbria in 1055 should probably be seen as an attempt to bring the far north into line with the rest of the realm. The attempt collapsed in a revolt of the Northumbrians and the expulsion of Tostig after he had dealt ruthlessly with Northumbrian law and the levying of taxes. That he could assert an authority over both is significant. Norman control of the north was established only after a generation of piecemeal effort. The consequence of piecemeal effort was the dismembering of the old earldom into tightly-knit, territorially compact lordships organized as 'castelleries' around a major stronghold. The lords of the castelleries were solely responsible for local defence, the keeping of the peace and the execution of justice. There was, indeed, at the time no one else who could do it. The pattern of government was thus grounded in a kind of martial law; but more than that, several of the lordships had been fitted into the shells of former chieftainries and administrative districts which carried with them remnants of the regalian jurisdiction of the former earldom. So the kind of jurisdiction which by special dispensation belonged to the abbot of Peterborough in his Soke and to the abbot of St Edmunds in his eight and a half hundreds, belonged as of right to the archbishop of York in Hexham-'shire', to the bishop of Durham in Durham-'shire', and to the lords of Richmond-'shire', Hallam-'shire', Lancaster, Holderness, Pontefract, Pickering, Tickhill, Coupland, Clitheroe, Skipton, Conisburgh, Kendal, Allerdale, Tynemouth and Tynedale.[68]

The northern castelleries were jurisdictional enclaves which long impeded effective shire government. Even at the end of the sixteenth century it could be said that sheriffs north of Trent 'had but small force'.[69] The shire organization through hundreds or wapentakes and the lordship endowed with powers of government were alternative ways of keeping the peace and executing justice. In the far north in the early twelfth century there was no practicable alternative to the exercise of virtually all government through lords. What is striking about the rest of England, however, is that the alternatives do not stand as two separate, contrasted or competing systems; instead they were woven together. A major achievement of the pre-Conquest kings of the English was the integration over much of the realm of the

---

[68.] W.E. Kapelle, *The Norman Conquest of the North* (London, 1979), especially chapters 3–4, G.W.S. Barrow, 'Northern English society in the early Middle Ages', *Northern History* 4 (1969), 1–28, and 'The pattern of lordship and feudal settlement in Cumbria', *Journal of Medieval Studies*, 1 (1975), 117–38, J.E.A. Jolliffe, 'Northumbrian institutions', *EHR* 41 (1926), 1–42, R.R. Reid, 'Barony and thenage', *EHR* 35 (1920), 161–99, W. Page, 'Some remarks on the Northumbrian palatinates and regalities' *Archaeologia* 51 (1888), 143–55; the footnotes to Hurnard, 'The Anglo-Norman franchises', are a mine of information.

[69.] R.R. Reid, *The King's Council of the North* (London, 1921), p. 8 n. 16. For the situation in the later twelfth century see J.C. Holt, *The Northerners* (Oxford, 1961), especially chapter XI.

interests of the crown and of landlords, and the vehicle of that integration was the shire. Even the greatest of the 'private' jurisdictions were reckoned as 'hundreds', and, with the exception of some of the 'special jurisdictions', did not stand apart from the shire, but shared its work and bowed to its superior jurisdiction. The exceptions should not distract us: they stand out because they were exceptional, and are better known because their privileges needed to be protected by frequent charters of confirmation. More important was what was normal, and about that less is recorded. We should not, however, suppose that the greater the lord the greater his franchisal powers. One of the greatest baronies of the twelfth century was the honor of Mowbray, with 46 mesne tenants of knightly rank, and numerous manors scattered over seven shires; yet in none of these extensive estates did the lord of Mowbray have more than *sac and soc*, *toll and team*, and *infangthief*.[70] We should not conclude that Mowbray, his officials, and his mesne tenants were of less importance in the government of the realm than the holders of more substantial franchises. Certainly they had more of their interests to protect in the courts of the hundred and shire where the Mowbray estates lay; but we should not forget that Mowbray's men and their neighbours *were* the hundred court, that the hundred court was a 'branch office' of the shire, and that the shire court was, basically, an assembly of the estate-holders of the shire deliberating under the guidance of God's representative and the king's representative. To draw distinctions between royal authority and landlords' authority, or between 'public' and 'private' is unreal.

Co-ordination and control

England in 1066 was a united kingdom but it was not a unified state. Government in the shires may have been reasonably well articulated through the subordinate structure of hundreds and tithings, but there was no central direction of the shires themselves, no system of supervision by visitation, no central office for controlling the king's officers in the shires. This was not decentralized government; it was merely uncentralized.

The shires were virtually self-contained units for all purposes. There was no larger unit of management, not even, in any real sense, the realm itself. In theory the king himself presided at the twice-yearly meetings of each shire; in practice he was represented by two surrogates, the earl and the bishop, the one speaking for the secular aspects of royal authority, the other for the spiritual, for the shire compre-

---

[70.] *Charters of the Honour of Mowbray*, ed. D.E. Greenway (Oxford, 1972), p. lviii.

hended all aspects of the life of the community. There were seven earls on the eve of the Norman Conquest, each responsible for a group of shires, but dealing with each separately. The earls were in effect provincial governors, and there was some danger that the provincial earldoms might develop along the lines of continental duchies; but the danger was minimized by frequently changing the groupings of shires which earls managed. In consequence provincial earldoms did not develop an institutional structure intermediate between shire and king. Although the earl represented royal authority in all normal business of the shire, he was not the intermediary for special business: matters which needed to be brought to the attention of the shire were conveyed directly by a royal writ addressed to the earl, bishop and thegns of the shire (sometimes also, and with increasing frequency to the sheriff). The writ seems to have been an English invention, developed at the same time as the organization of the realm into shires as a convenient means of communicating the royal will. It differed markedly from the written instrument known as the diploma, which on the continent made known the will of the ruler. The diploma was in Latin and designed to impress by the solemnity of its rotund and grandiloquent phraseology and its invocation of the Almighty. The writ, by contrast, was in the vernacular and was remarkably terse and simple: 'Edward, king, to his men in the shire, greeting. I make known to you my will that . . .' was the standard formula. The short business-like format is the mark of a device frequently in use;[71] and it is not surprising that the one element in the royal Household which seems to have taken on the character of an organized administrative service was the 'writing-office'.[72]

Matters which went beyond the competence of a shire or concerned the policy of the kingdom were considered in conferences of leading men from the shires, known as meetings of the *witan* (that is to say 'counsellors', literally 'wise men'). From meetings of the witan might issue edicts or statements of general policy in the form of 'Laws'. It was customary for pre-Conquest kings to issue codes of laws not infrequently reiterating old rules as well as making new ones, and interlaced with exhortations: 'It is a wise precaution to have warships made ready every year soon after Easter' (VI Ethelred, 33), 'And let us uphold the security and sanctity of the churches of God and frequently attend them' (I Cnut, 2), 'Assuredly, he who pronounces a more severe judgement on the friendless man or stranger than upon an acquaintance harms himself' (II Cnut, 35.1). Although the witan were consulted before the issue of laws, the authority to make and change

[71.] G. Barraclough, 'The Anglo-Saxon writ', *History* 39 (1954), 193–215, Harmer, *Anglo-Saxon Writs*, P. Chaplais, 'The Anglo-Saxon chancery from the diploma to the writ', *Journal of the Society of Archivists*, 3 (1965–6), 160–76.
[72.] Loyn, *The Governance of Anglo-Saxon England*, pp. 106ff.

law rested solely with the crown, and gave it the power to mould social institutions (such as the powers of the kindred), to shape administrative institutions, and to regulate the balance between lordly and communal jurisdiction.

The king's laws also regulated the monetary system of the realm. Elaborate rules defined the crown's exclusive control of the coinage, in contrast to the seigneurial and episcopal coinages of the continent. Its management was remarkably sophisticated. Coins could be struck only by licensed moneyers working in approved mints at specified places, about 60 in number and distributed so that few people lived more than 15 miles from a mint. The coins were of prescribed design, bearing on the obverse a 'portrait' of the king, and on the reverse the name of the moneyer and the mint; and they were also to be of prescribed fineness of silver and of prescribed weight. The dies from which the coins were struck were issued to the moneyers from a central base in London, thus ensuring a uniform type throughout the realm. Every few years, usually before the dies had worn down and standards began to decline, the design was changed and frequently also the prescribed weight; coins of the old design then ceased to be legal tender and had to be exchanged at a mint for new coins struck from new dies. The system had numerous advantages. It gave the crown control of the moneyers; it made counterfeiting more difficult or at least easier to detect; it facilitated commercial transactions by giving everyone confidence in the value of the coin by standardizing it and minimizing depreciation by long use; and it protected the royal revenue by ensuring that coin tendered in payment of taxes would be worth a close approximation of its face value. A controlled coinage was indeed a useful concomitant to the levy of geld. Moreover, although the system was expensive to administer it could be made to pay for itself and yield a profit in two simple ways: first by allowing the moneyers to levy a discount on exchanging old money for new, and secondly by charging the moneyers for the dies they were obliged to use and for their licences to operate. It permitted even more sophisticated controls, for by varying the weight and hence the number of coins which could be struck from the limited resource of bullion silver, a measure of influence could be exercised over inflationary or deflationary pressures in the economy. It is a striking testimony to the efficiency of the royal officials directing the system that in the eight months between the death of King Edward the Confessor and the battle of Hastings, new dies had been cut bearing the image of King Harold and coins of his short reign survive from 42 different mints.[73]

73. M. Dolley, *Anglo-Saxon Pennies* (London, 1964), Campbell, 'Observations on English government', pp. 39–41.

Besides its obvious trading and fiscal advantage, a controlled coinage also served a more subtle and vital political purpose. It advertised the universality and effectiveness of royal authority. While leaving administration largely to the shires, pre-Conquest kings kept in their own hands the minimum necessary means of co-ordination and control. They may not have created a unified state, but they had gone a long way to circumventing the disadvantages of not having one.

The Normanization of England

The Norman conquest of England did not take place in 1066. The victory of Hastings gave Duke William the crown, and for a short time the illusion of triumph; but effective control of the kingdom was won only in a series of increasingly bitter campaigns against local revolts between 1068 and 1072. William seems at first to have expected to rule England through co-operative Englishmen, much as the Danish king Cnut had done from 1016 to 1035. The resistance changed his attitude and his policy. He was, as the Anglo-Saxon chronicle says, 'a stern and violent man, and no one dared do anything against his will'. Englishmen were swept away from all positions of power and influence. At all but the lowest level of the landlord class they were deprived of their estates. The consequence was a tenurial revolution. Every surviving Englishman acquired a Norman lord. William claimed that all land in the kingdom belonged to the crown. He was everyone's lord. Domesday Book shows about a fifth of the realm still held directly by the crown in 1086. Rather over half had been distributed to the king's principal followers in huge estates, which they then partitioned among their own men. They were all, directly or at one or two stages removed, tenants of the crown, holding their lands as fiefs, and owing military service, usually in the form of knight service. About a quarter of the land remained in the hands of the Church, but William insisted that the bishops and the abbots of the greater monasteries should hold their estates as fiefs, doing him homage and rendering knight service. It obliged them to reorganize their estates and apportion manors to men of the knightly class. In this way the church lands were prevented from remaining pockets of Englishry.

The new landlords were fewer in number and generally wealthier than their predecessors. In pre-Conquest England there had been a few very great families and a large number of thegns holding relatively small estates. The new fief-holders probably did not number more than 1500, of whom about 100 came to be reckoned as 'barons'. It was a narrower, more tightly knit, hierarchical ruling class. It was a ruling class of foreigners, speaking a language the natives did not understand. It sat like a carapace on the realm. The duality of William's rule is reflected on his seal: the side which shows him crowned and enthroned bears the legend 'king of the English', the side which shows him as a mounted warrior bears the legend 'patron of the Normans'.

The dependence of the new ruler for control of England on his barons with their castles and knights might have meant that the realm would be organized upon the great baronial fiefs (the 'honors' as the fiefs of tenants-in-chief were termed) instead of upon the shires. It did not happen. William was determined to be an effective king, not simply a feudal suzerain, as, in effect, was the king of France. One sign of his determination is the oath of allegiance which he took from the barons' men at Salisbury in 1086. Moreover, he abolished the provincial earldoms. In the hands of a Norman with vast estates and a retinue of knightly vassals an earldom could, under a feeble ruler, have turned into an autonomous province like the duchy of Normandy itself. It can never have been far from William's mind that the man who had taken the throne on the death of Edward the Confessor in 1066, and who had nearly overcome his invading army at Hastings had himself been a provincial earl, Earl Harold of Wessex. On the Bayeux Tapestry Earl Harold was described as 'duke of the English' (*dux Anglorum*).[74] But most important of all in preventing the consolidation of governmental power upon fiefs was the dispersal of the estates which constituted the honors of the tenants-in-chief: instead of being granted in compact territorial blocs, the honors consisted of numerous parcels of manors scattered over several shires and interspersed with the holdings of other barons.[75] The greatest landlord in the realm in 1086 after the king himself, Robert, count of Mortain, held 793 manors distributed over 20 shires.[76] The honor of Peverel with its headquarters in Nottinghamshire had manors spread over 10 shires. The medium-sized honor of Stogursey was based in Somerset but had some of its major holdings in Northamptonshire and Oxfordshire, and some manors in Devon, Wiltshire and Essex.[77]

There can be little doubt that dispersal was deliberate policy: it was already the practice in Normandy. Some barons adopted a similar policy with their own men, forming fiefs comprising separated manors.[78] But although the dispersal of estates disrupted the territorial integrity of an honor, its feudal integrity was maintained by oath-

[74.] The Bayeux Tapestry, *EHD* ii. 239.

[75.] Cf. R. Lennard, *Rural England, 1086–1135* (Oxford, 1959), pp. 33–5.

[76.] *VCH Cornwall*, ii. 57.

[77.] These examples are from W. Farrer, *Honors and Knights' Fees* (London and Manchester, 1923–5), i. 146–259 and 103–45.

[78.] Bates, *Normandy Before 1066*, p. 170, Douglas, *William the Conqueror*, p. 268.

takings and suit of court. The principle applied was this: 'Every lord may summon his man for the purpose of doing justice in his court. If he is resident at a remote manor of the honor from which he holds, he must nevertheless answer his lord's summons. But if a lord holds more than one fief he cannot compel the man of one to go to the court of another.'[79] The dispersal of an honor did not simply mean the disruption of the territorial power of a great lord; it had the concomitant advantage of giving him interests and influence in different parts of the country. In consequence the great barons did not acquire a provincial outlook: they were more inclined to think in terms of the realm as a whole. It made the king's court the focus for the politics of the realm. The networks of the honors, with the threads of vassalage and homage reaching out like spiders' webs across the country, gave the realm a new kind of unity. It was no longer necessary for the crown to advertise itself as the co-ordinating factor in a compartmentalized kingdom. Norman kings showed no interest in publicizing their authority by issuing law codes as their predecessors had done. There was no formal law-making in the old style under the Normans, only edicts.

The abolition of the provincial earldoms and the territorial dispersal of great honors were important features of the Normanization of England; but qualifications have to be entered on both points. There were 'earls' in post-Conquest England, and there were some concentrations of territorial power. Some of the king's barons were given the title and dignity of 'count'. Their titles were linked to shires, which the Normans called 'counties'. Historians are accustomed to call these counts 'earls' for this is the word which ultimately prevailed in English usage, although, perversely, we still today call an earl's wife a 'countess'. The word 'count' is reserved for those who drew their title from a county in Normandy. This is a convenient usage but we should recognize that post-Conquest 'earls' were just like Norman counts. The latter were recent creations in Normandy: none was older than the beginning of the eleventh century. Although they acquired territorial designations they were not normally governors of administrative counties.[80] Those who managed the counties on behalf of the dukes were the 'vice-counts', in Latin *vicecomites*, which is the word applied in post-Conquest England to the sheriffs. Countships (or 'earldoms') were created in England for those men who stood close to the king/duke but who did not already hold countships in Normandy. Conversely those who were counts in Normandy did not acquire an English title however great their holdings in the kingdom (the most

[79]. *Leges Henrici*, 55. 1, 1a, 1b.
[80]. D.C. Douglas, 'The earliest Norman counts', *EHR* 61 (1946), 129–56.

notable being the counts of Mortain, Eu and Aumale). The counts of Normandy and England constituted one body of men whom the king/duke wished especially to honour, and who by their title acquired a precedence at his court. Although the earl (adopting now the customary usage) would share in the royal profits of jurisdiction in the shire from which he drew his title, he was not accorded an administrative function. Not all shires acquired an earl: there were only seven earldoms in 1086. Essentially the title was a personal dignity. It is significant that some earls preferred to use their family name. It was a habit which persisted with new creations in the twelfth century: even in royal records we encounter for example Earl Warenne (Surrey), Earl Giffard (Buckingham), Earl Ferrers (Derby).[81]

Although it was usual for an earl to have a major landholding in the shire from which the earldom was designated, he was not necessarily the most prominent landholder there. There were, however, some earls with so preponderant a landed interest in the shire from which they drew their title that it could be said that the shire had virtually been handed over to them. King William made his half-brother Odo, bishop of Bayeux, earl of Kent and gave him all the former royal estates there. Of Shropshire, Domesday Book says of Earl Roger that he 'holds of the king the city of Shrewsbury and the whole county and the whole of the demesne rights which King Edward held there, with 12 manors which the same king held there and 57 berewicks pertaining thereto'. There were five other tenants-in-chief in Shropshire but between them they held only one-eighth of the county, and three of them were also sub-tenants of the earl. Herefordshire was similarly dominated by William FitzOsbern and his men.[82] In Cheshire there was only one tenant-in-chief besides earl Hugh and he was the local bishop. To these we should add similar concentrations of landed power in the hands of the count of Poitou in what subsequently became the county of Lancaster, in the hands of the bishop of Durham in what became county Durham, and in the hands of the hands of the Count of Mortain who as part of his vast holdings throughout England held fully two-thirds of Cornwall.[83] It is commonly said that the purpose was defensive, and it was obviously sensible to create a well endowed local command in the marchlands, and in strategically

---

[81]. When an earldom of Wiltshire was created in the 1140s for Patrick, son of Walter of Salisbury, it was as 'Patrick, earl of Salisbury' that he was commonly known. An earldom of Sussex was created for William d'Aubigny in 1141, but in royal charters he is twice styled 'earl of Sussex', four times 'earl of Chichester', six times 'earl of Arundel' and once even as 'Count d'Aubigny'. See R.H.C. Davis, *King Stephen* (London, 1967), Appendix 1.

[82]. See the introduction to the Domesday survey of the county by J. Tait in *VCH Shropshire*, i, and by J.H. Round, *VCH Herefordshire*, i.

[83]. For an analysis of concentrations of power see J. Le Patourel, *The Norman Empire* (Oxford, 1976), pp. 307ff.

important Kent. But this cannot be the whole of the explanation. It cannot account for the concentration of a feudal power in Cornwall; and conversely there were no such 'defensive' earldoms where they might have been expected in the vulnerable coastal regions of the Danelaw. It should be observed that all the districts under dominant lordship had, in one way or another, unusual forms of local government, and this was probably the key reason for giving them special treatment (there were also briefly earldoms of East Anglia and Northumbria). We may then say that the kingdom was managed in a quite different way under William the Conqueror than it had been before the Conquest: instead of being arranged into provincial earldoms there was a heartland of dispersed lordship managed by royal officers, the sheriffs, without any intermediary, and a periphery of distinctive regions under dominant lordship. Several of the earls who had effective control of a shire-earldom proved troublesome; they were deprived and the earldoms lapsed within a generation of the Conquest.[84] Two survived intact: the earldom of Chester, and the lordship of the bishop of Durham which constituted an earldom in fact if not *eo nomine*. Both soon developed into jurisdictional 'immunities', the sheriffs were answerable to the lord and the king's officers could not normally enter.[85] Here is an indication of what might have happened: the organization of post-Conquest England was to a marked degree a matter of historical accident.[86]

It is, however, significant that the units of government were the shires, whether under royal officers or dominant lordship. There was one very good reason for not tampering with the shire organization: it yielded taxation in the form of the geld. Levies of geld were very important to William the Conqueror. He was preoccupied in his later years with the defence of Normandy against neighbours alarmed by his accretion of power. The wealth of England was made to pay for it. Geld was levied so frequently that it became virtually an annual tax, and at increased rates. Domesday Book illustrates the conjunction of shire organization and fief-holding, and the importance of geld. Domesday Book is arranged by shires; but under the heading of each shire the information is organized not in terms of vills but in terms of estate-holders. To reconstruct the information relating to vills under divided lordship it is necessary to look for it under the names of the lords. On the other hand to find out about honors one has to fit

84. The earldoms of Hereford and East Anglia were forfeit in 1075, Kent in 1088, and Shropshire in 1102.
85. G. Barraclough, *The Earldom and County Palatine of Chester* (Oxford, 1953), J. Scammell, 'The origins and limitations of the liberty of Durham', *EHR* 81 (1966), 449–73.
86. Cornwall was not drawn into the normal administrative framework until late in the reign of Henry II. The administration of Shropshire, Herefordshire and Kent remained unusual, but conducted by a sheriff answerable to the king.

together the information given for each shire about the holdings of tenants-in-chief. The intermediaries in the payment of geld were the estate-holders, and Domesday Book presents clearly the relationships of geld liability to the assets and productive capacity of the estate.

Within the shires the existing organization persisted because there was no alternative, and for the most part it had to be managed at the lower levels by Englishmen. The new masters were few in numbers, a few thousand in a population of about one and a half million. Many of the new landlords were absentees, residing on one of the scattered manors of which their fiefs were composed. The great lords co-operated with the king's commissioners in the making of the Domesday survey because it gave them, probably for the first time, a clear assessment of the assets of their estates.

The dependence of the Normans on English methods of local government is illustrated in a curious way in a new law for the protection of the incomers against the hostility of the natives. This was the law of *murdrum*. The author of the twelfth-century *Dialogus de Scaccario* explains its origin as follows:

> In the period immediately following the Conquest what were left of the conquered English lay in ambush for the distrusted and hated Normans and murdered them secretly in woods and unfrequented places as opportunity offered. Now when the kings and their ministers had for some years inflicted the most severe penalties on the English without effect, it was finally decided that the hundred in which a Norman was found killed, without his slayer being known or revealing his identity by flight, should be mulcted in a large sum. . . according to the locality of the murder and the commonness of the crime.[87]

The only escape from the fine, apart from delivering up the assassin immediately, was by proving that the victim was English (known as 'presentment of Englishry'). The problem of protecting the Conqueror's alien followers of course abated in time, and French and English became difficult to distinguish, but the *murdrum* survived as the best available means of coping with the category of homicide known as murder. As a legal text of the later twelfth century explains: 'murder, being done secretly, out of sight and knowledge of all but the killer and his accomplices, cannot be immediately followed by the hue and cry'.[88] As part of the normal processes of criminal law in the twelfth century the collective fine was usually less than that exacted under the Conqueror but was still large enough to persuade the hundred in which the body was found to use all its resources to identify the slayer; it was levied for the death of any freeman whatever his

---

[87]. *Dialogus*, pp. 52–3.
[88]. *Glanvill*, XIV. 3.

racial origins (so that 'presentment of Englishry' became simply proof of serfdom), but was remitted if the slayer was handed over to justice within seven days. The *Leges Henrici Primi* gives some indication of how elaborate were the rules and procedures which had gathered around it within 50 years of its introduction. First of all there had to be rules to guard against the body being quietly disposed of or spirited away into another hundred. As soon as a murder victim was discovered pledges had to be taken both from the lord on whose land it was found and from the headman of the hundred that the fine would if necessary be paid. The hundredmen had to be assembled at the spot where the body was found, and the corpse itself raised upon a hurdle and kept there for seven days 'with logs burning about it at night'. Announcements had to be made throughout the vicinity with liberal promise of reward for information leading to an arrest. If the fine became payable assessing liability was complicated: in the early years a lord could be held liable if the victim were found in his manor house or its environs, and the money would be raised by selling off the crops and livestock. If this did not suffice the hundred had to make good the deficiency, and the hundred was wholly liable if the manor happened to be the king's. If, however, 'the *murdrum* is discovered in fields which are open and accessible from all directions, the fine shall be made good by the whole hundred in common, not by the lord to whom the land belongs; if it takes place on the boundaries between estates, the liability shall fall on the lands on either side; if it occurs on the king's highway, the lord whose land is found to be adjacent shall pay the penalty for it.' If a suspect could be arrested within seven days, the hundred had to try to keep him alive to stand to justice for then the slayer's property would be forfeit to the king and the hundred escape liability; but a particular danger, it seems, was that the relatives of the murdered man would take vengeance on the slayer before he could be handed over to the sheriff; if the hundred allowed that to happen it would still have to pay the fine.[89] We are not, however, told how the hundred discharged the obligations imposed upon it: how, if the fine became payable by 'the hundred in common' it was apportioned, or how it went about identifying a suspect and establishing at least *prima facie* proof of his guilt. That it had to establish some presumption of guilt is suggested by the rule on what should happen if the suspect unfortunately died of natural causes before the presumption could be tested by trial in court. Then, we are told, 'his accusers shall demonstrate his guilt and summon support for their assertions at his graveside'.[90] This is tantalizingly vague: if we knew who acted as 'accusers' and what kind of support they summoned for their assert-

[89.] *Leges Henrici*, 91, 92.
[90.] *Ibid.*, 92.3a.

ions we might better understand how King Henry II was later able to fashion a standard procedure for the public indictment of criminal suspects by juries of presentment.

It is striking confirmation of the strength of the hundredal organization at the time of the Conquest and of the effectiveness of communal policing powers that the Normans could lay the burden of *murdrum* upon it. But what is even more striking is that they were unable to apply the law of *murdrum* to about a third of the country where either there was no hundredal organization or the hundreds had not developed a communal policing function. These regions were the whole of old Northumbria including Yorkshire, and the Welsh border shires of Cheshire, Shropshire and Herefordshire. What is to be found there instead of communal policing are para-military forces of 'sergeants of the peace' acting under the authority of local lords.[91] There were bitter complaints about their crude methods of law enforcement in the early thirteenth century when at last the royal government made some effort to introduce more sophisticated methods. So the Conqueror's drastic exercise of royal authority came to nothing where there were no established communal methods of enforcing it.

The survival of the institutional framework of Anglo-Saxon local government should not, however, mislead us into thinking that there was no break in continuity. Institutions may survive simply as shells into which new notions are fitted. William the Conqueror seriously undermined the traditional working of the shire in three ways. First, the establishment of feudal tenure as the only way in which members of the ruling class held their lands meant that the greater part of litigation over land moved out of the shire courts into the honorial courts of the barons. Secondly, the abolition of the old-style earldoms robbed the shire court of its principal layman who had presided as the king's surrogate. Thirdly, under the influence of church reformers, William thought it wrong that laymen should be involved in the hearing of cases concerning 'the cure of souls', and in 1072 decreed that henceforward bishops should have sole jurisdiction when and where they chose, secular authority being restricted to assisting the Church in enforcing its jurisdiction.[92] This decree did not immediately mean that the hearing of cases against 'God's law' moved away from sessions of the shire, but in promoting a distinction between the bishop's synod and the shire court it set in motion a line of development which was to

[91.] Stewart-Brown, *The Serjeants of the Peace*, and D.C. Cox, *VCH Shropshire*, iii. 20–3. Neither the Anglo-Saxons laws nor the Norman lawbooks mention alternatives to hundredal policing and frankpledge.

[92.] *EHD* ii. 604–5, *Select Charters*, pp. 99–100. For the interpretation of this edict see C. Morris, 'William I and the Church courts', *EHR* 82 (1967), 449–63, and F. Barlow, *The English Church 1066–1154* (London, 1979), pp. 150–5.

lead to the creation of a wholly separate system of ecclesiastical courts. In these ways the old unity of the shire was shattered, and the meetings of the shire court ceased to be the occasions on which the whole life of the shire community was brought into focus. In the old days disputes about land and inheritances, the reading out of charters, and the public witnessing of land transactions were of the deepest interest to all the upper strata of society in the shire; and God's business, such as accusations of adultery, had all the fascination of public scrutiny of other people's lives. It was hardly necessary to require attendance at meetings of the shire. It was different after the Conquest. There was no longer a great earl to grace the sessions with the semblance of royal majesty; bishops ceased to attend as a matter of course; the greater landlords did not put in an appearance, but were represented by their stewards. Attendance at the shire court became a chore and a burden which, significantly, frequently became a duty attached to the holders of certain tenancies. Sessions of the shire were now principally for the conduct of the king's business and criminal matters under the direction of the sheriff. This is what the Normans would have expected. To them the shire was equatable with the continental *pagus*, and the sheriff with the *vicecomes*, who in Normandy was the all-powerful administrator of the *pagus* as the duke's official. The old shire had been, as it were, the realm in little; it was now changing into an administrative subdivision of the realm.

Bibliographical Note

The Problems of Governing

Basic to an understanding of the period is J. Le Patourel, *The Norman Empire* (Oxford, 1976), especially chapter 5 on 'The practical problems of government'. For a shorter survey incorporating more recent work see M. Chibnall, *Anglo-Norman England 1066-1166* (Oxford, 1986), especially chapter 3. Detailed studies of reigns are D.C. Douglas, *William the Conqueror* (London, 1964), and F. Barlow, *William Rufus* (London, 1983), in the English Monarchs series; a succeeding volume on Henry I by C. Warren Hollister is forthcoming, in the meantime see his 'Normandy, France and the Anglo-Norman *regnum*', *Speculum* 51 (1976), 202-42, and C. Warren Hollister and J.W. Baldwin, 'The rise of administrative kingship: Henry I and Philip Augustus', *American Historical Review* 83 (1978), 867-905. There are important contributions to an understanding of the period and the problems of governing in J. Campbell, 'Observations on English government from the tenth to the twelfth century', *TRHS* 25 (1975), 39-54, and 'The significance of the Anglo-Norman state in the administrative history of western Europe', in *Beihefte der Francia*, 9, *Histoire Comparée de l'Adminstration* (Munich, 1980), pp. 117-34; J.A. Green, *The Government of England under Henry I* (Cambridge, 1986); J. Le Patourel, *Normandy and England 1066-1144* (Stenton Lecture, Reading, 1971); J. Prestwich, 'War and finance in the Anglo-Norman state', *TRHS* 4 (1954), 19-43; R. Southern, 'Ranulf Flambard and early Anglo-Norman administration', *TRHS*, 4th series, 16 (1933), reprinted in *Medieval Humanism and Other Studies* (Oxford, 1970), pp. 183-205, and 'The place of Henry I in English history', *Proceedings of the British Academy* 58 (1962), 127-56, reprinted in *Medieval Humanism*, pp. 206-33. An amplification of some of the arguments of this chapter will be found in W.L. Warren, 'The myth of Norman administrative efficiency', *TRHS* 34 (1984), 113-32.

Royal Finance

The main source of information is the Pipe Roll 31 Henry I: *Magnus Rotulus Scaccarii de anno 31 Henrici I*, ed. J. Hunter (Record Commission, 1833, reprinted in facsimile 1929). For an analysis and commentary see J.A. Green ' "Praeclarum et magnificum antiquitatis monumentum": the earliest surviving Pipe Roll', *BIHR* 55 (1982), 1-17, and *The Government of England under Henry I* (Cambridge, 1986), especially chapter 4 and pp. 220-5. For an understanding of the workings of the exchequer the *Dialogus de Scaccario* by Henry II's treasurer, Richard FitzNigel, is indispensable, though it must be used with caution for the earlier period; there is a convenient edition, with a translation and a helpful introduction by C. Johnson (London, 1950); there is a complete translation in *EHD*, ii. 490-569. On financial administration see: C.Warren Hollister, 'The origins of the English treasury', *EHR* 93 (1978), 262-75; Green, *Government under Henry I*, chapter 4; B.D. Loyn and A.E. Verhulst, *Medieval Finance: a Comparison of Financial Institutions in Northwestern Europe* (Providence, Rhode Island, 1967); E. Mason, 'The Maudits and their chamberlainship of the exchequer', *EHR* 49 (1976), 1-23; H.G. Richardson and G.O. Sayles, *The Governance of Mediaeval England* (Edinburgh, 1963), chapters XI and XII; G.H. White, 'Financial administration under Henry I', *TRHS*, 4th series, 8 (1925), 56-78.

Central Government and Local Administration

Earlier work on this difficult period in the history of government is subsumed in or superseded by J.A. Green, *The Government of England under Henry I* (Cambridge, 1986), which includes a comprehensive bibliography. There are useful shorter surveys in C.Warren Hollister and J.W.

3

The Origins of Central Government *c.*1087–*c.*1135

The Problems of Governing

In the half century following the Norman Conquest there was a major shift in the balance between the elements of the Anglo-Saxon legacy. Whereas pre-Conquest kings had organized their realm into self-managing parts and concerned themselves largely with matters which transcended the parts or involved the kingdom as a whole, post-Conquest kings were much more actively interventionist. Centralized institutions were developed for monitoring the crown's rights in the localities, and for linking the parts to the centre. By the earliest years of the twelfth century there had emerged a royal administrative service separate from the royal Household. The principal elements in this administrative service were a chief minister with a wide authority to act in the king's name, a variety of royal commissioners, some with a local or regional jurisdiction, and some who were described by contemporaries as 'justices of all England', and a management device which it would be premature to call an 'office' but which had already by 1110 acquired the nickname of *scaccarium*, 'the exchequer'.[1] The most visible, but by no means the only function of the exchequer was to subject the sheriffs to an annual audit. The origins, relationships and precise nature of these developments are not easy to establish, partly because they began as improvisations and *ad hoc* arrangements

Baldwin, 'The rise of administrative kingship: Henry I and Philip Augustus', *American Historical Review* 83 (1978), 867–905 (the relevant section of which is by Hollister), and M. Chibnall, *Anglo-Norman England 1066–1166* (Oxford, 1986), chapter 4. The most detailed study of judicial processes is the long introduction by R.C. Van Caenegem to his edition of *Royal Writs in England from the Conquest to Glanvill* (Selden Society, 1959). There are interesting examples of law in action in D.M. Stenton, *English Justice between the Norman Conquest and the Great Charter, 1066–1215 (London, 1965)*. Particularly illuminating is R.C. Van Caenegem, 'Public prosecution of crime in twelfth-century England', in *Church and Government in the Middle Ages*, ed. C.N.L. Brooke, D.E. Luscombe, G.H. Martin, and D.M. Owen (Cambridge, 1976), pp. 41–76.

[1.] Green, *Government under Henry I*, pp. 40–2.

which only gradually took on a settled form, and partly because the evidence for them is sparse. There are no records of royal administration for this period except for the chance survival of one record of an exchequer audit, the Pipe Roll for 1129–30, which reveals the existence of an elaborate system of financial management, but which casts only an oblique and fitful light on the administrative structure behind it. Additional, though inadequate, information has to be gleaned from incidental statements of chroniclers who had no intimate knowledge of the operations of royal government, and from references in royal writs and charters which happen to survive. Instead of approaching this important but obscure phase of the development of royal government by attempting to piece together such fragmentary and inconclusive evidence, it would be better to try to reach an understanding of what was involved by considering first the circumstances out of which the developments arose, and the problems to which they were a response.

The Norman kings were constantly preoccupied with the defence of their frontiers and the discomfiture of their enemies. In his early days Duke William had embarked upon a policy of aggression against Normandy's neighbours, partly to establish his own prestige and ascendency over the factious Normans, and partly to divert their ambitions from internecine strife within Normandy itself. The conquest of England was the grand culmination of this policy, and should in theory have made William unassailable, but in practice it intensified the fearful hostility of threatened neighbours. In particular it sundered the long tradition of co-operation between the rulers of Normandy and the Capetian kings and set a new pattern by which the kings of France strove for over a century to neutralize Normandy, undermine its stability, and separate it from the kingdom of England. The government of England in consequence became harnessed to an insistent militarism, and revenue raising to the needs of servicing a war economy.

The situation was exacerbated in the short term by the strife between the Conqueror's sons. On his deathbed, King William I assigned the duchy of Normandy to his eldest son, Robert Curthose, and the kingdom of England to his second son, William Rufus. Each was intent on ousting the other. William Rufus, with greater resources and a harder determination, established a foothold in Normandy. Duke Robert, wearying of several years of indecisive struggle, abandoned it to go on the First Crusade, encouraged to do so by his brother with a loan of 100,000 marks for which he took the duchy as security. When Duke Robert was on his way home from the Holy Land, King William Rufus was in August 1100 killed while hunting in the New Forest, and the throne of England was seized by the youngest of the Conqueror's sons, Henry. He thwarted an attempted invasion of England by Duke Robert, took the struggle to Normandy, defeated and captured his elder brother at the battle of Tinchebrai in 1106, and kept him prisoner for 28 years until his death in 1134. But King Henry did not hold captive Robert's son, William Clito, who, befriended by those who feared the permanent union of Normandy and England, became the rallying point of opposition. Henry I's hold on Normandy was perilous until he defeated a formidable coalition of his overlord, King Louis VI, with the counts of Flanders and Anjou, at Brémule in 1119. Though not seriously challenged thereafter Henry could not, with William Clito still hovering in the wings until his death in 1128, feel really secure, and cowed opposition with the deterrent effect of his military might.

The opposition was not simply external. Most of the barons holding lands on both sides of the Channel favoured the political union of Normandy and England; but many of them, including some of those most highly favoured by William the Conqueror, would have preferred to see them united under the affable, easy-going and open-handed Robert Curthose rather than either of his hard-headed, domineering younger brothers. 'The king', says the chronicler Symeon of Durham of Henry I in 1123, 'was more fearful of the treachery of his vassals than apprehensive of external attack'.[2] Divided loyalties undermined the cohesion of the feudal structure fashioned by the Conqueror. Feudal military service could not be relied upon. Both William II and Henry I utilized the old English obligation to army service. King Henry, we are told, when mustering forces against Duke Robert's threatened invasion, trained his English foot-soldiers to use their shields against mounted warriors.[3] But after 1102 little more is heard of the English obligation to fyrd service, which disappeared not only because it was inadequate for fighting continental wars but also, it seems, because of a general breakdown of the old public service obligations based on the hidage assessments and organized in the shires.[4] Increasingly military reliance was placed on mercenary knights and archers. William Rufus was described by Abbot Suger of St Denis as 'a pourer out of English treasure and a wonderful dealer in and paymaster of knights.'[5] Henry I recruited mercenaries in large numbers from Brittany and Flanders. In 1101 he arranged with the count of Flanders for the supply of 1000 knights in return for an annuity of 500 pounds. Even in the later years of the

---

[2.] Symeon of Durham, *Opera Omnia*, ed. T. Arnold (Roll Series, 1882-5), ii. 274.

[3.] William of Malmesbury, *De Gestis Regum*, ed. W. Stubbs (Rolls Series, 1887-9) ii. 472.

[4.] C. Warren Hollister, *The Military Organization of Norman England* (Oxford, 1965), pp. 253-7.

[5.] *Vie de Louis VI le Gros*, ed. H. Waquet (Paris, 1964), p. 8.

reign when there was no immediate threat, large forces were quartered in frontier districts. In addition to the payment of mercenaries huge sums were expended on defensive fortresses: Henry I erected at least 45. Henry is said to have preferred diplomacy to war; but that too was expensive as money was poured out in pensions to supporters, subsidies to allies, and bribes to the vassals of his enemies. The marriage of his daughter Matilda to Emperor Henry V of Germany was part of the diplomatic offensive against the king of France, but her dowry cost at least 10,000 marks.[6]

It is not surprising that a major element in revenue raising was the English geld. The Anglo-Saxon Chronicle asserts that it had not been necessary to take geld in the later years of Edward the Confessor's reign; but it was reimposed shortly after the Conquest, frequently levied, and sometimes at abnormally high rates.[7] The evidence of the Pipe Roll of 1129–30 suggests that it had by then become an annual levy at a standard rate of two shillings on the hide. But for the purposes of regular instead of emergency taxation the English geld had serious defects. It was levied on an assessment system designed for other purposes, which bore no real relationship to the wealth of those liable, or to changing land values. To bring it into line with the real wealth of England and the financial needs of the Norman kings required a reassessment of liability. One of the main intentions of the Domesday survey was to tackle problems connected with the geld.[8] The most immediate was a consequence of the replacement of pre-Conquest landowners by Normans, and the disputes and confusions over landholding which ensued. The geld collectors might know from the shire records how much they were supposed to collect, but could not always be certain from whom to collect. The first purpose of the Domesday commissioners was to identify definitively the rightful holders of estates. The primary questions were: who holds this land and for how many hides does it geld? It was indeed because of the resolution of tenurial questions that the record of the survey acquired the nickname of Domesday Book, 'because its decisions, like those of the Last Judgement are final'. But besides this pressing purpose the survey also tackled the wider problem of the relationship of geld assessment to real value. It listed the assets of estates in terms of available manpower, plough-teams, natural resources and livestock. It attempted some sort of valuation, and asked what the estate had been

6. Prestwich, 'War and finance', p. 32, Green, *Government under Henry I*, p. 17.
7. On geld after the Conquest see J.A. Green, 'The last century of danegeld', *EHR* 96 (1981), 141–58. For the complexities of geld levying see R.W. Welldon Finn, *The Domesday Inquest* (London, 1961), p. 44.
8. S. Harvey, 'Domesday Book and Anglo-Norman governance', *TRHS* 25 (1975), 175–93, Warren, 'The myth of Norman efficiency', pp. 128–30.

worth in times past, what it was worth now, and whether more could be got from it. The valuations in Domesday Book are makeshift and inconsistent, understandably so given the remarkably short time of a few months in which the survey was conducted; but they served to identify disparities and indicate the potential for more thorough taxation. The next step should have been reassessment; but it never happened. Undoubtedly some thought was given to it. The chronicler Orderic Vitalis has a garbled story of a project by Ranulf Flambard, William II's chief minister, for having all fields measured 'by the rope'.[9] In Henry I's reign there were some local surveys supplementary to Domesday Book in Lindsey, Leicestershire, and Northamptonshire, of uncertain purpose but related to geld assessments.[10] There were some piecemeal revisions to judge from the Pipe Roll of 1129–30 which records a few payments for the privilege of having manors remain at the old assessment. But the failure to carry through a thorough reform of the old English system not only left the geld as an arbitary and inadequate tax but also forced the crown into finding other means of raising revenue. A general reassessment would of course have been a major undertaking, and the failure to embark upon it may be attributed to the political difficulties of the Conqueror's successors and an understandable reluctance to encourage support for Duke Robert and his son. Henry I in particular, whom many regarded as a usurper king, had to pay a high price for being allowed to levy geld at all by remitting payments to his barons on their demesne lands. He seems to have been able in time to convert the concession from being general into a favour for named individuals (a powerful piece of discriminatory patronage), but even so the shortfall on the theoretical return of a geld levy was substantial: the Pipe Roll of 1129–30 reveals that of a total geld demand amounting to £4356 no less than £1811 (over 40 per cent) was 'pardoned'.[11]

Administering the geld was not the only problem faced by the Norman kings in managing their English inheritance. Sparse as is the information available, it seems that at least by Henry I's reign the fabric of Anglo-Saxon local government was coming apart at the seams. One indication is a writ of Henry I attempting to arrest the transformation of the shires, already grievously if inadvertently weakened in their traditional functioning by William the Conqueror.

9. *The Ecclesiastical History of Ordericus Vitalis*, ed. and translated by M. Chibnall (Oxford, 1969–80), vi. 22; see also Chibnall, *Anglo-Norman England*, p. 117.
10. J.H. Round, *Feudal England* (London, 1895, reset ed. 1964), pp. 149–81, *The Lincolnshire Domesday and the Lindsey Survey*, ed. C.W. Foster and T. Longley, with an introduction by F.M. Stenton (Lincoln Record Society, 1924), *The Leicestershire Survey*, ed. C.F. Slade (Leicester, 1956).
11. Green, *Government under Henry I*, p. 223.

It cannot be precisely dated but probably derives from the end of the first decade of the reign. It begins:

> Know that I will and command that my shires and hundreds shall meet in the same places and on the same occasions as they met in the time of King Edward and not otherwise. And I will not allow that my sheriff shall convene them otherwise on account of his own convenience as he sees it. But I myself, whenever I wish it, may summon them to deal with royal business at my will.

We can only guess at what had been happening in the shires; but the implication is clear that there was a danger of the customary courts becoming 'sheriffs' courts'. The writ goes on to say something about the land law:

> If a plea about land shall arise between two of my barons it should be heard in my court. If it is between the vassals of one of my honorial barons let it be heard in the court of their lord. And if it is between the vassals of two lords let it be heard in the shire court.[12]

This last provision flew in the face of feudal custom, for a contemporary law book states that such a case should be heard in the court of the defendant's lord.[13] The king's ruling was no doubt a solution to an awkward problem, more likely to secure justice and less likely to provoke hostility between vassalage groups; but we may suspect that its primary purpose was to recover for the shire some jurisdiction over the kind of business which would engage the interest and attract the attendance of local landholders.

Another indication of the Normans' difficulty in managing the Anglo-Saxon inheritance concerns the coinage. An edict of Henry I at the very beginning of his reign required all burgesses 'to swear to maintain my money in England and countenance no falsification'. It prescribed penalties for anyone in possession of false money, insisted that moneyers should not recast coin except in their own shire and in the presence of two lawful witnesses, and banned the exchanging of new coin for old by anyone but licensed moneyers.[14] These were basic rules which had operated under English kings for over a century; but that the elaborate Anglo-Saxon system was foundering is suggested by other pieces of evidence. One of the advantages of the old rules and of frequently requiring old money to be exchanged for new had been the reliability of coins tendered in payment of royal dues and taxes; but Henry I's treasury had to resort to expedients to guard against losses to the revenue from coins of diminished or suspect value. Sometimes

---

12. *EHD* ii. 433–4.
13. *Leges Henrici*, 25.2.
14. *The Laws of the Kings of England*, ed. A.J. Robertson (Cambridge, 1925), pp. 284–5, *Regesta*, ii, no. 501.

the coins were weighed instead of being accepted at face value; sometimes payments were discounted at a standard rate; and in the case of major payments it became the normal practice to assay a sample for silver content and discount the whole payment by any shortfall in the sample.[15] That standards were declining is revealed by a royal decree of 1108 insisting that coins should be round and increasing the penalties for debasement to blinding and castration.[16] Traders commonly nicked the edges of coins to check that they were not merely plated with silver; and it is a measure of the government's desperation that it resorted to the tactic of having all coins nicked. The crisis came in 1124 when the king's mercenaries on the continent refused payment in English coin because, they said, it was barely one-third silver. In its humiliation the crown exacted a fearful retribution on the licensed moneyers: 94 of them were blinded and castrated. It is significant that the reprisals were not conducted by the sheriffs responsible for the local mints but by the king's chief minister, Roger, bishop of Salisbury, who summoned the moneyers before him at Winchester.[17]

The problems which these examples highlight were not unrelated; underlying them is a withering of traditional practice, and a decay of the in-built checks and balances of the Anglo-Saxon system. One effect was to leave the sheriff so untrammelled in the exercise of local power that his own interests threatened to take precedence over the king's. Coping with this problem was not difficult. The annual audit of sheriffs' accounts at the exchequer was one of the new methods. Another was the requirement that payments by the sheriff of the money he owed in respect of shire revenues – the *farm* of the shire – should be assayed for silver content: this, we are told, was a decision of the king's council 'in order to protect both the king and the public', for 'the sheriff, finding that he suffers on account of the loss on inferior money, takes good care that the moneyers who work under him do not exceed the established proportion of alloy.'[18] Ingenuity was the hallmark of Henry I's government; and the difficulties with the coinage which for so long had seemed intractable abated in the later years of the reign. But *ad hoc* measures of this kind did not go to the deeper level of the problem.

---

[15]. Cf. *Dialogus*, pp. 41–3.
[16]. Eadmer, *Historia Novorum*, ed. M. Rule (Rolls Series, 1884), p. 193, Symeon of Durham, ii. 239, Florence of Worcester, ii. 57.
[17]. *Gesta Normannorum Ducum*, ed. J. Marx (Rouen, 1914), p.297, *Annales Monastici*, ii. 47. On the coinage generally see M. Dolley, *The Norman Conquest and the English Coinage* (London, 1966), G.C. Brooke, *A Catalogue of English Coins in the British Museum, The Norman Kings* (London, 1916), T. Bisson, *Conservation of Coinage* (Oxford, 1979), P. Nightingale, 'Some London moneyers and reflections on the organization of English mints in the eleventh and twelfth centuries', *Numismatic Chronicle* 142 (1982), 34–50.
[18]. *Dialogus*, p. 43.

The deeper problem was the state of local government. It may well have been the most serious, but it is the hardest to discern for lack of concrete evidence. There are nevertheless signs to be read which suggest that a crisis in the management of the Anglo-Saxon legacy had developed by the beginning of the twelfth century. The Normanization of the upper levels of society in the reign of William the Conqueror and the changes wrought by him in the management and operation of the shires had shaken and weakened but had not dissolved the old structures and methods. There was a high degree of continuity in local government across the divide of the Conquest because it continued to be run by Englishmen. But by the beginning of Henry I's reign a generation had passed; those who had first-hand experience of pre-Conquest practice were dying off and were almost everywhere being replaced by Normans. It may be thought that there had been time enough for the necessary knowledge and expertise to be transmitted; but language was a barrier to an easy transition from English to Norman administration. Anglo-Saxon government had been conducted in the vernacular, and such records as must once have been kept at least at shire level have disappeared because they were unintelligible and hence useless to Normans who spoke French and wrote Latin. It is probably for this reason that Henry I found it necessary to reiterate in Latin the old rules on the coinage which had hitherto circulated in English. And it is presumably a defective transmission of know-how as well as a weakening of effective supervision which is responsible for the declining standards of the coinage both in workmanship and quality which so seriously threatened the royal finances in Henry I's reign.

At the level of estate-management the transition from English to Norman seems generally to have happened about the same time for it was in the early twelfth century and not before that some of the better-run estates produced surveys and statements of manorial custom in Latin.[19] Similarly it is in the reign of Henry I that there appears a small crop of tracts for the use of middle-ranking administrators: the *Quadripartitus*, the *Leges Henrici Primi*, the *Instituta Cnuti* and the *Consiliatio Cnuti*, parts at least of the *Leges Edwardi Regis*, and perhaps also the *Leis Willhelmi*.[20] Some of these are simply collections and translations of Anglo-Saxon laws. Some attempt to grapple with unfamiliar aspects of Anglo-Saxon practice. One, the so-called *Leges Henrici Primi*, bravely if not very lucidly attempts an exposition of legal principles and practice in the shire and hundred courts. These are signs and hints only that there was a problem; we cannot know for

[19.]Warren, 'The myth of Norman efficiency', p. 118 and n. 3.
[20.] H.G. Richardson and G.O. Sayles, *Law and Legislation from Aethelbert to Magna Carta* (Edinburgh, 1966), pp. 41–9.

certain what was happening in the shires; but a recognition that the Normans had difficulty in mastering Anglo-Saxon practice may help to explain why, for example, the sophisticated pre-Conquest methods of tithing and borh became transmuted into the cruder frankpledge. The author of the *Leges Henrici Primi* vehemently denounces 'rapacity and evil and hateful novelties' in the administration of the law, but unfortunately does not specify what they were. In contrast to the confusion which he saw in the shires he extols the firmness and consistency of royal jurisdiction.[21] This was to be the new factor in the situation. It is significant that Henry I, in his ordinance on the shire and hundred courts, required the sheriffs to observe traditional practice, but declared that the king himself might convene them in extraordinary session for the purposes of royal government.

Ignorance of the workings of English local government must for a generation after the Conquest have been most profound at the highest level of Norman government – in the king's court itself, and this must have severely limited its capacity to prevent the erosion and decay of the traditional mechanisms through which was discharged the fundamental royal duty 'to defend his people and Holy Church from those who seek to injure them, and to destroy and extirpate wrongdoers'. Henry I, who gained the throne by dubious means, had to work harder than his predecessors to prove that he was worthy of it. He earned the soubriquet of 'the Lion of Justice'. This is one reason for the extension of central government into the localities. Another is that royal jurisdiction was profitable.

Royal Finance

The most striking achievement of Norman government was to keep the crown solvent despite its enormous expenditure. Henry I died with a treasury full to overflowing, and a huge credit balance in the form of outstanding debts. The chance survival of the Pipe Roll of 1129–30 enables us to identify the sources of income. A Pipe Roll was a record of an audit of the accounts of each sheriff held at Michaelmas each year at the exchequer. Only one survives from Henry I's reign, and no more until 1155, but thereafter in almost unbroken sequence. In 1178 Henry II's treasurer wrote a treatise on how the audit was conducted, known as *The Dialogue of the Exchequer* (*Dialogus de Scaccario*), which took the form of a discussion on exchequer procedure between an expert and an apprentice. Richard FitzNigel was the son of Nigel, bishop of Ely, who had been treasurer under Henry I, and was able to speak of the origins of the practices of his own day, though what he

21. *Leges Henrici*, 6.3a and 7.2, 6.2a and 9.10a.

says is more in the nature of office tradition than altogether reliable history. He was devoted to traditional procedures, which he describes as 'the ancient course' of the exchequer, so that what he says helps to make sense of the otherwise bald information of the isolated Pipe Roll drawn up at Michaelmas 1130 and relating to the previous year. When the Pipe Rolls began we do not know, but it was certainly much before that of 1129–30 for it already exhibits the established procedures familiar to Richard FitzNigel and refers to debts carried over for several years.

Some royal revenues were probably paid directly into the financial department of the king's Household, the Chamber, and do not figure in the Pipe Rolls, but the bulk of royal revenues reached the treasury through the sheriffs and were recorded at the annual exchequer audit. The exchequer got its name from the chequered cloth which was spread on a table at which sat the king's representatives and before which was brought the sheriff. On the chequered cloth were set counters representing sums of money and moved after the manner of an abacus, so that it was possible for all at the table to see at a glance the state of the account which was being audited. The sheriff was questioned on two categories of royal revenue: first those items of revenue for which the sheriff himself was responsible, and secondly the payments for which individuals had personally contracted and for which the sheriff acted as debt collector.

The sheriff contracted to manage the shire, taking the revenues of the royal estates there and the profits of jurisdiction, for a lump sum known as 'the farm of the shire'. He was allowed to deduct payments he made on behalf of the king provided he could satisfy the exchequer that he had acted in accordance with instructions. He was personally responsible for collecting, transmitting to the treasury, and account-ing at the exchequer for the 'public' debts, as distinct from those incurred by individuals. These included taxation and *murdrum* fines on vills. The geld was augmented by levies on boroughs; and the author of the *Dialogus* refers to 'common assizes', which seem to have been supplementary taxation on shires to make up for the unevenness of geld assessments.[22] In these ways the shortcomings of the geld were to some extent redressed, though as improvisations they testify to the failure to establish a satisfactory system of taxation. In the Pipe Roll of 1129–30 'aids of shires and boroughs' amounted to £725 which was equivalent to less than half of the remissions of geld to individuals.[23]

The most substantial and regular item of revenue was that from the farms of the shires. The Pipe Roll of 1129–30 puts it at about £15,000,

---

[22.] *Dialogus*, pp. 47–8, 57, 108.

and records that over £10,000 had been paid in, amounting to about 40 per cent of the receipts of the treasury that year. If a royal manor was granted to someone by the king, its value had to be deducted from the farm owed by the sheriff. On later Pipe Rolls such deductions for *terrae datae* steadily accumulate. There are very few references to *terrae datae* on the Pipe Roll of 1129–30, but this is probably because the shire farms had recently been revised and the deductions for alienations of royal estates consolidated. It is difficult to know how the royal estates under Henry I compare with the lands listed as belonging to the king (*terra regis*) in Domesday Book, but recent studies suggest that alienations had been very extensive, presumably in grants to buy support and reward loyalty.[24] It is significant that very few of the numerous forfeitures of those broken for disloyalty remained for long in the king's hand. The scale of alienations since the Conqueror's day is such that there can be little justification for describing the royal estates as 'royal demesne' in the sense of a permanent landed endowment intended to provide a regular income sufficient to enable the king in normal circumstances to 'live of his own'. The notion of a permanent endowment for the crown was not alien to the period: it may be seen in the royal *domaine* of the French kings, consisting largely of Capetian family estates prudently augmented whenever possible. It may be that William the Conqueror had some such intention when he retained in his hand many more manors than those which Edward the Confessor had held, amounting indeed on the evidence of Domesday Book to about one-fifth of the realm; but if this were the intention it did not survive the political necessities of William II and Henry I. They seem to have regarded the Domesday *terra regis* simply as 'land in the hands of the king' and principally as a reserve of capital assets from which grants could be made as required. Nevertheless the income from the royal estates indicated on the Pipe Roll of 1129–30 is not appreciably lower than the income at the time of the Domesday survey, and since this cannot be explained by accretions in the form of forfeitures and escheats, it suggests that careful attention was paid to the proper stocking, management and exploitation of the manors which remained in the king's hand.

At an exchequer audit the treasurer questioned the sheriff about the payments he himself owed, and then handed over to the chancellor (or his deputy) who questioned the sheriff about the payments he had been instructed to collect from individuals who owed money to the crown. Some of these were feudal dues, that is to say they were owed in

[23] Green, *Government under Henry I*, p. 225.
[24] J.A. Green, 'William Rufus, Henry I and the royal demesne', *History* 64 (1979), 337–51.

respect of fiefs held of the crown, such as the payment to succeed to an inheritance known as the 'relief', or money paid in lieu of military service known as 'scutage'. But there are also many individual debts listed on the Pipe Roll under the heading of *Placita et Conventiones*, that is to say 'Pleas and Agreements'. The *Dialogus* explains that *placita* are 'pecuniary penalties into which delinquents fall', and *conventiones* are 'what is voluntarily proffered'. Some examples from the Pipe Roll of 1129–30 will illustrate what was involved.[25]

> The earl of Warwick renders account of £72.16s.8d and two warhorses for pleas concerning stags.
> (He has been hunting without permission in the royal game reserves).
>
> William of Fécamp owes 100 marks of silver in respect of the land of his father which Robert FitzNigel holds.
> (He claims to have been cheated of his inheritance and wishes the king to secure it for him; there is a price to pay).
>
> Guy Maufe owes one warhorse that he may be justly treated in the court of his lord. He has paid 40 shillings in lieu of the warhorse.
> (He is at odds with his lord, and wishes to have the king on his side).
>
> The burgesses of Gloucester owe 30 marks of silver if they can recover through the justice of the king the money which was taken from them in Ireland.
> (They are enlisting the aid of royal diplomacy).
>
> Turgis of Avranches, renders account of 300 marks of silver and 1 mark of gold and 1 warhorse for the land and widow of Hugh d'Auberville, and to have wardship over his son until the latter is twenty years old.
> (Turgis is looking for profitable pickings from an estate in wardship; he will have to pay heavily for it).
>
> Lucy, countess of Chester, owes £266.13s.4d for the land of her father; also 500 marks that she need not take a husband inside five years. And the same lady owes 100 marks of silver that she may do justice in her court among her own men.
> (She has sought from the king a very special privilege: that though a woman she be allowed to manage the honor of Chester as its lord and not be consigned to a husband at the king's will; the price is high).

It should be explained that the amount stated as 'owed' is not the full amount of the original proffer unless it is a 'new agreement', that is to say that it has arisen in the current accounting year; if it is an 'old agreement' only the amount still outstanding at the beginning of the accounting year will appear on a Pipe Roll. Since there is only one surviving roll from Henry I's reign it is impossible to trace debts back to

25. *Pipe Roll 31 Henry I*, pp. 67, 77, 85, 106.

their origin. Those who entered into agreements to pay for the crown's help or for a privilege were allowed to pay in instalments often over many years. The Pipe Roll of 1129–30 records that £6045 had been collected on 'pleas and agreements' in the current year, amounting to about 25 per cent of the total brought in on all items of account of £24,608. It is the second most substantial item of revenue after the farms of the shire, which was 41 per cent of the total. But the amount still owed under 'pleas and agreements' was an astonishing £34,693, amounting to 50 per cent of all outstanding debts to the crown. The total amount of outstanding debt carried forward to the next year was £68,850. It was a convenient 'reserve' against contingencies; and the debts of numerous individuals kept them in leading strings.

The wholly new element which distinguishes Norman government from that of pre-Conquest kings is, as the Pipe Roll of 1129–30 clearly reveals, the exploitation of the crown's feudal lordship. There were two aspects to this. One is the sharing of rights which is characteristic of feudal lordship but which in the case of the crown was of far greater scope and magnitude than that of other feudal lords, for the king was lord of all. Even bishops were fief-holders of the crown, and when a bishop died the episcopal estates would be taken into the king's hands until a successor was appointed. Every great baronial honor would sooner or later have to yield to the crown's exploitation for no heir could enter upon the inheritance without doing homage and promising to pay an inheritance duty (the 'relief') fixed arbitrarily by the king. Estates with no heir reverted to the crown and could be rented out or sold off. Estates with an heir under age were in wardship, and the right could be turned to financial advantage by selling the wardship to the highest bidder. The marriages of widows and their daughters were for sale. There were numerous small ways in which the king could turn his lordship to profit, for confirmation of a charter, for example, for permission to fence off land to make a game preserve, for permission to assign land to a church, for permission to a vassal to arrange a marriage for one of his children. Conversely the king could levy penalties for breach of his rights, for example for marrying off a daughter without his prior assent.

The other aspect of exploitable feudal lordship was the crown's jurisdiction in all matters pertaining to fief-holding, for although the king's court was primarily a tribunal for settling disputes between his tenants-in-chief, it was also the resort for anyone who was unjustly treated by his lord, or could not obtain justice, or had a grievance for which there was no ready remedy. It might in theory be the duty of the king as feudal overlord to see that justice was done, but in practice his intervention was treated as a privilege for which the petitioner was expected to pay.

Those who rose to the rank of the king's chief minister were those who were most adept at turning royal authority to profit. Ranulf Flambard under William II was variously described by the chroniclers as 'chief manager of the king's wealth and justice', 'judge and tax collector of the whole of England', 'manager of the whole kingdom', 'chief agent of the king's will'.[26] But the effective exploitation of royal authority required not merely a manager but also an organization or at least some agencies through which to manage.

Central Government and Local Administration

The Household of the Norman kings did not, in most respects, differ greatly from that which had served William the Conqueror and his predecessors as dukes of Normandy. After the Conquest it served in both England and Normandy, for the king/duke did not switch from one set of household officers to another when he crossed the Channel: he took his Household with him. The titles of its officials derived from the traditional practice of the Frankish court; but its structure was similar to the household of any great lord, although its subordinate officials and lesser servants were more numerous.

The royal Household serviced the domestic, military, financial and leisure needs of the king and his court and performed some administrative functions almost as a sideline. There were five principal departments. That of the steward superintended the hall, the supply of provisions, the laundry, and the butchery. The butlery looked after the wines and the kitchens. The constabulary was the military side of the Household, and on campaigns the constables acted as quartermasters to the king's army; they also and more regularly superintended the stables and the hawks and hounds for the king's hunting; and under the subordinate office of the marshal provided the royal guard, the ushers, the watchmen who looked after the fires and the hornblowers. The Chamber saw to the king's personal needs, kept his moneys and valuables, and made payments on his behalf. The chapel was serviced by several chaplains who provided not only religious services but also, under a chief clerk, wrote whatever documents were required.

We should not exaggerate the importance of household officers in the counsels of the king and in the operations of government. They did not achieve the eminence, dignity and decisive role in administration of their counterparts in Germany. They were not usually men of high social standing, and though the king's benevolence raised them up it was rarely to the higher ranks of the feudal hierarchy. They were of

26. Southern, 'Ranulf Flambard', p. 184.

course close to the king and are the most regular witnesses to royal charters. In the counsels of the king they were overshadowed by the great men who frequented the court, and those, whether great or not, whom he chose to keep by him because he respected their advice and skills but who held no office. Government until at least the very end of the twelfth century operated as much through trusted men as through constituted offices.

A major change in the Household shortly after the Conquest was the development of the secretarial services under a chancellor. The dukes of Normandy had not needed to have much writing done for them and did not even have a seal. As kings of England they had to depend much more on written communications. The English seal was adopted and the English writ, for which more varied uses were found, until it became a protean device for almost all expressions of the king's will. The chancellors ascended to the first rank of household officials in terms of pay and perquisities and outclassed the others in the rewards of office – most of them being appointed to bishoprics.

Another development, less striking but equally significant, was on the financial side.[27] The Chamber had deposits of coin and valuables in convenient strongholds, but the main store of treasure in England was where it had been under English kings, at Winchester. From there the Chamber and its deposits were replenished as required under the superintendance of two chamberlains who each held a key to one of the two locks with which the treasure chests were secured. But as finance became big business under the Norman kings, the treasury became much more than a storehouse, regularly receiving payments due to the king, directly paying creditors on instructions from the Household, and keeping meticulous accounts. By Henry I's reign the two chamberlains were outranked by a new officer, the treasurer. The origins of the office are obscure. It may have been invented or have evolved as financial business became more sophisticated. The treasurer seems to have been thought of still at the end of Henry I's reign as a detached member of the Household, but he had by then become a specialist part of an administrative service separate from the Household. A major part of the treasurer's duties came to be the drawing up of the summonses to the sheriffs to a session of the exchequer, at which the treasurer himself examined the sheriff on the public debts. The summons specified in detail the debts both public and private for which the sheriff had to answer, and was the basis on which the audit was conducted.

The political union of Normandy and England was not an admini-

---

[27.] On the treasury see Richardson and Sayles, *Governance*, chapter XI, Hollister, 'The origins of the English treasury', Green, *Government under Henry I*, pp. 32-5.

strative union. The centre of government was the king's court wherever that might be, for that was where decisions were made, set into writing in the chancery and conveyed by the marshal's servants; but they were executed by administrative services separately managed in England and Normandy.

It seems to have been thought proper that when the king was out of England there should be a vicegerency of some kind. There was no consistency in the methods employed: sometimes members of the royal family were appointed as regents, sometimes a group of trusted counsellors, sometimes one.[28] Similarly when the king was in England ducal authority was deputed in Normandy. Inevitably the ruler was always absent from one or other of his dominions, sometimes for long periods. William the Conqueror was out of England for four years from 1076 to 1080. Henry I was twice out of England for a year, and twice for two years; altogether he spent more of his reign in Normandy than in England. But although the absences entailed the appointment of deputies they did not of necessity entail the development of separately managed administrative services. Absences did not mean that the ruler was out of touch. Efficient cross-Channel courier services were established; and Rouen and Caen were closer to London and Winchester than either London or Winchester was to York. And, in practice, although when the king was in Normandy he would deal with English business through appointed regents, he might by-pass them to act through a minister responsible for some particular aspect of royal business (whether or not he was also a regent), or even communicate directly with local agents. The real reason why there were separate administrative services was not the ruler's absences but the differences between the administrative structures and the sources of revenue in Normandy and England which could be effectively managed only by men on the spot who were knowledgeable about the ways they worked. So behind the regents or in association with them were a group of ministers who did not travel with the king but were permanently based in either England or Normandy to look after the king's business. They were usually men experienced in the king's service as former members of the Household, or counsellors or sheriffs. They held no formal office, but at least by the early years of Henry I's reign were officially addressed as 'barons of the exchequer' for they were authorized to attend its sessions. The king's foremost financial adviser presided at the exchequer sessions and was identified by the chroniclers as chief minister though it is not always clear that he had an overriding authority. For many years of Henry I's

---

28. F.J. West, *The Justiciarship in England* (Cambridge, 1966), chapter 1, D. Bates, 'The origins of the justiciarship', *Anglo-Norman Studies* 4 (1981), 1–12, Hollister, 'The rise of administrative kingship', pp. 873–7, Green, *Government under Henry I*, pp. 38–40.

reign it was Roger, bishop of Salisbury, and the king reposed so much confidence in him that after 1123 he was appointed sole regent during the king's absence. This has led some historians to equate him with the later 'chief justiciar' who had a formal function as the king's deputy and head of the administration; but it does not seem that an office crystallized about Roger. His remarkable authority was personal.[29]

Before the conquest of England the dukes of Normandy had conducted their ducal business directly as they perambulated their duchy; but in compartmentalized England the king's business was chiefly discharged by instructions conveyed in writs to the officers and men of the shires. Perambulation, though it remained the habit of rulers until the thirteenth century, was an inadequate method for extended dominions. The king's itinerary indeed rarely took him west of Bath, north of Northampton, or east of Huntingdon. Writs to the shire no longer sufficed to discharge the king's business after the former comprehensiveness of shire jurisdiction under the triumvirate of earl, bishop and sheriff was dissolved. The removal of the earl and the withdrawal of the bishop created a particular problem because their presence had been necessary for the proper hearing of the *regia placita*, those pleas which were reserved for royal jurisdiction. They could not be left to the supervision of the sheriff alone because he had a financial interest in the outcome, since the pecuniary penalties were part of the income for which he farmed the shire. The gap was filled by the appointment of 'local justiciars' to act as royal justices in the shires.[30] Usually, it seems, they were men of local prominence, though the evidence for everything about them apart from their existence is very meagre. Next to nothing is known of their supervision of major criminal pleas in the shires for that was not a matter of record. They emerge occasionally into the light in surviving royal writs authorizing them to discharge another function, that of hearing or taking action in civil pleas which had been brought to the king's attention by petitioners. Royal intervention in the operations of the feudal courts needed agents acting on royal authority. The fact that they required an authorizing writ to hear pleas shows that it was not a normal function of their office. Sometimes they were instructed to act jointly with the sheriff or other royal commissioners and to hold hearings in the shire court. It is difficult to speak precisely not only because of the paucity

[29]. E.J. Kealey, *Roger of Salisbury* (Berkeley, California, 1972), Green, *Government under Henry I*, chapter 3.

[30]. H.A. Cronne, 'The office of local justiciar in England under the Norman kings', *University of Birmingham Historical Journal* 6 (1958), 18–38; but see the reservations expressed by Hollister, 'The rise of administrative kingship', pp. 882–5, and Green, *Government under Henry I*, pp. 107–8. The duties of local justiciars in respect of crown pleas are demonstrated in R.F. Hunnisett, 'The origins of the office of coroner', *TRHS* 8 (1958), 89ff.

of the evidence but also because it was an era of expedients constantly varied.

It was presumably in order to remedy an unsatisfactory situation in the administration of justice in the king's name that the activities of the local justiciars came to be supplemented and perhaps even superseded by officials described by the chroniclers as 'justices of all England' with wide-ranging and permanent instead of *ad hoc* commissions.[31] Although the evidence is again too slight, they were clearly established by the middle years of Henry I's reign. Seven of the commissioners can be named with certainty, and another four with less confidence. They seem to have been empowered to hear all kinds of judicial business, and to cut into the jurisdiction of both sheriffs and local justiciars. A chronicler reports that in Leicestershire in 1124 Ralph Basset hanged 44 thieves, more than anyone could remember having been executed before, and to have had six men blinded and castrated.[32] It seems that he was engaged on a major drive against prevalent crime parallel to the prosecution of the moneyers by Roger of Salisbury. Significantly the financial proceeds of criminal pleas heard by a visiting royal justice had to be paid into the treasury and not appropriated by the sheriff. It is from the accounting details of such payments on the Pipe Roll of 1129–30 that the activities of visiting justices can be detected. How they operated is far from clear. Attempts to equate them with the later justices itinerant operating systematically with well-defined commissions of limited duration lack the support of firm evidence. What does seem unmistakable, however, is that this was an attempt to reinforce a defective local administration by carrying royal authority directly into the shires.

The visiting justices and the exchequer were separate but complementary means of centralizing control over the king's business in the shires. There was much more to the exchequer than the auditing of sheriffs' accounts. It was the necessary mechanism for co-ordinating the dispersed elements of the king's government. In essence an exchequer session was a joint meeting of members of the royal Household with those responsible for managing the king's business in England (with parallel sessions in Normandy). The chancellor, the two chamberlains, the constable and the marshal had appointed places at the exchequer table. As the treasurer's scribe made entries on the Pipe Roll at the treasurer's dictation, the chancellor's scribe wrote an identical version for the use of the Household. Much of the

31. W.J. Reedy, 'The origins of the general eyre in the reign of Henry I', *Speculum* 41 (1966), 688–724, and 'Were Ralph and Richard Basset really chief justiciars of England in the reign of Herny I?', *Twelfth Century*, *Acta* 2 (1975), 73–103, Hollister, 'The rise of administrative kingship', pp. 882–5, Green, *Government under Henry I*, pp. 108–10.
32. *The Anglo-Saxon Chronicle*, sub anno 1124.

business which came to audit orginated in the Household. From there issued instructions by writs to the sheriff to expend money from his farm on the king's business. He had to produce the writs at the exchequer to warrant his expenditure. These would then be checked against the chancery's copies, and only if all was in order would the sheriff be given his quittance. 'Pleas and agreements' usually originated in the king's court. A man seeking a favour would have to negotiate with the king's officers. When terms were agreed a record would be made of it in the chancery. The treasurer would then have to be notified so that he could enter it on the summons to the sheriff, for the summons was the sheriff's authorization to collect the debt. A clerk of the chancery took over the questioning of the sheriff when the private debts were reached, and with the aid of the chancery's records could check if the original intention had been properly carried out. There were two formal sessions of the exchequer each year at Easter and Michaelmas. At Michaelmas the Pipe Roll was drawn up and the year's account closed. At Easter there was a 'view of accounts' at which the sheriff paid in half the farm and reported any difficulties he had encountered in discharging his duties. It might be that a debtor had died, and the sheriff would have to be given fresh instructions to pursue payment from whoever held the estate. Recalcitrant debtors could be summoned before the exchequer and held in the custody of the marshal until they offered satisfaction. Aggrieved persons might appear before the exchequer board to complain, for instance, that they had not obtained the favour for which they were indebted, or that they were victims of official malfeasance. The exchequer was a judicial tribunal. As the *Dialogus* explains, 'the highest skill at the exchequer does not lie in calculations but in judgements of all kinds', and that only expert knowledge could determine 'whether the sheriffs have acted wrongly'.[33]

The division of the exchequer audit into two parts – the examination of the public debts conducted by the treasurer, and the examination of the private debts by the chancellor's clerk – is symbolic of the old and the new ways of revenue raising for the crown. The quest to raise money on a large scale by marketing the crown's prerogative to grant privileges, concessions and favours, had prompted Norman government to find ways of dealing effectively with individuals, instead of, as hitherto, of approaching the king's lesser subjects simply as members of communities. It was a major breakthrough not simply in revenue raising but in the art of government.

Henry I's government was precocious; but we should restrain admiration for it. It was not so much a matter of governing the realm

33. *Dialogus*, p. 15.

as of better management of the crown's interests. Its exploitation of feudal lordship was in many respects an unsavoury and abusive response to the failure to reform the geld. Ingenuity rather than reform is the hallmark of administrative developments under Henry I. Control of the far north was effectively established in his reign, but surprisingly it was not accompanied by the introduction of a shire organization. The Norman kings' neglect of reform in the structural organization of their realm is very striking and historically important for it meant the fossilization of the existing structure.

Contemporary monastic chroniclers were favourably disposed to Henry I because of the peace, order and justice which his rule brought. What they meant by 'justice' was that the church could protect its landed interests. Petitioners could be sure of a hearing because the exercise of royal jurisdiction was profitable. But at a time when much of the old law was dissolving, when jurisprudence was a subject of eager study in the schools, and church councils were addressing themselves to revision of ecclesiastical law and proce-dures, it is astonishing that there was no royal legislation in Eng-land. Change was afoot but it seems to have been unregulated. It was most marked in the direction of authoritarian prosecution of crime by royal officials without any of the customary safeguards against unsupported accusations.[34] This is how, it seems, government attem-pted to cope with the weakening of older forms of communal forms of peace-keeping and law enforcement. The author of the *Leges Henrici Primi* sharply criticized arbitrary innovations: 'to the greater confusion of all a new method of impleading is sought out, a new trick for inflicting injury is devised, as if too little damage follows from what has been done before, and he who does most harm to most people is valued the most highly.'[35] Bishop Hervey of Ely complained bitterly to King Henry I that everyone, rich and poor alike was afflicted with injurious persecution by the accusations of royal officials. The king's response was to grant to the church of Ely the privilege that its men should not be impleaded by official pro-secutors.[36] But the grant of a privilege was no substitute for adequate safeguards against official oppression and extortion. There was a failure both to lay down rules and to supervise adequately the activi-ties of the servants of sheriffs and local justiciars. Similarly, although the sheriffs were controlled in the sense that the king's govern-ment made sure that the king got what was due to him, there was no control or supervision of how sheriffs went about doing it. The only principle which operated, it seems, was what was to the king's advan-

---

34. Van Caenegem, 'Public prosecution of crime', pp. 41–76.
35. *Leges Henrici*, 6.4.
36. Van Caenegem, p. 56.

tage. The king's wealth was the product of a vast foraging operation; and his government, it had been aptly said, was 'predatory'.[37] Richard FitzNigel, Henry II's treasurer, writing in the *Dialogus* of the rules which operated in his day to control distraint upon a defaulting debtor's chattels, remarks that is was not always so: 'I myself, though not yet hoary-headed, have seen not only a lord's chattels lawfully sold for his personal debts, but those also of his knights and villeins.'[38]

Earlier historians made much of a remark by the chronicler Orderic Vitalis that under Henry I, 'Many illustrious men were snatched from the summit of exalted power and irremediably sentenced to the forfeiture of their inheritances; while others of lowly origin for their obsequious services were, so to speak, raised from the dust and exalted above counts and illustrious castellans and given multiple opportunities.'[39] It is necessary to qualify his assertions. There was nothing new in raising up useful servants; vigorous rulers were always doing it; and it has to be said that Henry I's cautious benevolence to his servants was outstripped by his lavish patronage of baronial families who supported his cause, and on whose political counsel he chiefly relied.[40] But that there was tension and resentment between the two sides of Henry I's government – the political and the administrative – can hardly be doubted. The history of the honor of Pontefract is instructive. It was held by the Lacy family, richly rewarded for services to William the Conqueror. After Henry I gained the throne by *coup d'état* Robert de Lacy was instrumental in holding the North for him, and exercised an authority which seems to have derived from holding the office of local justiciar or perhaps that of sheriff of Yorkshire. But about 1114, for reasons which are obscure, he incurred the king's disfavour and was banished from his English estates. Henry I then gave Pontefract to Hugh de Laval who controlled lands on the border between Normandy and Anjou and whose support was politically desirable. When Hugh died about 1129, King Henry sold his widow with her dowry to William Maltravers, an assiduous if not very distinguished servant of the crown, and granted him custody of the honor itself for 15 years. He had to pay the very heavy price of 1000 marks. He was a man of low social standing, did nothing to establish a favourable reputation in the honor, and seems, it has been said, to have been nothing more than 'a land speculator'. No sooner was King Henry I dead than Maltravers was murdered by a knight of the honor. Under Henry's successor, King Stephen, a veil was drawn over the crime and

[37.] Southern, 'Henry I', p. 231.
[38.] *Dialogus*, p. 112.
[39.] *The Ecclesiastical History of Ordericus Vitalis*, vi. 16–17.
[40.] B.McD. Walker, 'King Henry I's "old men" ', *Journal of British Studies* 8 (1968), 1–21, Hollister, pp. 889–90, Green, chapter 7.

the Lacys recovered Pontefract.[41] The hostility of the 'feudal' towards the 'official' elements of Henry I's entourage was to be the mainspring of change after his death.

---

41. W.E.Wightman, *The Lacy Family in England and Normandy* (Oxford, 1966), pp. 65–73.

Bibliographical Note

The Reign of King Stephen

R.H.C. Davis, *King Stephen 1135-1154* (London, 1967) and H.A. Cronne, *The Reign of Stephen 1135-1154* (London, 1970) are complementary; neither are responsible for the views expressed here. See also: F.M. Stenton, *The First Century of English Feudalism* (Oxford, 1937, 2nd ed., 1961), chapter VII; E. King, 'The anarchy of King Stephen's reign', *TRHS* 34 (1984), 133-53, and 'King Stephen and the Anglo-Norman aristocracy', *History* 59 (1974), 180-94; T. Callahan, 'The notion of anarchy in England 1135-1154: a bibliographical survey', *The British Studies Monitor* 6 (1976), 23-35. The principal source for royal government is *Regesta Regum Anglo-Normannorum*, 3, ed. H.A. Cronne and R.H.C. Davis (Oxford, 1968).

The Restoration of Royal Government

This topic is treated more fully in W.L. Warren, *Henry II* (London, 1973), chapter 7.

4
Alternative Forms of Government, 1135–1166

The Reign of King Stephen, 1135–1154

King Henry I, whose only legitimate son had been drowned in 1120, intended that he should be succeeded by his daughter Matilda, widow of Emperor Henry V of Germany, and remarried to Geoffrey, count of Anjou. In fact the succession was settled by a *coup d'état*. The throne was seized by the old king's nephew, Stephen, count of Mortain, and by Henry I's benevolence one of the greatest land-holders in England and Normandy. He was the son of William the Conqueror's sister, Adela, who had been married to the count of Blois to cement an alliance between Normandy and Blois. Stephen's elder brother, Theobald, had already succeeded to the countship; his other brother, Henry, was bishop of Winchester. Stephen was accepted, rather hastily, by the barons as a preferable alternative to Matilda and her husband. Matilda protested in vain at the court of Rome that they were all oath-breakers, and Stephen an usurper. But although Stephen was accepted by the barons, and recognized as king by a cautious papacy, he was only briefly in undisputed control. It was not easy for him to satisfy the aspirations of the diverse interest groups which tried to get his support by offering him theirs, and he became, though capriciously, a tool of faction. Matilda had hopes of turning the tables. Her major asset was the decision by her half-brother, Robert, earl of Gloucester, to champion her cause. He was the most distinguished and powerful of the old king's bastards. What ensued was a struggle which in one respect was a contest between the grandchildren of the Conqueror for the throne of England, and in another was a struggle between the house of Blois and the house of Anjou for control of Normandy.

Matilda attracted some of those who were indebted to her father, and those whose hopes Stephen failed to satisfy, but never enough influential support among the barons to achieve an ascendancy. Stephen lost control of parts of England, mainly in the west, and had to suffer the humiliation of an outlying stronghold held for Matilda far down the Thames at Wallingford; but the allegiance of the majority of the barons was generally very steady and he usually held the military initiative. He suffered one disaster: while trying to curb the ambitions of the earl of Chester in the Midlands he was defeated at the battle of Lincoln and held captive for nine months. He bore his reverse with fortitude and dignity, while Matilda behaved with the imperious arrogance which confirmed the fears of those who had never wanted her on the throne.

Matilda's husband, Geoffrey, count of Anjou, played no part in the civil war in England. He concentrated his campaigning efforts on Normandy, and after a dour struggle lasting 10 years conquered it, and was recognized as duke by the king of France. King Louis VII hardly knew which side to support: for two generations the Capetians had allied with Anjou against the alliance of Normandy with Blois; but Henry I's strategem for buying off the hostility of Anjou had been deeply alarming. King Louis married his sister to King Stephen's son Eustace; but in recognizing Geoffrey of Anjou as duke of Normandy, he was happy to accept a *fait accompli* which looked like separating Normandy from England. So indeed it must had appeared after the death of Earl Robert of Gloucester in 1147. Matilda virtually abandoned the attempt to dislodge a Stephen restored to freedom and general support, and retired to Normandy. Her supporters in England were hard pressed to defend themselves, and some drifted back to the king. The situation was dramatically changed by the appearance on the scene of the young son of Matilda and Geoffrey – Henry of Anjou. He revealed himself as courageous, enterprising, a born leader of men, and above all determined to secure the 'rights' which the 'usurper' Stephen was denying him. In his earliest charters he described himself as 'Henry, son of the daughter of King Henry, and right heir of Normandy and England'.[1] Geoffrey astutely handed over Normandy to Henry in 1149 when he was 16, for the Normans could more readily bear the rule of a descendant of the ducal house than that of a conquering Angevin. Geoffrey, retiring to Anjou, died unexpectedly in September 1151, and the young Henry became count of Anjou as well as duke of Normandy. A few months later he married Eleanor, duchess in her own right of Aquitaine, and the cast-off wife of King Louis VII. In her name Henry became overlord of the sprawling duchy of Aquitaine which embraced most of France south of the Loire.

These developments were decisive for the barons in England. Most of them held lands in Normandy which, even if less profitable than their English estates, were esteemed as their patrimony. So long as it seemed possible that King Stephen's loss of Normandy could be

[1] *Recueil des Actes de Henri II*, ed. L. Delisle and E. Berger (Paris, 1906–27), i. 6ff, *Regesta*, iii, no. 635.

reversed they could bear the temporary inconvenience of a divided allegiance; but with the emergence of Henry of Anjou as overlord of much of France, his control of Normandy began to look permanent. The arguments which had swayed them in supporting Stephen against Matilda, did not extend to supporting Stephen's son, Eustace, against Matilda's son, Henry. Duke Henry forced them to reappraise their position by landing in England in 1153. His forces were by no means formidable, even with the support of some who took a chance on declaring for him. The majority of the barons stood by the allegiance to King Stephen but were very reluctant to confront Henry's challenge by fighting him. Honour was satisfied and the reunion of England and Normandy assured by a sensible compromise: Stephen was to hold the throne of England until his death, and Henry was to succeed him.

King Stephen's reign has commonly been characterized as period of 'weak' government. For this some historians have held King Stephen responsible. He was a man more of the stamp of the Conqueror's eldest son, Robert Curthose, than of William II or Henry I. He preferred to be liked rather than feared, and respected for his martial arts and open-handed generosity than for stern rule. He is said to have had no settled policy, to have shifted irresolutely from expedient to expedient, and to have baulked at hard decisions. He allowed himself to be manipulated by those at court with stronger wills, and his affability was exploited by the greedy and the power-hungry. Other historians have exonerated Stephen from at least part of the responsibility for faltering government by pointing to the difficulties of his position. His title to the throne was tainted by perjury and his hold on it seriously challenged. He had to court popularity to hold off the challenge, and the obvious way was to relax the harshness of his predecessor's rule. Since he could not be sure of the loyalty of Henry I's administrative servants he had to rely on friends and reward them handsomely, and it was only prudent to win waverers with concessions and favours. Civil war dislocated the normal operations of government and loosened central control over the localities. It was an understandable if unwise response to the situation to put responsibility for keeping order into the hands of those who had territorial power.

Neither of these lines of argument is entirely convincing. Stephen was certainly less ruthless than his predecessors and prone to take the path of least resistance; but he was doggedly successful in his defence of his throne and there is no reason to believe that he was any less resolute in defence of his kingly status. He fended off those who sought to manipulate him; and although he favoured some barons, building up their territorial power and conferring offices upon them, he obstructed the ambitions of others. His insecurity has been exaggerated. He could count on the loyalty of the majority of his barons even in adversity. The civil war was intermittent and left much of the realm untroubled. It is true that royal government under Stephen was reduced in scope, vigour and effectiveness; but it cannot be assumed that either through incompetence or preoccupation with political problems it simply atrophied. Had that been so his successor would have needed only to revitalize it; in fact he found it necessary to reconstruct it. An interpretation of Stephen's rule which better fits the facts is that he deliberately pursued a policy of decentralization, and the case for it will here be argued. With hindsight Stephen's reign may be seen as an interruption in the development of royal government; but it should not lightly be dismissed as a hiatus for it is particularly interesting in offering not simply a different style but a different form of government.

There are no surviving records of government from King Stephen's reign, indirect evidence from charters and chronicles is neither plentiful nor easy to interpret, and much has to be inferred from the problems encountered by his successor. Nevertheless it is possible to identify two features which marked a significant change from the policy of his predecessor. One is an upgrading of the role of the earl (who still, in the terminology and understanding of the period was a 'count'). The number of earls increased markedly. There were seven at the beginning of the reign; Stephen created new earldoms freely, and made 19 appointments, and not simply to confer honorific titles and enhanced status upon his supporters. There are clear signs that, in principle, at least, each shire or county (*comitatus*) was to have an earl or count (*comes*) who was to be both its military and administrative head. The earl was to exercise real power in right of office, and even more through control over the county sheriff and local justiciar. Several of the new earls had previously been sheriffs, and some even retained shrieval office after being given an earldom.[2] The other notable feature, which may be seen as a corollary of the first, was a downgrading of the role of central government. This may be detected not merely in a reduced scale of activity, but also in the lower status of Stephen's chief officials. None of them achieved the prominence of their predecessors under Henry I, and none were as richly rewarded. Roger of Salisbury had no successor as royal surrogate. No more is heard of the 'justices of all England' at least as a regularly functioning group of experts. Stephen undoubtedly had royal justices who could act for him in any part of England under his control; but they were few in number and seem to have been seconded for a special purpose from other duties. Most of the royal justices who had served Henry I went over to Matilda sooner or later.[3] Taken together these two develop-

---

[2.] Cronne, *Reign of Stephen*, pp. 138–47, 149, Davis, *King Stephen*, pp. 32–3 and Appendix 1.
[3.] Cronne, pp. 202, 269.

ments bespeak a shift of executive power from the centre to the provinces.

It might be supposed that these developments were simply a practical response to a state of war, which required that 'civil authorities' be subordinated to military governors; that a king preoccupied with saving his throne had of necessity to entrust wider executive functions to those with effective power in the localities; and that it was prudent to reward those on whose loyalty he needed to rely. But although the state of war undoubtedly hastened the trend it cannot be said to have begun it. It is true that the onset of civil war saw a spate of new earldoms created by King Stephen, but these should be seen as the urgent culmination of a process already set in train from the beginning of the reign. As early as 1137 the creation of an earldom of Bedford for Hugh de Poer, a member of the influential Beaumont family, provoked the rebellion of Miles de Beauchamp, sheriff of the county, who refused to surrender Bedford castle and had to be besieged.[4] This strongly suggests that a real transfer of power from sheriff to earl was involved, not merely the bestowal of an honorific title. Moreover, the crucial event in the downgrading of the central administration occurred three months before Matilda landed in England to pursue her challenge for the throne. In June 1139 Roger of Salisbury, still head of the administrative service in England as in Henry I's day, and his nephews, who between them controlled the chancery, treasury and exchequer, were arrested on patently trumped up charges and freed only on condition that they resigned their offices and surrendered their castles. It is commonly argued that their loyalty could not be trusted, and they had to be removed in anticipation of Matilda's challenge; but if so it was rash and counterproductive. It alienated the ecclesiastical authorities, for three of them were bishops; it provoked distrust of the king among the rest of those in the royal service; and it raised Matilda's hopes of a major desertion of Stephen. It must instead be seen as a move intended from the beginning and delayed only until it could be conveniently contrived. It is significant that the dismissed officials were not replaced by men of equal standing, influence and authority. The royal seal was changed.[5] It was the proclamation of a new dispensation.

The creation of earldoms for virtually every shire involved something more than interposing a military governor between the central government and its local agents. Of the greatest significance is the way that the new earls addressed themselves to 'their' counties.[6] Typical is the following salutation of an earl's charter:

[4.] *Gesta Stephani*, ed. and translated by K.R. Potter (London, 1955), pp. 31, 33, 77, Stenton, *First Century*, pp. 235–7, Cronne, pp. 141, 172.
[5.] Cronne, pp. 94–8, Davis, pp. 31–2, and for an illustration of the seal facing p. 52.
[6.] On the nature of the earldoms in Stephen's reign, Davis, pp. 129–32, and Appendix 1.

Roger, earl (*comes*) of Warwick to all his barons and his sheriff, bailiffs and ministers, and his tax collectors (*collectores*) of Warwickshire, greeting. . .[7]

Here is implied a conception of the earl as surrogate for the king ruling an autonomous county, which was certainly novel in the context of earlier post-Conquest 'earldoms', but normal in contemporary Germany or Italy or France. What was involved in the shift of power from central to local control was an alternative conception of government. It should not be seen as forced upon a weak, incompetent king under the stress of war but as a deliberate choice by Stephen and his preferred advisers among the greater barons (of whom he had himself until recently been one). It was a conscious rejection of the trend towards centralization, bureaucracy and government by servants of the state.

It is significant that Matilda found the new policy irresistible. Though she showed respect to her father's servants, she too created earldoms freely, some in direct competition with King Stephen's creations. In her brief period of ascendancy she confirmed to Geoffrey de Mandeville, earl of Essex, custody of the Tower of London and the offices of justice and sheriff of London and Middlesex; and she granted him the office of justice in Essex and Hertfordshire, and permission to build a castle anywhere on his lands.[8] We should not see this simply as a matter of baronial greed nor merely as a baronial reaction against the centralization of control in the hands of Henry I's officials. It may be observed that in ecclesiastical circles there was a comparable opposition to the trend towards centralization in church government as in many respects an unwarranted invasion of traditional local authority. A polemicist of Henry I's time spoke up strongly for a decentralized church of episcopal equals, and disapproved of direct intervention by the papacy in the life of local churches.[9] Until well into the reign of Henry II there was sentiment even among church reformers against the undermining of the authority of the bishops in their dioceses by what could be regarded as wanton appeals to higher authority.[10] On the other hand there seems to have been growing unease at the policy of putting local govenment into the hands of some great magnates. It too readily fostered partisanship, and obliged those who did not have the favour of the local earl and his friends to defend their interests or pursue their ambitions by resort to arms. Private war did more to

---

[7.] *Ibid*, p. 131, with other examples.

[8.] *Regesta*, iii. 274–5.

[9.] F. Barlow, *The English Church 1066–1154* (London, 1979), pp. 293, 296.

[10.] W.L. Warren, *Henry II* (London, 1973), pp. 442–4.

undermine Stephen's kingship than civil war. There was, if not a breakdown of law and order, a widespread belief that law and order were not impartially enforced, and that justice was a casualty not so much of war as of royal inertia. Henry I began to seem, in retrospect, a 'lion of justice.' Even Battle Abbey, the Norman war memorial for the victory at Hastings, had acute difficulty in defending its property against the encroachments of petty local landlords who enjoyed protection in the right places. The abbey's chronicler did not mince his words: 'Stephen became king but his justice was little regarded and he who was strongest got most.'[11]

Even the strongest began to have second thoughts. The most richly endowed barons had the most widely dispersed estates, and it was not easy to protect widespread interests simultaneously. Particularly instructive is the example of Robert de Beaumont, earl of Leicester. He and his twin brother Waleran, count of Meulan, were the sons of Robert of Meulan, the confidant of Henry I, and had been brought up at the royal court. They were friends of Stephen of Blois and the principal influence upon him in the early years of the reign. They and other members of the family were among the earliest recipients of his favours, and Waleran was the prime mover in the downfall of Roger of Salisbury and his clan of administrators. In their competition with the earl of Chester for control of the Midlands they had the support of King Stephen and it led him to the disaster at Lincoln. Thereafter Earl Robert tried to limit the civil war by arranging private treaties with a network of earls on both sides of the political divide; the most striking was a treaty with the earl of Chester.[12] When Henry of Anjou landed in England in 1153 Earl Robert went over to him; it was a major factor in obliging King Stephen to a compromise peace. It must not be supposed that in agreeing to have Henry of Anjou as king the barons were abandoning their preference for the kind of government Stephen had offered them; they probably expected that Henry would be preoccupied with his widespread continental dominions and would be obliged to defer to their wishes. But enough of them, it seems, were prepared to see a restoration of effective royal authority. Earl Robert of Leicester himself presided at a restored exchequer.

The Restoration of Royal Government, 1154-1166

Henry II (1154-1189) made no secret of his intention to rule as his grandfather had done. At every opportunity he let it be known that what has been customary in Henry I's day was to be the touchstone of

11. *The Chronicle of Battle Abbey*, ed. E.Searle (Oxford, 1980), p. 212.
12. Stenton, *First Century*, pp. 249-52.

what was right and proper. The chronicler of Battle Abbey described the policy succinctly as 'the restoration of ancestral times'; the author of the *Dialogus de Scaccario* called it 'renewing the golden days of his grandfather'.[13] But how much 'restoration' or 'renewal' was necessary is a perplexing question which has long divided historians.

In principle there was clear policy that all grants by the 'usurper', Stephen, were invalid; but in practice some accommodation with recipients was politically unavoidable. So far as the incidental consequences of the time of disorder were concerned less temporizing was necessary, and the relentless pursuit of usurped royal property and perquisites was the counterpart to the restoration to their rights of subjects who had been unable to defend their own. The hearing of pleas of the deprived was a major occupation of Henry II in the early years of his reign, and the settlement of complaints earned for him a reputation for strict justice. This is what contemporaries regarded as the justification for strong monarchy, and is probably what the chronicler of Battle Abbey meant by 'ancestral times'.

The harder questions to answer about restoration are how much damage had been done to the administrative institutions of royal government, and how seriously royal authority had itself been undermined. Chroniclers of Stephen's reign give graphic examples of the breakdown of royal government; but their evidence is not easy to interpret. In particular it is difficult to determine whether the alleged breakdown was general and persistent, or localized and confined to particular periods of the reign.[14] The documentary evidence, on the other hand, though insufficient for a definitive judgement, suggests that Stephen's administration did not differ markedly from that of Henry I. It certainly indicates that King Stephen had a small but efficient secretariat which issued writs in the same peremptory tones as his predecessor, that officials acting in his name heard pleas in the shires, and that it is probable that exchequer sessions were held. But the surviving evidence is not incompatible with the view that executive power had shifted to the provinces under the authority of the earls, with the king retaining direct responsibility for those matters which transcended provincial administration, and the residual authority to intervene in response to petitioners. How effective his intervention was must remain an open question.

Although the available evidence does not allow us to see government at work under Stephen, there is sufficient relating to the coinage and to the exchequer to allow us to appraise the situation confronting Henry II. The chronicler William of Malmesbury alleges that

---

13. *Chronicle of Battle Abbey*, p. 213, *Dialogus*, p. 77.
14. Discussed by King, 'The anarchy of Stephen's reign', pp. 133–53.

under Stephen the coinage became utterly untrustworthy not only because of widespread counterfeiting but also because of a deliberate policy of debasement; but surviving examples of Stephen's coins cannot be said to give credence to his accusations.[15] There were indeed fluctuations in weight but not more marked that in Henry I's time; and although there may have been a period of lightweight coins in the middle of the reign, Stephen's first and last issues were as good as the best since the Conquest. Moreover, there were seven distinct issues with changes of design which argues that the established practice of frequent recoinages was maintained. The most serious criticism is not that Stephen debased the coinage but that he failed to uphold the principle that only the king's money should circulate in the realm. It was understandable and perhaps necessary that Empress Matilda and her adherents should have had coins struck for districts under their control; but in the areas supposedly subject to Stephen's jurisdiction at least four magnates are known to have had coins struck to distinctive designs and bearing their own names, with a strong possibility that several more did so.[16] At the official mints the dies from which coins were struck bearing the king's head were supplied by the crown; but who controlled the moneyers? The traditional practice was that the moneyers were licensed by the crown and supervised by the sheriffs. Stephen, however, is known to have granted to two bishops and one abbot the right to appoint their own moneyers, and it may reasonably be suspected that some of the moneyers in the county boroughs passed, whether by grant or not, under the control of the earls, together with the profits of exchanging old money for new. In the third year of Henry II's reign the coinage was overhauled. New dies were issued for coins bearing the new king's image, and a new uniform type for the whole realm re-established; but it seems that it was not thought opportune to reassert total royal management of the coinage. For over 12 years the design of the coins remained unchanged, and during that time the number of licensed mints was allowed to decline from about 30 to 10, so that it became no longer normal for a county borough to have a mint, and control of the local mint could no longer be a valued perquisite. Then in 1180 there was a radical reform of the whole system. At the surviving mints new buildings were erected to house 'royal exchanges' (*cambii regis*). The production of coins was divorced from the business of exchanging worn coins for new of good weight. The moneyer was a craftsman who contracted for the job of striking coins, but the exchanger was a royal official and the profits of exchanging passed to the royal treasury. New dies were issued to a

[15]. *Historia Novella*, ed. and translated by K.R. Potter (London, 1955) p.42; Stephen's coinage is discussed by Cronne, *Reign of Stephen*, pp. 236-44.
[16]. Cronne, p. 241.

much improved design, and thereafter the type of coin remained unchanged not merely until the end of Henry II's reign but right through the next two reigns also – for a total of 67 years.[17] The decision to adopt the continental custom of an unchanging coin type, and to abandon the traditional English practice of frequent recoinages, with the demonetizing of the previous issue, may suggest a less sophisticated attitude to the management of the coinage; but there was a major justification for it in the fostering of international trade. A consistent type of reliable quality could become more widely recognized and accepted; and after 1180 English coins did in fact become the major trading currency of northern Europe, setting a standard which the coinages of other countries sought to emulate.[18]

So Henry II did restore effective royal control of the profitability of coining; but the length of time taken to do it suggests that the consequences of Stephen's reign were not easily overcome. Stephen had upheld, so far as he could, the principles that the crown should license mints, issue coins and prescribe standards; but practice had fallen short of principle, and he had, it seems likely, relinquished control of local minting and the profits of exchanging. It may be observed that in re-establishing a royal monopoly Henry II did not simply 'restore ancestral times': the traditional practices were reviewed and major changes were introduced. In this respect the history of the coinage was to typify Henry II's approach to government as a whole.

Sessions of the exchequer may have been held in Stephen's reign, but there is good reason to believe that they were no more than a shadow of exchequer sessions under Henry I. Unless an entirely new financial system were to be introduced, exchequer sessions were necessary at the very least for the review of sheriffs' accounts of revenue due to the crown from royal manors and perquisites in the shires. Allowances would have to be made for grants which the king made from royal estates, and for the expenditure which sheriffs incurred in attending to royal business; that exchequer sessions under Stephen involved anything more than this is extremely unlikely. Although there are no exchequer records surviving from Stephen's reign to prove the point, those from the early years of the next reign make such a conclusion inescapable. The early Pipe Rolls of Henry II are both slim and limited in scope. They deal almost exclusively with the county farms, with *murdrum* fines, and with the proceeds of geld and the 'gifts' tendered by counties and boroughs. There was no carry over of debts in respect of 'proffers and agreements' from the previous reign, and several years elapsed before items under this heading comparable

17. On Henry II's coinage see D.F. Allen, *A Catalogue of English Coins in the British Museum: The Cross-and-Crosslets Type of Henry II* (London, 1951), Warren, *Henry II*, pp. 264–5.
18. J. Porteus, *Coins in History* (London, 1969), p. 71.

to those of Henry I's day reappear. In comparison with the Pipe Roll of 1130 the early rolls of Henry II appear uncertain and incompetent; and although there was a steady improvement it was not until the eleventh year of the reign that ancestral practice could be said to have been fully restored. The earlier Pipe Rolls, indeed, fully support the contention of the author of the *Dialogus de Scaccario* that 'the science (*scientia*) of the exchequer had almost perished during the long years of civil war'.[19]

The *scientia* of which Richard FitzNigel speaks had many facets. One of them may be termed 'know how'. He reports that Nigel, bishop of Ely, (his father), who had been treasurer under Henry I and dismissed by Stephen, had been matchless for his knowledge of exchequer practice, and had to be recalled at the urgent entreaty of Henry II to help in restoring it.[20] Stephen probably paid dearly for the dismissal of Bishop Roger of Salisbury and Bishop Nigel of Ely, for the expertise of the exchequer was lodged in their experience. The *Dialogus de Scaccario*, written in 1178, was the first attempt to put such experience into writing. The prologue explains that one of the treasurer's colleagues said to him one day: 'Why do you not teach others that knowledge of the exchequer for which you are famous, and have it written down lest it die with you?' The author demurred: 'Why brother, you have long sat at the exchequer yourself and nothing is hidden from you, for you are so precise; and the same must be true of others who sit there.' But the other was well aware of the limitations of oral tradition and learning by apprenticeship, and countered: 'But as those who grope in the dark without light often stumble, so there are many who seeing do not see, and hearing do not understand.'[21] Here was the new attitude to the transmission of experience bred in the Schools, which would have surprised the older generation of administrators, and from which Stephen's servants could not benefit. The *scientia* was not simply a matter of accounting practice; it included what the *Dialogus* calls 'the customs and laws of the exchequer' – that experience crystallized into customary rules or formulated into ordinances – in which the author says 'the more noble, valuable and esoteric science of the exchequer consists'.[22]

For those who constituted the exchequer board – the 'barons' as they were termed – the application of the *scientia* had to be supported with up-to-date information if the king's best interest were to be served: information, for example, about the state and profitability of royal manors, about estates which reverted ('escheated') to the crown

[19.] *Dialogus*, p. 50, G.J. Turner, 'The sheriff's farm', *TRHS*, new series, 12 (1898), pp. 127–31.
[20.] *Dialogus*, p. 50, cf. pp. 2–3.
[21.] *Ibid.*, p. 5.
[22.] *Ibid.*, p. 65.

for default of heirs, about the value to be put on baronial inheritances, about widows and heiresses, and minors in the king's gift, about Jewish moneylenders, for after their deaths the crown took over their loan accounts. The quest for information, and with it a firmer grip on the crown's rights, was a marked feature of the period of restoration. Barons of the exchequer, including household officers such as the chancellor and the constable, went out into the shires. The full scope of their activities is hidden from us, but their visitations left incidental traces on the Pipe Rolls, from the payments they authorized for the re-stocking of royal manors, and from the financial penalties they levied in the shire courts as they took over the hearing of pleas of the crown.[23]

There were two notable systematic inquiries. The first, beginning early in the reign and lasting for several years, was conducted by special commissioners who sought through the testimony of local men to re-establish the full extent of royal estates, recovering what had been lost through the grants of King Stephen and the carelessness of sheriffs in failing to prevent encroachments on royal property.[24] The second, in 1166, turned a spotlight on estates which were held from the crown as fiefs. The king required his barons to supply the names of their sub-tenants holding by knight-service. The crown already knew how much knight-service each tenant-in-chief owed, but many barons had created more tenancies by knight-service than they needed to discharge their military obligation. They had done so for various reasons: it might be that a large retinue of knights was deemed fitting for their dignity, it might be that other military commitments such as the constant garrisoning of castles required more knights than they had to render for royal campaigns; but more commonly they were simply responding to the desire of their deserving retainers and kinsfolk to be rewarded with the more honourable form of land tenure. One purpose of the inquiry was, as the return of the archibishop of York noted, 'because you wish to know if there are any who have not done you allegiance'.[25] This was an important reaffirmation of the principle established by William I in the oath taken at Salisbury in 1086 that homage to a lord could not override allegiance to the crown. It is probable that under William II and Henry I, but only laxly or not at all under Stephen, all those newly entering upon homage to the lord had to swear allegiance to the king, and that their names were enrolled. But there was another purpose to Henry II's inquiry. The information about sub-fiefs gave the crown a fair indication of the feudal resources of an honor, so enabling a realistic price to be put upon it when charging *relief* to an heir, putting it out to wardship, or

23. Warren, *Henry II*, pp. 284–5.
24. *Ibid.*, pp. 61–2, 273–4, cf. *Dialogus*, p. 93.
25. *EHD* ii. 906, followed by other examples.

marketing an heiress. Moreover, if by reason of escheat, or forfeiture or wardship an honor came into the hands of the crown, all the fief-holders on it became liable to the exchequer for the feudal dues which they would previously have rendered to their lord.[26]

Restoration took more than a decade; but it would be unreasonable to take this length of time as a measure of Stephen's laxity for it was also a consequence of political circumstances. The civil war had not ended in a victory for either side. Henry II had to enlist the co-operation of those who had supported Stephen if the realm were to be at peace. Resolving disputes between the grantees of Stephen and Matilda, and restoring those who had been despoiled in the time of disorder were probably the most delicate problems confronting him in the early years of his reign; but they had to compete for his attention with even more pressing political problems in his continental dominions. In the first eight years of his reign Henry II was in England for no more than 17 months, and most of that in one spell from April 1157 to August 1158. He did not thereafter set foot in England again, so far as is known, until January 1163. He was not of course out of touch, and was often in Normandy within convenient reach of ministers and messengers; but given the huge size of his continental dominions, his peripatetic habit, and the difficulties and hazards of land travel at the time, the government of England had to be able to function without him.

A man left in charge was Robert de Beaumont, earl of Leicester. The author of the *Dialogus de Scaccario*, who served under him, described him as 'a man of sound judgement, well-educated, expe-rienced in legal business, and by nature strong-minded'. Henry II, he adds, who was acute at discerning a man's inner qualities, 'had such high regard for him that he appointed him to preside not only over the exchequer but also over the whole kingdom'.[27] When the queen was in England in the king's absence writs were issued in her name on the king's behalf; but when she too was absent Earl Robert had authority to act in his own name. It does not seem that he was accorded an official title; nor had Bishop Roger of Salisbury when he deputized for Henry I. In Henry II's continental dominions, in Normandy for example, or Anjou, there was already a well-established office of deputy with the title of *senescallus*, a seneschal, or in English parlance a steward. Every great lord had a steward who supervised the manage-ment of his estates and collected his revenues. As duke of Normandy and count of Anjou Henry II was himself a great lord; but in England he was a king and the deputy of a king was something different from

26. Warren, *Henry II*, pp. 275–7, T.K. Keefe, *Feudal Assessments and the Political Community under Henry II and his sons* (Berkeley, California, 1983).
27. *Dialogus*, pp. 57–8.

the deputy of a great lord. Earl Robert's successors as chief minister, who acted as regent in the king's absence, were styled 'justiciar'; but Earl Robert's authority was not quite so extensive as that of later justiciars. He could hear judicial proceedings, but could not initiate them, nor pronounce a final judgement except on the express orders of the king at the request of a plaintiff. In the recorded writs which he issued he conveyed instructions 'by order of the king from overseas'. Moreover, his authority was not undivided: he had a colleague in Richard de Luci, a man like himself of the fief-holding laity but of very different background. Robert de Beaumont had been born into the highest rank of the baronage and had been brought up in the entourage of King Henry I. His grandfather was already count of Meulan before being given the earldom of Leicester by Henry I. Richard de Luci was born into the lower end of the feudal hierarchy of a relatively humble knightly family. He was however rising rapidly in feudal society and acquiring favours and fiefs which were to elevate him to the baronage by making himself useful to greater men and especially to the king. He had served King Stephen loyally and when Henry II came to the throne was constable of the Tower of London and of Windsor castle. Whether there was a formal division of authority between the two colleagues is not clear; but Richard de Luci was to prove himself an able administrator and it seems likely that he was the overseer of the administrative service while Earl Robert performed the more public functions of royal deputy. In appointing the two to act for him, with the well-born earl taking the lead, and neither of them open to the charge of being the young king's creature or crony, Henry II seems deliberately to have been avoiding creating another Bishop Roger, whose viceregal authority and clan of clerical administrators had provoked hostility among the baronage. Earl Robert and Richard de Luci were intermediaries of royal authority not substitutes for a king.[28]

If in this respect the young Henry II was cautious about following his grandfather too closely, and was prepared to repose his confidence and his government in an earl, there can be no doubt of his determination to reduce earldoms to the status they had had in his grandfather's day. A direct assault upon entrenched local power would have been foolhardy, but the policy was resolute and applied whenever opportunity offered. It was the same for his mother's creations as for Stephen's. Those earldoms which were as yet weakly established, or whose holders had no claim upon his favour or forbearance were simply not recognized. Others were allowed to lapse when their first

---

[28.] F. West, *The Justiciarship in England, 1066–1232* (Cambridge, 1966), pp. 31–45, D. Crouch, *The Beaumont Twins* (Cambridge, 1986), pp. 89–95.

holder died. Ten of the earldoms created by Stephen or Matilda disappeared. Those earldoms which survived were shorn of governmental powers. Not even Earl Robert's family were exempt. One of the earldoms to lapse was that of Worcester created for his twin brother, Waleran, count of Meulan. Another was the earldom of Bedford created for his younger brother Hugh. Earl Robert himself was denied that control of 'the city, castle, and the whole county of Hertfordshire' which Stephen had granted him in 1140. This consistent and resolute policy must, more than anything else at the time, have spelled the restoration of royal authority over the government of the realm.[29]

29. *Regesta*, iii. 437, Warren, *Henry II*, pp. 364–5.

Bibliographical Note

The Transformation of Royal Government

The arguments presented in this chapter are discussed more fully in W.L. Warren, *Henry II* (London, 1973), chapter 9. J. Boussard, *Le Gouvernement d'Henri II Plantagenêt* (Paris, 1956) is a storehouse of information. On legal developments see also: R.C. Van Caenegem, *Royal Writs in England from the Conquest to Glanvill* (Selden Society, 1959), *The Birth of the English Common Law* (Cambridge, 1973), and 'Public prosecution of crime in twelfth-century England' in *Church and Government in the Middle Ages*, ed. C.N.L. Brooke, D.E. Luscombe, G.H. Martin, and D.M. Owen (Cambridge, 1976), pp.41–76; N.D. Hurnard, 'The jury of presentment and the Assize of Clarendon', *EHR* 56 (1941), 374–410; F.W. Maitland, *Forms of Action at Common Law*, ed. A.H. Chaytor and W.J. Whitaker (Cambridge, 1936); D.M. Stenton, *English Justice between the Norman Conquest and the Great Charter, 1066–1215* (London, 1965).

5

The Transformation of Royal Government *c.*1166–*c.*1180

After his prolonged absences from his kingdom in the first decade of his reign, King Henry II spent almost the whole period from January 1163 to March 1166 in England, with only one short break of a few weeks in Normandy. To contemporary chroniclers it was a period chiefly notable for a campaign against the Welsh, and the notorious quarrel between the king and his former chancellor, now archbishop of Canterbury, Thomas Becket; but the king's chief concern was with the state of the realm and its governance. Those years saw the culmination of restoration, and major changes in the criminal law and in how it was to be applied. The quarrel with the archbishop itself reflected the king's concern with the governance of the realm. Becket's first public defiance of the king was over a proposal at the council of Woodstock in 1163 to enhance the royal revenue from the shires.[1] The quarrel found a focus in the vexed question of the appropriate punishment for members of the clergy who were guilty of serious crime. The king's response to claims to greater autonomy by the ecclesiastical authorities was to call for a reaffirmation of the customs of his grandfather's day, set out in the 'Constitutions of Clarendon' of 1164. Indeed, at a deeper level of the quarrel it may be said that the king was seeking to reassert royal control over the bishops as he had over the earls. It should, however, be observed that in the clause of the Constitutions which dealt with criminous clerks the king did not insist on a return to past practice, but proposed a novel compromise whereby the ecclesiastical courts were to try accused clergy but were to hand over those found guilty to the secular authorities for punishment.[2] As with the reform of the coinage the reassertion of old principles of royal control was not thought to be incompatible with innovations in practice.

With hindsight many historians have believed that the measures taken in these years to reform the state of the realm inaugurated a line

[1.] Discussed by J.A. Green, 'The last century of danegeld', *EHR* 96 (1981), 255–7.
[2.] Constitutions of Clarendon, cl. 3, *EHD* ii. 719–20, Warren, *Henry II*, p. 481.

of development which was to transform royal government. The change was indeed astonishing. Early Norman royal government, from the time of the Conquest, had intervened occasionally and selectively in the shires; by the later years of Henry I's reign it was attempting to monitor the shires more regularly by frequent visitation. The early years of Henry II, however, were more like early Norman government with forays into the shires by royal officers; and it was not until 1166 that a systematic visitation of the whole country by two royal commissioners was embarked upon. Yet within twenty years, possibly within twelve, Henry II's government had moved far beyond anything attempted under Henry I: it had taken over direct management of much of the work of government in the localities and in particular had undertaken a major part of the dispensation of justice both criminal and civil. It is, however, unlikely that this change was intended or even envisaged in 1166; it was rather the consequence of a series of intelligent and decisive responses to the problems of government as they were progressively perceived.

The intention of this chapter is to trace the steps by which this transformation occurred. In the longer perspective of the history of the governance of England, the way that reform came about was even more important than the reforms themselves, for it established a pattern for the future development of English government. Essentially this was by adapting, modifying and supplementing existing practices rather than by radical change and the devising of new institutions. To call it an evolutionary process would be misleading, for the blending of old and new, while giving an appearance of continuity, left English government riddled with anomalies, antiquities, exceptions, and less than rational practices, but nevertheless with a momentum of reform; it was development by incremental change.

The problem to which the king addressed himself during his unusually long stay in England was lawlessness. It was a reproach to his kingship for the repression of wrong-doing was second only to the defence of the realm in the catalogue of royal duties. The problem was two-fold: there was an unprecedented crimewave, and the methods of prosecuting crime were in disarray. The crimewave may have been a by-product of the years of disorder in Stephen's reign, though there were those at the time who attributed it to rising prosperity and the drunkenness for which the English were notorious.[3] Under customary law the initiative in bringing criminal proceedings rested largely with the aggrieved party who personally made an accusation in court. Frivolous or malicious accusations were guarded against by putting

---

[3.] *Dialogus*, p. 87, M.T. Clanchy, *England and its Rulers 1066–1272* (London, 1983), p. 248.

the accuser in peril of standing trial himself or suffering a penalty if he could not substantiate his accusation. On the other hand, there was a strong incentive to make justifiable accusations by a system of compensation elaborated into detailed tariffs for specific injuries. Additional monetary penalties were payable to those whose authority had been insulted, commonly the lord, or the bishop, or the king, or to more than one of them. Some more serious crimes could not be satisfied by monetary payment – they were 'unemendable' – and the guilty suffered in life or limb and forfeiture of land and chattels; such crimes were among the 'pleas of the crown' and could be tried only in the presence of a representative of the king. In the course of the first half of the twelfth century, however, an essential piece of the old system dropped out: the practice of a fixed tariff for compensation and penalty disappeared with, as Maitland has written, 'marvellous suddenness'.[4] How and when is difficult to say: it was still being described in the lawbooks written in Henry I's reign, but the *Leges Henrici Primi* speaks also, with barely concealed disapproval, of 'a new method of impleading' by a local official who prosecuted suspected criminals in the king's name but on his own authority and without the necessity of bringing other accusers or witnesses to support the charge.[5] The author calls such an official a *iudex fiscalis* by which he seems to mean the local justiciar, although other sources indicate that official prosecutions were brought by lesser officials, commonly the 'sergeants' of the hundreds (or wapentakes).[6] *The Leges Henrici Primi* indicated some safeguard against unwarranted prosecution in that an accused who had not been caught in the act, and who had been brought to trial by an official 'acting with the authority of his independent jurisdiction in the absence of any other accuser or informer' could clear himself 'by his own oath and that of two neighbours'; but there was obviously scope for corruption as well as unjustified prosecution, and the evidence for the activities of prosecuting officials is almost entirely of complaints about over-zealousness, arbitrary oppression and corruption. At the same time the ecclesiastical authorities were moving in a similar direction. Offences against 'God's law' had of old been a matter for private accusation in the public courts leading to trial before the bishop. Alternatively the bishop on a visitation of his diocese might convene a synod and act on the testimony of sworn members of a parish. But as the church began to develop a more formal system of jurisdiction through ecclesiastical courts it looked to more efficient methods of identifying transgressors and delegated an inquisitional authority to

[4.] P & M, ii. 458.
[5.] *Leges Henrici*, 6.4, cf. 6.3a, Van Caenegem, 'Public prosecution of crime', pp. 53ff.
[6.] *Leges Henrici*, 63.1.

local officials, most commonly archdeacons. The protests about ecclesiastical prosecutors nosing out cases of moral turpitude were even louder than against secular prosecutors, and it was a bitter jest of the time to speculate on whether archdeacons could go to Heaven.[7]

Although the practice had become common in the later years of Henry I's reign as well as Stephen's, Henry II seems to have had a rooted objection to prosecution by officials, whether ecclesiastical or secular, on their word alone. He is said by chroniclers to have made an edict early in his reign in England and Normandy prohibiting prosecutions by lesser officials, both ecclesiastical and secular, without the supporting testimony of worthy men of the neighbourhood; and he is reported as having protested bitterly to the ecclesiastical authorities in England about a rural dean who had blackmailed the wife of a burgess of Scarborough by threatening to accuse her of adultery, adding in his characteristically extravagant way that archdeacons and rural deans extracted more money by such means in a year than reached the royal treasury.[8] When the bishops asked how they were to be expected to proceed when no one wished or dared to come forward with supporting testimony, the king responded by offering royal assistance: in such a case the sheriff, when requested by the bishop, should cause 12 law-worthy men of the neighbourhood 'to swear before the bishop that they will manifest the truth of the matter to the best of their knowledge'; his novel proposal was embodied in clause 6 of the Constitutions of Clarendon.[9]

It is proof that the king was motivated not by anti-clericalism, as Becket's biographers alleged, but by firm conviction that he persisted in his attitude when confronted by the problem of the effective prosecution of serious crime: even in a situation of lawlessness which required drastic remedy, and which may at least in part have been a consequence of his edict, he refused to contemplate *ex officio* prosecution. Instead he proposed a method analogous to that which he had offered to the bishops but much more elaborately worked out. It was set forth in an 'assize' after taking counsel with his barons at Clarendon early in 1166. 'Assize' was a word which was shortly to acquire several uses, but essentially it was an alternative to customary law enforced by royal authority, differing from an edict in that it had baronial assent. The Assize of Clarendon begins:

King Henry, by the counsel of all his barons, has ordained that for the preservation of the peace and enforcement of justice, inquiry shall be made in every county and every hundred through 12 of the more law-abiding men of each hundred and through four of the more law-abiding

[7] Van Caenegem, 'Public prosecution of crime', pp. 66–8.
[8] Warren, *Henry II*, p. 434 and n. 4.
[9] *EHD* ii. 720.

men of each vill, put on oath to tell the truth, whether there is in their hundred or vill any man accused or publicly suspected as robber or murderer or thief or anyone who has harboured them since the lord king became king.[10]

This was not a trial jury – that did not appear for another half century; this was a panel of local men required to declare on oath what serious crimes had been committed in the neighbourhood and who was suspected of committing them: the sworn panel was said to 'present' suspects for trial and was known as a 'jury of presentment' or later as the 'grand jury'. Suspects indicted by the jury of presentment were, if possible, arrested by the sheriff and held in custody pending trial. Those who could not be arrested were condemned to outlawry. There was traditionally much variation in custom on the procedures and methods for testing accusations; but the Assize prescribed one method only for those indicted by the jury of presentment: the ordeal of water. By this the accused was bound and lowered by a rope into a deep pool of water; if he sank to the level of a knot tied in the rope at the distance of the length of his hair he was declared innocent, but if the water would not receive him and he floated he was adjudged guilty.

The Assize prescribed that in respect of those indicted by the jury of presentment 'no one shall have jurisdiction or judgement or forfeiture except the lord king in the royal court', and insisted that all the chattels of those who failed at the ordeal or who fled should be forfeit to the crown; but it allowed that 'with respect to those seized otherwise than by this oath, let whatever is customary and right be done.'[11] In other words the Assize did not abrogate customary law but supplemented it. At the same time, however it deterred lords from trying to protect their men from private accusations, for it was only if they allowed the normal processes of the law to take their course before the jury of presentment indicted suspects that they could retain the right to forfeitures imposed on their vassals and villeins. The Assize, moreover, insisted

that all should come to the shire court for the making of this oath, so that no one on account of any jurisdiction or soke that he may enjoy shall abstain from attendance. And let there be no one in city, or borough, or castle or elsewhere who shall prevent the sheriff from entering upon his land or jurisdiction for the purpose of arresting those who have been accused as robbers, murderers, or thieves, or those who harbour them, or outlaws; on the contrary the king commands that assistance be given in arresting them.[12]

[10.] Assize of Clarendon, cl. 1, *EHD* ii. 408.
[11.] *Ibid.*, cl. 5.
[12.] *Ibid.*, cl.s 8 and 10.

In short, in the assault on serious crime, royal authority overrode a wide variety of customary procedures, and also overrode franchisal jurisdiction, private privileges and exemptions; but it did so only on the basis of the jury's presentations; neither sheriffs nor royal justices could on their own authority set aside customary law or invade established rights. It was the local community which was made responsible for law and order, and was given the backing of royal authority and the assistance of royal officials.

There were other provisions for the punishment by mutilation of those found guilty, and for dealing with vagabonds and outlaws, provisions which might subsequently be modified; but the aspects described above were the enduring heart of the Assize. It was at first assumed that it would be of temporary application, to be enforced so long as the king would wish it; but its main provisions, with an extension to other serious crimes, such as forgery and arson, and with revised punishments, were incorporated in the Assize of Northampton in 1176, and thereafter came to be regarded as a normal part of the law of the realm.[13] Indictment by the grand jury was to be fundamental in the prosecution of crime under English law until the creation of the Office of Director of Public Prosecutions in 1879; thereafter the grand jury's functions became largely ceremonial until it was abolished in 1933. In the United States of America it retains to this day its essential function of declaring whether there is a *prima facie* case to answer and which suspects should be sent for trial. It was to be of singular importance in legal history that England, having experimented with *ex officio* prosecution, should have abandoned it just when the Church, having refined the procedures, formally adopted it and when the general trend in European states was to do the same.

Early in 1166, at the same time as the Assize of Clarendon was promulgated, two of the king's principal counsellors were commissioned to visit the shires. They were Geoffrey de Mandeville, earl of Essex, and Richard de Luci, the king's chief administrator. Historians have seen this either as a revival of the general visitations of Henry I's day or as the forerunner of the new kind of visitation shortly to be commissioned by Henry II. It was neither. It is difficult to equate these two top-level commissioners with either the 'justices of all England' of the early twelfth century or the 'justices itinerant' who were to follow later; moreover their activity was limited to hearing pleas of the crown. Rather they seem to be *ad hoc* commissioners (in the same way that the Domesday Survey had been conducted by *ad hoc* commissioners) charged with monitoring the application of the Assize. When

13. Assize of Northampton, *EHD* ii. 411–13.

they visited a shire the presentments were made to them, and they presided at the trials; otherwise the new procedures were applied by the sheriffs and local justiciars. After 17 shires had been visited the commission ceased because Earl Geoffrey took sick and died at Carlisle in October 1166. At Michaelmas 1166 the financial consequences of the Assizes began to be recorded on the Pipe Roll as the sheriffs accounted 'for the chattels of those fled or who perished at the judgement of water'. Significantly the sheriffs of shires which had been visited by the commissioners reported the names of more felons whose chattels were forfeit than the sheriffs of shires which had not been visited. For example the sheriff of Essex and Hertfordshire accounted for 31 felons, the sheriff of Lincolnshire for 39, the sheriff of Norfolk and Suffolk for 101, and the sheriff of Yorkshire for 127. All of these were on the route of the commissioners. By contrast the sheriff of Gloucestershire accounted for eight felons, the sheriff of Hampshire for four, the sheriff of Wiltshire for three, and the sheriff of Worcestershire for one.[14] The efficacy of visitation could not have been more clearly demonstrated. The implication was that the sheriffs were either remiss or corrupt or both. The sheriffs who had been visited could not cheat the exchequer by pocketing the proceeds of the sale of felons' chattels because the commissioners would have a record of the cases which was returned to the exchequer so that when the sheriff appeared he could be examined as to what he had done about each of them; if he claimed that the convicted felon were a pauper with no chattels to auction he would be required to swear an affidavit.

There were two consequences from this experience. The first was that visitation became frequent and regular. Starting in 1168 several teams of commissioners were sent out, each covering a prescribed circuit of shires; they came to be known as 'justices itinerant' or more formally as 'justices in eyre'. They differed from Henry I's visiting justices in that they did not hold a permanent commission: they were separately appointed for each visitation or 'eyre' and their authority as royal justices lasted only for the duration of the eyre. Moreover their authority to act in the king's name was defined and limited by the terms of their commission: at the beginning of each eyre they were given a set of instructions which empowered them to act in specified ways. These instructions came to be known as 'the articles of the eyre.' As the eyres became established the authority to conduct the trials of those indicted by juries of presentment, together with hearing of the other pleas of the crown, was assigned solely to them, and the local justiciars disappeared.

The second consequence of the experience gained by visitation was a

14. Warren, *Henry II*, pp. 284–6.

thorough review of the operations of local government. In 1170 a special eyre was commissioned to inquire into what the officials of local government had demanded from people under their jurisdiction, whether properly or improperly, 'by reason of which the land and people have been oppressed.' The inquiry was immediately dubbed 'the Inquest of Sheriffs', but it ranged much wider than the activities of sheriffs and their subordinate officials, extending also to what all landholders had exacted from their tenants through their stewards and manorial officials. The commissioners were to inquire particularly into the administration of the Assize of Clarendon:

> concerning also the chattels of those who fled or were convicted through that assize, let inquiry be made as to what has been done and what has issued from it in the several hundreds and vills, and let it be accurately and carefully written down. And inquiry is to be made whether anyone has been unjustly accused in that assize for reward or promise or from hatred or other unjust cause, and whether any accused person has been released or any accusation withdrawn for reward or promise or favour, and who received the reward for it, and let this similarly be written down.[15]

It is unfortunate that only a few records of this inquiry survive, all relating to baronial officials; but one consequence was quickly manifest: 20 sheriffs were dismissed.[16] Thereafter the sheriffs were more usually appointed from those who made a career of the royal service than from those with a local power base and a standing in feudal society. It was a turning point in the history of the office: thereafter the sheriff's capacity to act at his own discretion was to be steadily restricted, and instead of being a virtually autonomous governor of a county he was to become the local agent of a centralized administration which watched him closely.

At the same time as tackling the problem of the prosecution of serious crime, King Henry II and his ministers tackled another aspect of lawlessness – what was known at the time as 'disseisin', that is to say, the forcible dispossession of a man from his enjoyment of rights in land or other valuable perquisites. Disseisin was not necessarily wrong: it could be used for example to enforce compliance with decisions of a court in civil actions, and was the proper penalty for a man who withheld the services due to his lord from the land. But it might also be employed unjustifiably to enforce the will of the strong against the weak, for example, or to gain a procedural advantage in a disputed claim, for the law quite properly made it easier for the man in possession to defend himself than for a challenger to press his claim. The king

15. Inquest of Sheriffs, *EHD* ii. 438–40.
16. *EHD* ii. 437–8; for some of the surviving returns see *ibid*, pp. 441–8.

had indeed given extra protection to the man in possession by insisting that a claimant had to have a royal writ authorizing him to bring a legal action before the defendant could be obliged to answer.[17] The origins of this rule are obscure, but it may have been introduced to quell wanton or unwelcome claims in the aftermath of the civil war. One consequence, however, may have been to prompt some to resort to disseisin instead of having recourse to law. Early in his reign King Henry II issued an edict which drew a distinction been a proper and an improper or 'unjust' disseisin by defining the latter as one made 'without the judgement of a court'.[18] Then, as one of the several measures taken in the remarkable year of 1166, he made an assize on the matter declaring an unjust disseisin to be a breach of the king's peace and thereby punishable as a plea of the crown.[19] Presumably offenders were at first prosecuted by the sheriffs and local justiciars, but with the establishment of the regular eyres jurisdiction passed to the justices itinerant. The clearest indication of this is one of the instructions to the justices about to set out on eyre in 1176: 'Let the justices of the lord king cause an inquisition to be made concerning disseisins made contrary to the assize.'[20] The king's primary concern was obviously to quell the disorder of self-help; but what of the man disseised, how was he to secure redress? The normal procedure would be for him to be given a royal writ (the 'writ of right') authorizing him to bring an action for recovery in his lord's court. But this was unsatisfactory. Actions for right over land were cautiously protracted for the final judgement if properly reached would be irreversible. The customary law required that claimant and defendant should confront each other in court, and there were numerous allowable excuses for non-attendance (known as 'essoins') which could be exploited to delay proceedings. And if no other satisfactory proof could be adduced the dispute would have to be put to the hazard of trial by battle – a duel fought between the parties to the action or their champions. In the case of an unjust disseisin what was needed was a swift way of restoring possession to the man disseised, so that he could at least continue to enjoy the property pending a final resolution of the dispute. Soon after the itinerant justices began to prosecute unjust disseisors someone seems to have asked, why not help the man disseised at the same time? But it was not so easy to do this: it would be necessary to identify beyond dispute who had been disseised, and even more critically of what precisely he had been disseised. The best answer to this problem was: let the disseised man take the

---

17. *Glanvill* XII. 25, p. 148, cf. XII. 2, p. 137.
18. Warren, *Henry II*, p. 336 n. 1.
19. *Ibid.*, p. 337 and n. 1.
20. Assize of Northampton, cl. 5, *EHD* ii. 412.

initiative – let him make a specific claim, and then ask a jury of local
men whether he is telling the truth. But having reached this solution
what then had to be done was to devise a foolproof procedure for
giving effect to it. A solution to the whole problem of unjust disseisin
was provided in the assize of *novel disseisin*, and the story long circulated that the king and his advisers had spent many sleepless nights
formulating a writ to give effect to it.[21] The writ was in standardized
form (itself an advance on current practice) requiring only the addition of names, places and times. The writ was a model of conciseness,
precision, and effectiveness. Its wording, in translation, was as
follows:

> The king to the sheriff, greeting.
> X has complained to me that Y unjustly and without judgement has
> disseised him of his free tenement in [such and such a vill] since [my last
> crossing to Normandy]
> Therefore I command you, that if X gives you security for proceeding
> with his claim, you are to see that any chattels removed from that tene-
> ment are restored to it, and that the tenement and the chattels remain in
> peace [until the Sunday after Easter].
> And meanwhile you are to see that the tenement is viewed by 12 free and
> law-abiding men of the neighbourhood and their names endorsed on
> this writ; and summon them by good summoners to be before me or my
> justices on [the Sunday after Easter] ready to make the recognition.
> And summon Y or his bailiff if he himself cannot be found, on the
> security of gage and reliable sureties, to be there on that date to hear the
> recognition. And have there the summoners, and this writ, and the
> names of the sureties.[22]

To appreciate the ingenuity involved, let us follow through the
procedure. The plaintiff first sought the writ from any agency of the
king's court. Unlike other judicial writs at the time, which were issued
only at the discretion of the king or his chief minister and in
consideration of a proffer, the writ of *novel disseisin* was issued without quibble and for a small payment for the clerk's trouble. The plaintiff then took the writ to the sheriff to whom it was addressed, and
gave security that he seriously meant to pursue the claim (and was not,
for example, simply attempting to intimidate his opponent into
surrendering or offering a compromise). This was the real beginning
of the action, and the writ gave the sheriff both instructions and
authority to act – he was powerless in the matter without it. First he
laid the property in question under the protection of the king's peace,
temporarily and for a specified period, until the matter could be

21. Bracton, iii. 25.
22. *Glanvill* XIII. 33, pp. 167–8.

brought to trial. Then he empanelled a jury of 12 worthy men of the neighbourhood and had them 'view' the property, to make sure they knew what was in question and had considered what was involved before they appeared before the king's justices. Then the sheriff arranged for the parties and the jurors to be formally summoned to attend in court at a specified time. When the king's justices arrived the sheriff handed over the writ (it was said to be 'returnable', itself a new idea) which then became the justices' authority to act. The writ provided the justices with the information they needed to conduct the case. They could first check that the parties and the jurors (whose names the sheriff had written on the back of the writ) were present; and if not they could penalize defaulters, for the summoners were also required to be present and could if necessary be examined as to whether the summonses had been properly made. The justices then put to the jurors straightforward questions about the complaint as specified on the writ. Has the claimant been forcibly dispossessed, without the judgement of a court, within the time limit specified (that is to say, it had to be recent or 'novel' and so reasonably within the personal memory of the jurors)? Was the property in question possessed by the claimant as a 'free tenement' (that is to say that it was not a servile tenure and wholly subject to the jurisdiction of a manorial court)? Was the defendant named in the writ the person who had dis-possessed him? According to the tenor of the jurors' replies the king's justices gave judgement. If the jurors supported the plaintiff's claim the defendant would be penalized for having committed an unjust disseisin; if on the other hand the plaintiff's case was found defective, he would be penalized for making an unjust claim. If the justices gave judgement for the plaintiff the sheriff would be instructed to restore him to possession. The rolls kept by the justices' clerks recording the cases heard and the decisions made would at the conclusion of a visitation be returned to the exchequer, which would then require the sheriff to account for the financial penalties levied.

The proceedings under the assize were remarkably expeditious. Since no pleadings were necessary it did not matter if the defendant absented himself; he was summoned to attend and could be penalized if he did not, but the action could proceed without him. No essoins were allowed. And it was made all the swifter by having the preliminaries conducted by the sheriff before the court hearing. It should, however, be observed that it succeeded in its purpose of promptly reversing a dispossession by isolating a straightforward concrete issue to put to a jury. The jurors were not asked the difficult question of whether the plaintiff had a good right to the property of which he had been dispossessed or whether the defendant had justi-fication for thinking he had a better right, but simply whether the plaintiff had recently been improperly disseised. A decision on this matter could not therefore be a bar to further litigation about who had the better right; though if the losing defendant had no good case the action of *novel disseisin* would in practice be decisive.

The importance of *novel disseisin* goes far beyond the invention of a new form of legal process, for in finding solutions to the twin problems of prosecuting serious crime and curbing unjust disseisin, Henry II's government had discovered a solution to the age-old problem of how to delegate the full force of royal authority without either losing control of it or putting too much discretionary power into the hands of subordinates. It was achieved by a combination of a division of functions, procedural rules, and the recruitment into the exercise of royal government of non-officials, the ordinary men who served on juries. The itinerant justices carried the king's court into the shires, but they were limited in two ways, by the commission which defined the scope of their authority and by the prescribing of procedures by which that authority was to be exercised. The sheriffs had executive power, made the justices' work possible and enforced their decisions, but they did not share in making judgements, and in levying financial penalties were held strictly to account by the exchequer by means of the records of the justices' decisions. Both executive power and judgement, however, had to wait upon the juries in 'presenting' suspects or 'recognizing' key facts.

The invention of the returnable writ, which, unlike earlier writs, did not simply command someone to do something but set in motion a prescribed procedure, opened the way to a rapid expansion of the judicial services which the crown could offer to its subjects. The expansion began not with the assize of *novel disseisin* (which was a 'mixed' action, partly civil in respect of the plaintiff and partly criminal in respect of an unjust disseisor) but with a cognate action, the assize of *mort d'ancestor*.[23] This was a remedy for a man who had been unable to gain possession of a rightful inheritance either because the lord was improperly witholding it or because someone else had mistakenly been given possession. The writ and the procedure were basically similar to *novel disseisin* but in addition to posing different questions to the jury, the law governing its operation was different. The first question was whether the previous holder had held the property 'in demesne as of fee', and the jury might reject the claim because the dead man had not had an hereditary title, being possessed of it, for example, as security for a debt or as custodian for an absent crusader. The other crucial question was whether the claimant was the deceased's nearest heir. A major difference, however, was that plead-

23. *Glanvill* XIII. 3, p. 50.

ings, though not usually necessary, might be allowed; and so the defendant was permitted three successive essoins to allow him an opportunity to answer the claim. Pleading was allowed because the questions could not cover all circumstances: it might be, for example, that the defendant would acknowledge that the claimant was the deceased's nearest heir, but would allege that the deceased held the property only in right of his wife, and that he himself was the wife's nearest heir. The defendant's counter claim would then throw up a question of fact which could be put to the jury. It was on this basis of pleading to the facts that the law became more sophisticated, and, incidentally, that the services of lawyers became useful.

Initially the new writ processes approached claims only on the basis of facts about recent possession. In most cases this would be sufficient to settle the matter: the man who ought to be in possession gained possession without the necessity of having to prove his right by the protracted and hazardous traditional procedures. But since these 'possessory' assizes did not go to the root of the matter, anyone who believed that injustice had been done had to be allowed to re-open the matter and prove his better right in the court of the lord of the property in question. Sometimes the royal justices, uneasy about the outcome of a case, would offer the losing party a 'writ of right' on the spot commanding the lord to do prompt justice. In 1179, however, King Henry II offered as an alternative to the traditional procedure culminating in trial by battle the use of a jury in the royal court. The line of argument seems to have been that for several years juries had been asked to give a verdict on facts about recent possession, which may be said to establish a presumption of right, and many people had been satisfied with this; but if someone is not satisfied, why not ask another jury to look more deeply into the matter and see whether the presumption was justified. Let the time limit be lifted and let the jury inquire as far back as they can, considering all kinds of evidence and testimony, so as to work out, if they can, the relevant history of the descent of the property. This was known as the 'grand assize'.[24] The procedures under it were very formal, cautious and protracted, properly so when a final judgement was to be reached. Great care was taken over the selection of the jury, which was to consist entirely of knights of the neighbourhood – the sort of men who would be interested in family histories and the tenure of local property. At least a year and perhaps several might elapse before a final judgement was pronounced by the king's justices on the basis of the jury's finding – hence the value of a swift possessory action as a preliminary so that the man who had a presumptive right might enjoy possession in

[24.] *Ibid.*, II. 6, pp. 26–8.

the meantime. The procedure of the grand assize was available in cases which were brought initially into the royal court, but also to a defendant in a lord's court, who when challenged to prove his right could, if he wished, 'put himself upon the king's grand assize'. He would seek a 'writ of peace' from the sheriff to gain the king's protection, and the case would be transferred for hearing before royal justices.[25] This was, of course, to deny to lords the jurisdiction of their courts, though at the option of the defendant not at the will of the king. Nevertheless the grand assize was said at the time to be 'a royal boon conferred by the clemency of the king acting on the advice of his magnates'.[26]

The quotation is from a lawbook written about the end of Henry II's reign, entitled *Tractatus De Legibus et Consuetudinibus Regni Anglie* (The Treatise on the Laws and Customs of the Kingdom of England). Its authorship was credited to the king's chief minister at the time, Ranulf de Glanville, and is usually known by the short title of *Glanvill*. Just as the *Dialogus de Scaccario* was a guide and handbook for administrative apprentices and those who had business at the exchequer, so *Glanvill* was for apprentices at law and those who had business in the royal courts. Despite its full title *Glanvill* does not deal with the traditional procedures in lords' courts because their customs 'are so diverse and numerous that they cannot readily be reduced to writing.' Instead it dealt with the new procedural law of the royal courts which was clear, rational, precisely formulated and common to the whole country – the common law of the realm as distinct from customary law. There are 19 writs in *Glanvill* initiating actions before royal justices and about 30 governing steps in the conduct of cases more complicated than those under the possessory assizes. Even the old writs by which the king had responded to petitioners by commanding someone to make restitution or the like were given a new formulation and subjected to the new procedures. The old 'executive' writ commanding something to be done for the petitioner would have been addressed to the lord of the property in question, and threatened that if he did not do as required it would be done by some agent of the king – the local justiciar, perhaps, or the chief minister. The new 'judicial' form of the writ, as it appears in Glanvill was addressed to the sheriff instructing him to command (*praecipe*) whoever was denying to the petitioner his rights to render them to him, and if he refused to set in motion an action in the royal court: 'If he does not do so, summon him by good summoners to be before me or my justices on [the day after the octave of Easter] to show why he has not done so. And have there the summoners and this writ.'[27] Such a procedure

25. *Ibid.*, II. 8–11, pp. 29–31.
26. *Ibid.*, p. 28.
27. *Ibid.*, I. 6, p. 5.

eliminated the need for the king to hear the petitioner's arguments before issuing a writ, although a distinction was still drawn between writs 'of course', which were issued freely and cheaply, and writs 'of grace' which conferred a favour and for which a payment would have to be agreed with the king's ministers.

The new procedures for judicial actions before royal justices were enormously popular, and especially *mort d'ancestor*. So much so that by the time the grand assize was introduced the justices in eyre were overwhelmed with business, and being unable to conclude all the cases before them in one shire before their schedule required them to move on to another, they deferred cases for later consideration at the exchequer, where of course another manifestation of the king's court could be found. This problem was tackled in two ways. One was by having, in addition to the 'general eyres' for all kinds of royal business, more frequent visitations by teams of justices with a narrower commission to hear the swift possessory actions and uncomplicated pleas. The other was by detailing off some justices to remain at Westminster to hear the pleas of those who did not wish to wait for a visitation and the cases which could not conveniently be concluded before the itinerant justices. *Glanvill* speaks frequently of the 'chief court' (*capitalis curia*) at Westminster, but it should not be thought of as a superior court, but rather as a 'headquarters' court from which the circuit justices set out and to which they returned on completing their commission, and as a court in regular session with always a nucleus of resident justices.[28]

These developments over a period of less than twenty years could not have been imagined in 1166; and the rapidity of the transformation is all the more remarkable in that it was interrupted by a serious political crisis. The late 1160s and early 1170s were a time of troubles for Henry II: he was faced with resistance to his aggressive assertions of lordship over the Welsh, the Scots, the Bretons and the Poitevins, he was embroiled in a quarrel with the Church which reached a terrible climax with the murder of Archbishop Becket at Christmas 1170, he was drawn into a threatening situation in Ireland in 1171, and his troubles culminated in a widespread rebellion against his rule in 1173–4. It was indeed more than a rebellion for it was actively supported by the king of France and the count of Flanders. The ostensible purpose was to replace Henry II by his eldest son, Henry the Younger, who had been crowned as co-king in 1170. Henry the Younger was popular but feckless and improvident. He was a man of the stamp of William the Conqueror's eldest son Robert (whom many barons would have preferred to see as king of England), and of his grandson,

28. Warren, *Henry II*, pp. 295–8.

Stephen of Blois (who with baronial support did become king of England). We may see these three as representing or symbolizing an alternative type of governance to that which Henry I had imposed and Henry II had restored. It may be argued that the resistance of the bishops under Becket's leadership and the rebellion of the earls in 1173–4 were twin manifestations of hostility to the restoration. It is significant that the rebellion in England was led by Robert of Leicester, the son of the man who had governed the kingdom in the early years of the reign, Hugh, earl of Chester, whose earldom was a truncated version of that over which his father had held sway, and the aged Hugh, earl of Norfolk, who had been denied by Henry II the power in East Anglia for which he had fought against King Stephen. But it should be observed that just as there were some bishops who stood by Henry II and others who hesitated to side with Archbishop Becket, so there were some earls who were loyal to Henry II and others who hesitated to implicate themselves in rebellion. There was not so much a tide of baronial opinion as a choppy sea. Henry II's triumph over the rebels terminated the argument over whether the shires were to be managed by the crown or by the earls; but that is not to say that it opened the way to a totally unrestrained application of royal authority. Just as the king had been obliged to learn how to allay the anxieties of the bishops about the way royal authority was to be exercised over the clergy, so, it may be argued, he learned how to gain the co-operation or at least the acquiescence of the barons in the expansion of royal government.

One of the measures which in the earlier aggressive phase of the reassertion of royal authority most seriously aroused baronial fears and hostility must have been the so-called Inquest of Sheriffs of 1170. The most alarming aspect of it was that the searching enquiry into the activities of local officials of the crown was extended also to all land-holders: 'Likewise let inquiry be made concerning the archbishops, bishops, abbots, earls, barons, sub-tenants, knights, citizens and burgesses, and their stewards and officers as to what and how much they have received from their lands, since the lord king crossed to Normandy, from their hundreds and vills, and from each of their men, both with judgement and without, and let there be written down separately all these exactions and their causes and occasions.'[29] It is astonishing that such an inquiry was ever contemplated let alone carried out. It may be significant that it occurred after the death of Earl Robert de Beaumont in 1168. One of the few fragments of the returns to have survived concerns the earl of Arundel. It lists in detail with names and payments what he had received from his tenants for

---

[29.] Inquest of Sheriffs, cl. 3, *EHD* ii. 439.

his defence of the Welsh marches, to help him repay his debts to the Jews, to defray his expenses on the king's service, for the favour of succeeding to fiefs, and for being dubbed to knighthood. It includes this passage:

> Fifteen days before the Purification of St Mary next following, it will be four years since the servants of the earl seized 405 sheep of Matthew of Candos and transported them as far as Snettisham and kept them 14 weeks. In course of transit two died; they had in their charge 18 ewes and 80 lambs; and a sum of two shillings was paid over to these servants. In fact nothing was due to the earl. The earl's bailiffs reply that they seized the aforesaid chattels on account of default of service by Anelald of Bidon; the earl himself admits this and complains of Anelald.[30]

A fragment relating to the manor of Fakenham on the barony of Robert de Valognes lists fines levied in the manor court for the shortcomings of his servants in the management of the hay crop, the sheepfold, the piggery and the apiary.[31]

It is significant that no such inquiry was repeated, and it may have been part of the later accord between the king and his barons that it never would be. There are indeed grounds for thinking that a bargain was struck whereby the king was allowed to extend the scope of royal justice so far as freemen were concerned provided he retreated from interfering in landlords' jurisdiction over the unfree. This may be detected in the care taken in the new judicial procedures to ensure that pleas concerned free men and free tenures. One consequence was a sharpening of the distinction between the free and the unfree. Hitherto there had been degrees of freedom and unfreedom, but from this time the courts came to recognize a sharp cut-off point which could be identified by standard tests. At the time of Domesday Book the word 'villein' meant 'villager', but from now on it meant 'serf'. Royal assistance was put at the service of landlords in recovering fugitive villeins by the writ of 'naifty' addressed to the sheriff.[32] Many landlords in the later twelfth century were finding it economically advantageous to lease more of their land to peasants, to remit labour services for money payments, and to have their remaining demesnes worked by paid hands; but as their control over the peasantry through agricultural discipline slackened it was convenient for them to retain control through the jurisdiction of the manor court and such franchisal powers as they enjoyed in the hundreds. The extension of

30. *Ibid.*, ii. 442.
31. *Ibid.*, ii. 446.
32. *Glanvill* V, pp. 53ff., P. Hyams, 'The action of naifty in the early common law', *Law Quarterly Review* 110 (1974), 326–50, 'The proof of villein status in the common law', *EHR* 89 (1974), 721–49, and *King, Lords and Peasants in Medieval England* (Oxford, 1980).

franchisal powers over the peasantry by royal grant was indeed to be a marked feature of the later twelfth century. On the other hand the advantages to all free landholders of the new processes of royal justice were too great for the barons to resist.

Bibliographical Note

Central Government

For detailed studies of reigns see W.L. Warren, *Henry II* (London, 1973), and S. Painter, *The Reign of King John* (Baltimore, 1949). F.J. West, *The Justiciarship in England 1066–1232* (Cambridge, 1966) ranges widely over central government. J.E.A. Jolliffe, *Angevin Kingship* (London 1955) explores the workings of the king's government with searching insights. For a sketch of administrative developments see S.B. Chrimes, *An Introduction to the Administrative History of Medieval England* (Oxford, 1952), chapter III. For more specialized studies on the financial system see C. Johnson, introduction to *Pipe Roll 2 Richard I* (Pipe Roll Society, 1925); H. Jenkinson, 'Financial records of the reign of King John' in *Magna Carta Commemoration Essays*, ed. H.E. Malden (London, 1917), pp. 244–300; R.A. Brown, 'The treasury of the later twelfth century' in *Studies Presented to Sir Hilary Jenkinson*, ed. J. Conway Davies (London, 1957), pp. 35–49; H.G. Richardson, introduction to *Memoranda Roll 1 John* (Pipe Roll Society, 1943) on the financial system and developments in chancery practice. On the chancery see also: T.A.M. Bishop, *Scriptores Regis* (Oxford, 1961), and P. Chaplais, *English Royal Documents, King John – Henry VI* (Oxford, 1971). On the chamber see: J.E.A. Jolliffe, 'The *camera regis* under Henry II', *EHR* 68 (1953), 1–21, 337–62, much criticized by H.G. Richardson, 'The chamber under Henry II', *EHR* 69 (1954), 596–611; H.G. Richardson and G.O. Sayles, *The Governance of Medieval England* (Edinburgh, 1963), chapter XII; G.L. Harriss, *King, Parliament, and Public Finance in Medieval England to 1369* (Oxford, 1975), chapter VIII.

The King's Government in the Shires

For a survey of the workings of government in the localities see H.M. Jewell, *English Local Administration in the Middle Ages* (Newton Abbot, 1972). On the eyres see D. Crook, *Records of the General Eyre* (Public Record Office Handbooks, no. 20, 1982); H.M. Cam, 'Studies in the Hundred Rolls', in *Oxford Studies in Social and Legal History*, ed. P. Vinogradoff, viii (Oxford, 1921), chapter 1; and D.M. Stenton's long introduction to *The Earliest Lincolnshire Assize Rolls, 1202–1209* (Lincoln Record Society, 1926). On the royal justices see D.M. Stenton, *Pleas before the King and his Justices, 1198–1212*, 3 (Selden Society, 1967), Introduction, Appendix I, pp. xlvii ff., and R.V. Turner, *The English Judiciary in the Age of Glanvill and Bracton* (Cambridge, 1985). On the sheriff and local administration see W.A. Morris, *The Medieval English Sheriff to 1300* (Manchester, 1927, reprinted 1968), chapters V and VI, and I. Gladwin, *The Sheriff: the Man and his Office* (London, 1974). On the duties required of local people see A.B. White, *Self-Government at the King's Command* (Minnesota, 1933, reprinted 1974).

Revenue and Taxation

There is much valuable information in T. Madox, *The History and Antiquities of the Exchequer of England (1066–1327)* (2nd ed., London, 1769). J.H. Ramsay, *A History of the Revenues of the Kings of England 1066–1399* (Oxford, 1925) is defective in method and should be treated with caution. Detailed information is to be found in S.K. Mitchell, *Studies in Taxation under John and Henry III* (New Haven, Connecticut, 1914), and *Taxation in Medieval England* (New Haven, 1951). The best short study is G.L. Harriss, *King, Parliament, and Public Finance in Medieval England to 1369* (Oxford, 1975), chapters I, VI and VIII. For levies on the barons see S. Painter, *Studies in the History of the English Feudal Barony* (Baltimore, 1943), chapers II and III, and T.K. Keefe, *Feudal Assessments and the Political Community under Henry II and his Sons* (Berkeley, California, 1983).

6
Angevin Administration to c.1215

Central Government

By the later twelfth century central government had become a major factor in the governance of the realm, the number of men regularly employed in the royal service had greatly expanded, and the king's palace at Westminster had become the headquarters of an administration quite distinct from the royal Household. From the later years of the twelfth century there survive records of the business of chancery and the law courts whereas from earlier years there are only exchequer records. The accidents of survival may of course distort our impressions of when records began to be kept, but there are several indications that the closing years of the century saw a conscious attempt to improve administrative efficiency by more systematic record keeping. In the 1170s a standard formula had been devised for drawing up the agreements (known as 'final concords') by which litigants in the royal courts settled disputes over property by a compromise approved by the justices: two copies were made, one for each of the parties. In 1195 the justiciar, Hubert Walter, directed that a third copy was to be made and deposited for safekeeping in the treasury. Very many of them still

---

The Forest

A convenient and well-documented survey is C.R. Young, *The Royal Forests of Medieval England* (Leicester, 1979). See also: the introduction by G.J. Turner to his edition of *Select Pleas of the Forest* (Selden Society, 1901); M.L. Bazeley, 'The forest of Dean in its relations to the crown in the twelfth and thirteenth centuries', *Bristol and Gloucester Archaeological Society, Transactions*, 33 (1910), 153–286, and 'The extent of the English forest in the thirteenth century', *TRHS*, 4th series, 4 (1921), 140–72; J.C. Holt, *The Northerners* (Oxford, 1961), pp. 157–64.

Magna Carta as a Critique of Angevin Government

The principal work is J.C. Holt, *Magna Carta* (Cambridge,, 1965). See also: W.S. McKechnie, *Magna Carta* (2nd ed., Glasgow, 1914); J.C. Dickinson, *The Great Charter* (Historical Association pamphlet, 1955); S. Painter, *The Reign of King John* (Baltimore, 1949); J.C. Holt, *The Northerners* (Oxford, 1961); E. Miller, 'The background of Magna Carta', *Past and Present* 23 (1962), 72–83; J.C. Holt, *Magna Carta and Medieval Government* (London, 1985).

survive, and one is endorsed with the note that it is the first of its kind, made on 15 July 1195. In 1199 a schedule was drawn up of the several kinds of documents issued by the chancery, with the fees appropriate to each. Copies of charters had been kept in the past, but after 1199 they were systematically enrolled, and separate enrolments made of less formal grants and authorizations ('letters patent') and of instructions to officials ('letters close'). Not even the papal chancery could match the royal chancery of King John's day in the ordering of its archives.[1]

With an expanding bureaucracy devoting attention to its organization and methods, it might be expected that a more elaborate structure of offices would develop, and in particular that the justiciar would delegate some of his wide-ranging responsibilities to specialist deputies; but for a surprisingly long time this did not happen. There is a prime example in the history of the court of Common Pleas, otherwise known as 'the bench', a court for hearing civil litigation between subjects distinct from cases which lay between the crown and its subjects. It is reasonable to assume that a separate court for the hearing of common pleas had its origin in a decision of Henry II in 1178 that there were to be five justices who, in the words of the chronicler Roger of Howden, 'were to remain for the purpose of hearing the complaints of the people'.[2] There are indeed thereafter numerous references to 'the justices of the lord king at Westminster', or 'the royal court at Westminster', and it appears in *Glanvill* as 'the chief court'; but for 20 years this court is indistinguishable in practice from the king's court at the exchequer, the sessions of which were now normally held at Westminster instead of at Winchester. Phrases such as 'the justices of the lord king at Westminster', and 'justices of the exchequer', and 'barons of the exchequer' could be used as interchangeable terms in the same document.[3] There are at least as early as 1194 references to judicial business done *in banco*, 'in the bench', but these are references, it seems, to a secretariat which could appoint a day for litigants to have a hearing before the justices. It was not until the turn of the century that a tribunal separate from the exchequer and specializing in common pleas can be identified, but even then it was not given a distinct title. Its separate existence was short-lived for in

[1.] C.R. Cheney, *Hubert Walter* (London, 1967), pp. 95–6, 108–9. For final concords see C.W. Foster, introduction to *Final Concords of the County of Lincoln*, ii (Lincoln Record Society, 1920), and M.S. Walker, introduction to *Feet of Fines for the County of Lincoln for the Reign of King John* (Pipe Roll Society, 1954). On the development of chancery records see H.G. Richardson, introduction to *Memoranda Roll 1 John* (Pipe Roll Society, 1943), and V.H. Galbraith, *Studies in the Public Records* (London, 1948), pp. 64–77.

[2.] *Gesta Regis Henrici Secundi*, ed. W. Stubbs (Rolls Series, 1867), i. 207–8.

[3.] B. Kemp, 'Exchequer and bench in the later twelfth century – separate or identical tribunals?', *EHR* 88 (1973), 559–73.

1209 King John, then constantly in England, suspended the hearing of pleas at Westminster and had them transferred to the court which travelled about the country with himself (described as the court *coram rege*).[4] This then became the 'headquarters court' and not simply the court which heard especially important cases, or those which raised new points of principle, or in which the king's personal interest had been aroused. The inconvenience of obliging all litigants to pursue the peripatetic royal Household led to the provision in Magna Carta of 1215 that 'common pleas shall not follow our court but shall be held in some fixed place' (clause 17); but it was not until the revision of Magna Carta in 1217 that there are formal references to 'our justices of the bench' (clauses 14 and 15).[5]

There were probably two reasons for this slow differentiation of functions at the higher levels of the central administration. One was a habit of mind which saw the organization of government more as a network of men than as a structure of offices. This was what in the memory of the senior servants of the crown it always had been. It was not so long since government at the centre could be conducted by a few intimate counsellors of the king conferring together with the king personally or at twice-yearly sessions of the exchequer. A few held office in the peripatetic Household or, such as the treasurer, in the resident administration; but while office-holding provided for some fixed emoluments and designated a particular responsibility, it did not lead to a specialization of function, for office-holders like any other men close to the king might be called to other tasks; how a man was used depended on his capabilities and the trust reposed in him by the king. There were some who held no office but who were regularly intimate advisers and who might at any time be detailed off for a particular task. The only way of describing such a man is by the contemporary term *familiaris*, a 'familiar'. For the king to describe a man as his *familiaris* was sufficient to accredit him as an envoy to a foreign court. Much of the political and diplomatic aspects of government, as distinct from the administrative, were performed by *familiares*; but all, whether office-holders or not, might be commissioned for administrative tasks as barons of the exchequer or justices in eyre, to hold a sheriffdom or take charge of a castle or an escheated estate, to hold a special inquiry or to sort out a particular problem.[6] There had been few demarcation lines in the way the crown had hitherto managed its affairs. General competence was the way to the top in the

[4.] C.T. Flower, *Introduction to the Curia Regis Rolls*, (Selden Society, 1944), p. 33, D.M. Stenton, 'King John and the courts of justice', *Proceedings of the British Academy*, 44 (1958), pp. 107–18.
[5.] Magna Carta of 1215 clause 17, 1217 clauses 12,14,15, *EHD* iii. 319, 334.
[6.] Warren, *Henry II*, p. 305.

royal service and men of more specialized talents were likely to find themselves in the middle and lower ranks.

The other reason for the disinclination to admit specialized functions into the structure of the central administration was the notion of the unity of the king's government, grounded in the principle that there was only one source of authority and that was the king in his court. All extensions of government had to be represented as manifestations of the royal court. In the *Dialogus de Scaccario* of 1178 the exchequer was still not thought of as an institution but as a special session of the king's court convened twice a year at Easter and Michaelmas. Significantly, the management of the royal revenue had not devolved upon an expanded treasury – that was simply a servicing department acting under the instructions of the king's court of the exchequer. The itinerant justices did not hold a session of the shire court, they brought the king's court into the shire. The standardized judicial writs took the form of a summons from the king to attend before 'me or my justices'.

It was a long time before the king's chief minister in England was allowed to act as a vicegerent; still in the early years of Henry II's reign he was an intermediary conveying orders 'by writ of the king from oversea'. Even when he had become a deputy with authority to act on behalf of the king his capacity to issue executive and judicial writs in his own name was *pro tempore*: as soon as the king set foot in his realm writs ceased to be issued as instructions from the justiciar, his authority merged again into that of the king, and writs were issued as if they were personal expressions of the royal will. The unity of the resident administration as an aspect of the unity of all the king's government was preserved in the person of the justiciar. As a deputy in the king's absence he conducted all aspects of government, political as well as administrative, including, for example, the frequent task of leading campaigns against the Welsh. He presided at all manifestations of the royal court, so that in principle there was no difference between a session for financial and administrative business and a session to hear litigation arising out of disputes between subjects. Hence the lack of a differentiation between 'exchequer' and 'bench'. But just as the developing exigencies of government in the king's absence turned the chief minister from an intermediary into a deputy, so the expanding scope and volume of business in time forced changes in practice despite prevailing attitudes. By the time Richard FitzNigel retired as treasurer in 1196, about 18 years after writing his *Dialogus*, the business before the exchequer had grown so much and its sessions so prolonged that they could no longer in practice take the form of a joint meeting of Household officials and resident administrators to review the management of the king's business; Household officers had to have permanent deputies at Westminster, and communication was by memoranda, written instructions, and the exchange of enrolled documents. By the turn of the century, when information becomes available, a 'Michaelmas' session of the exchequer might go on until the following March and an 'Easter' session until the beginning of August. Similarly the hearing of common pleas became an almost daily business conducted by a developing corps of professional judges. The justiciar might be found at the exchequer or presiding over the hearing of pleas at Westminster or out in the shires with one of the teams of justices in eyre. He could not be everywhere at once, so the exchequer made notes on its Memoranda Roll with the heading 'to be discussed with the justiciar', and the justices hearing common pleas deferred awkward cases until he could be present. By the turn of the century the justiciar had a regular deputy whose work was confined to the exchequer and another who specialized in judicial business;[7] and it was probably this development which led to a distinction between exchequer and bench even though a separation was even then not formally recognized.

Although there are some slight indications of the use of the term 'justiciar' in reference to the king's chief minister from early in the reign of Henry II it was not until the 1180s that the justiciarship acquired its characteristic functions. Earl Robert of Leicester and Richard de Luci had shared authority not only with each other, but also with other ministers closer to the king than themselves, men such as Becket when he was chancellor, and had sometimes been subordinated to a formal regency of the queen or the king's eldest son. But later, after Earl Robert's death in 1168, Richard de Luci had become head of the government of England empowered in the king's absence as a viceroy.[8] No doubt Henry II's confidence in Richard de Luci had been fortified by the way that he had contained the great rebellion in England and had kept the government functioning while the king himself waged campaigns on the continent. His steadfast loyalty and indeed that of the whole administrative service was in marked contrast to the betrayal of the king by his wife and sons. The transition from intermediary to viceregal deputy was no doubt also facilitated by the perfection of methods of accounting and control and by standardized procedures which kept the agents of government on a tight rein. It was no longer necessary for the king himself to sanction the hearing of every petition for justice; he could henceforth confine himself to cases which required a decision at the very highest level and to requests for favours which involved the exercise of his grace. Nevertheless the

7. West, *Justiciarship*, p. 122, cf. p. 85.
8. *Ibid.*, pp. 31ff., Warren, *Henry II*, pp. 56 and n. 2, 261, 194.

endowment of the chief minister with viceregal powers did mean that the justiciar himself acquired a discretionary authority to decide which problems of government or thorny questions of justice to determine himself and which to refer to the king. It should however be observed that the authority to act as regent did not inhere in the justiciarship: it was conferred on the chief minister by special commission when required.[9] After the great rebellion it became normal for the justiciar to act as regent, but he did so only because of the confidence reposed in him personally by the king. Richard de Luci was succeeded after his retirement in 1179 by Ranulf de Glanville, a man of similar social background and with extensive experience of local government as a sheriff and as an itinerant justice.[10] His loyalty and competence were both brought to the king's attention in 1174 when he destroyed the hopes of the rebels in England by capturing the king of Scots before his invasion in support of Henry the Younger had got beyond Alnwick. As justiciar he left a reputation as the man who established the common law of England; but although the king was out of England for two-thirds of his justiciarship, Glanville went frequently to Normandy to consult with him.

At the beginning of the reign of Richard I (1189–99) there was a change in policy occasioned by the imminence of what might be termed an 'extraordinary absence'. Richard was already committed to the Third Crusade and impatient to be gone; but the distance of the Holy Land would make him and his Household virtually incommunicado. Acting with the advice of a council of magnates, King Richard appointed to be co-justiciars two men of a different kind from Luci and Glanville: one of the most powerful of the bishops and one of the most prominent of the earls, Hugh de Puiset, bishop of Durham, and William de Mandeville, earl of Essex. They were to act in concert with a group of colleagues or 'associates' (the chroniclers are vague about their precise status) consisting of professional administrators and magnates with administrative experience.[11] Richard's interests were safeguarded by including among them his long-standing *familiaris* William Longchamps; he had been Richard's chancellor in Aquitaine and now moved over to being royal chancellor, and by remaining in England with custody of the king's seal he had a *de facto* veto over the issue of writs and charters. These appointments constituted in effect a regency council, and a sensible arrangement in the circumstances, especially since there was a widespread fear that the unmarried king would not return from the Crusade and the succession was uncertain. Unfortunately Earl William died within a few weeks, and Richard,

9. West, pp. 189–90.
10. *Ibid.*, pp. 54–63, J.C. Russell, 'Ranulf de Glanville', *Speculum* 45 (1970), 69–79.
11. West, pp. 64–9.

who had no previous knowledge of the government of England and no interest in its administration apart from what could be raised for him in revenue, was swayed by expediency and pressure groups. By the time he departed on crusade he had allowed William Longchamps to assume a sole justiciarship, while retaining office as chancellor and also becoming bishop of Ely and papal legate.[12] But although his authority was extraordinary his power was not unchallenged, for the king had committed to his brother John, count of Mortain and lord of Ireland, control of seven counties which were in consequence withdrawn from the royal administration. Longchamps was a Frenchman unacquainted with English practice. He was accused of acting with autocratic arrogance. He was in fact a competent administrator, and it may be doubted if he were any more arrogant and autocratic than Glanville had been; but these qualities seem to have been even less acceptable in a foreigner. The discontent was exploited by Count John who aspired to make himself governor of the realm and entrench his claim to the succession. His ambition was thwarted, for although Longchamps was persuaded to resign, it was only in favour of a *de facto* regency council contrived by Queen Eleanor, the queen-mother, and Walter of Coutances, archbishop of Rouen, who had both returned to England after attending upon the king while he was in Sicily.[13] Count John committed himself to a dangerous but unsuccessful revolt. The political confusion had at least demonstrated the advantages of the previous arrangements for governing the realm in the king's absence, and King Richard was persuaded to revert to them. His return from the Holy Land was prolonged by his detention in Germany, held for ransom by Emperor Henry VI; but he was then within reach of his ministers and was freely allowed to take counsel with his advisers and communicate with England.

At Christmas 1193 Hubert Walter was appointed justiciar.[14] He had earned the king's respect on the Crusade and at his behest had recently been made archbishop of Canterbury. Much of his earlier life, however, had been spent in the higher reaches of the administrative service. He was a kinsman of Ranulf de Glanville and had probably acted as his personal assistant; he had served as a baron of the exchequer and as a justice in eyre. He resigned the justiciarship in 1198, to make way for his protégé, Geoffrey FitzPeter, but then took over the office of chancellor which he retained until his death in 1205. Geoffrey FitzPeter's career had been entirely in the resident administration in England.[15] For a dozen years Walter and FitzPeter took

12. *Ibid.*, pp. 69–74.
13. *Ibid.*, pp. 74–8.
14. *Ibid*, pp. 78–96, Cheney, *Hubert Walter*, chapter 5.
15. West, *Justiciarship*, pp. 98ff.

over the management of England with almost complete freedom to influence its workings, for after his release from captivity in 1194 King Richard spent two months in England and never visited it again before his death in 1199, and his successor, King John, was in the early years of his reign preoccupied with his continental dominions where his right to rule was disputed, and under threat from King Philip II of France.

In 1204 King Philip conquered Normandy and thereafter King John spent most of the rest of his reign in England. There was in consequence a major shift in the way the realm was managed.[16] The role of Geoffrey FitzPeter as justiciar diminished from being vicegerent to chief executive officer frequently in attendance upon the king. John had himself been trained in Glanville's household in expectation of his becoming king of Ireland, and he retained a keen interest in administration. He not merely transferred the hearing of pleas from Westminster to his peripatetic court but frequently himself sat with his justices to hear and decide cases, and from an incidental reference to his presence at an exchequer session it may be inferred that he personally intervened there too.[17] An even more significant change occurred on the death of Geoffrey FitzPeter in 1213. The king appointed to succeed him a *familiaris*, Peter des Roches, whose experience of government though of long standing had been entirely in the royal Household, and principally in the Chamber. In exercising the justiciarship he had two associates, Richard Marsh and William Brewer, and significantly they too were *familiares*.[18]

Although it is possible to explain these moves as a consequence of the deepening political crisis in England, and by John's paranoid suspicion of everyone, including royal officials, with whom he did not have personal ties, it is even more likely that they were intended to bring the government of the realm more directly into the king's hands, or at least under his personal supervision: he was absorbing the justiciarship. A chronicler of the next generation, Matthew Paris, asserts that John on hearing of the death of his chancellor, Hubert Walter, in 1205, exclaimed, 'By God's feet now at last I am king and lord of England.' He rather spoiled the effect of his anecdote by using it also on the occasion of the death of Geoffrey FitzPeter in 1213.[19] It was part of the legend, which Matthew Paris was largely responsible

16. *Ibid.*, pp. 125ff.

17. Stenton, 'King John and the courts of justice', p. 111, A.L. Poole, *From Domesday Book to Magna Carta* (2nd ed., Oxford, 1951), p. 429, R.V. Turner, *The King and his Courts: the role of John and Henry III in the administration of justice, 1199-1240* (Ithaca, New York, 1968), *Pipe Roll 6 John*, p. 147.

18. West, *Justiciarship*, pp. 178ff.

19. Matthew Paris, *Historia Anglorum*, ed. F. Madden (Rolls Series, 1866-9), ii. 104, *Chronica Majora*, ed. H.R. Luard (Rolls Series, 1872-83), ii. 559.

for popularizing, of the detestable King John. The ancedote is incredible because both men held office at the king's pleasure; but it is not inconceivable that it had its germ in John's view that the administrative service had come to interpose itself between the king and the government of the realm, and that while this had been unavoidable in the years of frequent and prolonged absences by the king it was improper when he was resident. Such a view would accord with the still prevailing notions of the unity of the king's government and the single source of authority in his court. With hindsight it may seem that King John's assumption of direct and personal involvement in the management of the realm was an aberrant interruption in a well-established trend to the development of an autonomous administrative service; but it seems so only because John's early death in 1216 was followed by a long minority in which the government of the realm, adapting itself to another kind of royal absence, rested upon a self regulating administrative service.

The King's Government in the Shires

The eyres and local government

The fundamental change in the governance of the realm after 1166 was that royal government came to deal directly and regularly with ordinary men in the shires. The change stemmed from the decision to transfer the adjudication of pleas of the crown from officials of local government to visiting royal commissioners. Royal government thereafter expanded by enlarging what constituted the pleas of the crown. Much of the expansion fell within the broad categories of the old pleas; but there were new categories as well, created by specific legislation in what were known as 'the king's assizes'. The most obvious of the new categories was civil litigation under the grand assize and the petty assizes such as *novel disseisin* and *mort d'ancestor*; but it should be observed that there were other assizes dealing with trade at the level of retailer and consumer. The earliest versions of these assizes are not well documented and have attracted little attention from historians; but they should be recognized as a significant extension of royal government into the life of the community.

There was an assize of wine in 1176, known only from the debts recorded on the Pipe Rolls for 'selling wine contrary to the assize'.[20] Its nature may be inferred from a revised version in 1199 which fixed maximum prices of wines by the tun and by the gallon according to their provenance.[21] There was an assize of ale at least from the reign of

[20] *Pipe Roll 22 Henry II*, pp. 126, 184.
[21] Howden, iv. 99–100.

King John which regulated prices according to the cost of the ingredients.[22] There was an assize of bread, attributed by the earliest surviving document to Henry II although the earliest evidence of its operation is from 1199.[23] It specified a formula for the fixing of prices which, with much subsequent elaboration, persisted until 1709. The earliest version of it, distinguishing between white bread and wholemeal, provided for a variation in the weight of the loaf according to the current price of wheat together with a fixed element of pricing for the baker's overhead expenses.

Within the same category though of a somewhat different kind was the assize of measures of 1196, of which a text is supplied by the contemporary chronicler Roger of Howden.[24] It required the use of standard measures for liquids and dry goods throughout the realm. The measures were to have iron pegs driven in to mark quantities. It also required the use of standard measures of length. It further required that all woollen cloths were to be of two ells width, 'and all are to be of the same quality in the middle as at the sides'. It forbade any trader to hang cloths outside his shop to deceive the prospective customer about the quality of the goods for sale. It prohibited the manufacture of any dye except black outside cities and county boroughs where the preparation of dyestuffs could be supervised. And it required the appointment of inspectors in cities and county boroughs who were to commit offenders to prison until they could be brought before the justices itinerant.

The assize of ale leaves little trace in the royal records and it may be that the assize did no more than prescribe the formula for determining prices, leaving the control of quality in what was then a rapidly perishable commodity as a matter for local regulation in the hundreds or, very often, by the lords of manors. The other assizes, however, were enforceable by the itinerant justices. The commission for the eyre of 1198 for example required the justices to check that the prescribed standard measures were being used, that the local inspectors were active and diligent, 'and if they have attached transgressors of the assize, and if they have not they are themselves to be punished as if they were the transgressors'.[25] This device of locally appointed officials acting in the interests of the community but strictly accountable to the king's justices for the enforcement of the king's law forged a new kind of link in the chain of government, and a new relationship between the crown and its subjects.

22. *Registrum Malmesburiense*, ed. J.S. Brewer and C.T. Martin (Rolls Series, 1879–80), i. 134.
23. *Pipe Roll 1 John*, p. 15, A.S.C. Ross, 'The assize of bread', *Econ. HR* 9 (1956–7), 332–42, E.David, *English Bread and Yeast Cookery* (London, 1977), pp. 226–9.
24. Howden, iv. 33–4; for the date see D.M. Stenton, introduction to *Pipe Roll 9 Richard I*, p. xxi.
25. Howden, iv. 62, cap. xix.

The appointment of inspectors of weights and measures was not, however, the first use of it: two years previously, in 1194, the shires were required to elect four men, three knights and one clerk, to be 'keepers of the pleas of the crown'.[26] This was the origin of the office of coroner, though the duty performed was not itself new. For as long as there had been pleas which could be determined only before a specified royal officer there had to be preliminary investigations and the collection of evidence which might be material to the hearing. It might first be necessary to identify whether a case was a plea of the crown. Robbery was a plea of the crown, but petty thieving fell within the sheriff's jurisdiction. Brawling belonged to the sheriff, but if it led to wounds it became a plea of the crown. House-breaking compounded a petty offence committed within a house, but the evidence for a break-in would have to be inspected. Cases which would normally be adjudged by the sheriff could, in the later twelfth century, be transferred for hearing to the royal justices if the injured party chose to add to his accusation that the injury of which he complained was done 'against the king's peace', but he would have to do it before competent witnesses; the surviving eyre rolls indicate that many did so, though they would have to count the cost, for the penalty for failing in an appeal to the royal justices could be severe. Allegations of wounding had to be looked into while the wounds were fresh, for months might elapse before a hearing by the justices itinerant. Dead bodies had to be viewed before burial, and 'presentments of Englishry' taken to determine whether the death fell within the law of *murdrum*. Rumours of treasure trove had to be investigated and the treasure impounded as material evidence. Confessions had to be received and subsequently reported. Few pleas of the crown, indeed, could have been effectively brought to trial unless relevant information was gathered and 'kept' by officials who could testify about it. How it was done before the reign of Henry II is not known for certain, although there are sufficient indications that in Henry I's day when pleas of the crown were heard by the local justiciars, the preparation and presentation of cases was done by subordinate officials of the local justiciars, and that they were the 'prosecutors' who aroused so much indignation.[27] From 1166 the juries of presentment removed the need for official accusers but not for preliminary investigations and the keeping of pleas; and although the responsibility for this may be assumed to have remained with the local justiciars they too soon disappeared with the transfer to the justices itinerant of the duty of hearing and determining pleas of

[26.] *EHD* iii. 304, cap. 20; see also R.F. Hunnisett, 'The origins of the office of coroner', *TRHS* 8 (1958), 85–104, 'Pleas of the crown and the coroner', *BIHR* 32 (1959), 117–37, and *The Medieval Coroner* (Cambridge, 1961).
[27.] See above, pp. 86, 107.

the crown. The duty of investigating then fell to the sheriffs' subordinates in the hundreds – usually though not invariably known as 'serjeants' and later as 'bailiffs' – though whether formal responsibility for the keeping of the pleas rested with the sheriffs or their serjeants is not clear. From 1194 it was laid upon the coroners, although the hundred serjeants continued to have a role in assisting them.

The appointment of coroners may be seen as a piece of administrative tidying: the completion of a train of reforms in the way that pleas of the crown were handled. It may be seen as a convenient solution to several administrative problems. It relieved the sheriffs and their subordinates of a serious duty at a time when they were increasingly burdened with routine tasks such as serving writs and empanelling juries under the new judicial procedures. It removed from the sheriffs a conflict of interest in distinguishing the crown's jurisdiction from their own. It lessened the opportunities for corruption, for knightly coroners serving the whole county were less likely than hundred serjeants to be subjected to persuasion to disguise a plea of the crown as a lesser offence or suppress information. Altogether it is typical of the ingenuity of the gifted administrators who ran the king's government at the end of the twelfth century, and especially of Hubert Walter who was responsible in his short justiciarship for several improvements in the operations of royal government; but quite apart from its administrative convenience the appointment of coroners was a major step in the development of what has been called 'self-government at the king's command'.[28] The trend began with the reforms which made juries of local men a regular and indispensable part of the administration of justice; the coroners too were local men called to assist in the king's government, but they differed from jurors in being continuously employed in an official capacity, and also in being elected by their peers in the shire court. The local community had always been involved in local government; now it was becoming an integral part of the king's government. To be elected as coroner was an onerous duty which individuals might seek to escape by proffering money to the crown to be excused service; but the principle was popular, and it would not be long before the men of the shires sought to have sheriffs elected.

The king's government in the later twelfth century was not remote from the men of the shires, commanding from a distance by impersonal writs: it descended on them in the visitations of the itinerant justices – the eyres. Nor were the shires remote from central government for barons of the exchequer, judges of the bench, the justiciar himself joined in the eyres. The visitations were of two kinds; the

---

28. The title of a book by A.B. White (Minnesota, 1933).

limited but frequent, and the comprehensive but at longer intervals. Visitations of limited scope were for purposes of taxation, or more often for judicial business, sometimes for both. The comprehensive visitations were intended in the later twelfth century to be at intervals of four years, and each took about two years to complete. For the comprehensive visitation W.C. Bolland popularized the term 'general eyre', but although historians have commonly employed it the term has no contemporary warrant: it was officially known as the eyre 'for all pleas' (*ad omnia placita*).[29] On a comprehensive eyre the professional judges and top-level administrators were joined by royal counsellors, including barons and bishops. It conducted a searching interrogation by a procedure laid down in 1194.

> Four knights are to be chosen from the whole county who, upon their oaths, are to choose two lawful knights from each hundred or wapentake, and these two are to choose upon their oath 10 knights from each hundred or wapentake, or free and lawful men if there are not enough knights, in order that those 12 together may answer to all the articles from every hundred or wapentake.[30]

The matters for enquiry as well as the functions which the itinerant justices were required to perform were specified in the commission known as 'the articles of the eyre' (*capitula itineris*). The range of business expanded at almost every comprehensive eyre until the articles became stereotyped in 1254, but the characteristic format of an eyre was already established under the justiciarship of Hubert Walter. We may distinguish five categories of business which, illustrated with examples of the articles from eyres at the end of the twelfth century, were as follows.[31]

(1) *Business of a judicial nature*
   For example:
   'Concerning pleas of the crown not yet concluded before the justices of the lord king.'
   'Also concerning recognitions [that is to say the petty assizes] and all pleas which have been summoned before the justices by the writ of the king or the justiciar or which had been remitted from the chief court.'
   'Also of grand assizes.'

[29]. W.C. Bolland, *The General Eyre* (Cambridge, 1922), now superseded by the works cited in the bibliographical note at the beginning of this chapter; for comments on the title see M.T. Clanchy, introduction to *The Roll and Writ File of the Berkshire Eyre of 1248* (Selden Society, 1973), pp. xix-xx, and Crook, *Records of the General Eyre*, p. 1.
[30]. *EHD* iii. 303.
[31]. Howden, iii. 262–7 translated in *EHD* iii. 303–6, Howden, iv. 61–2, *Munimenta Gildhallae Londoniensis*, ed. H.T. Riley (Rolls Series, 1859–60), i. 117–18.

'Also of malefactors and those who harbour and abet them [that is to say the procedures under the Assize of Clarendon.]

(2) *The interrogatories*
For example:
'Concerning escheats [that is to say fiefs reverting to the crown] and their values and who hold them and through whom.'
'Concerning daughters and sons of tenants-in-chief, and unmarried women, who are or should be at the disposal of our lord the king, and the value of their lands, and which of the males or females has married, and enquiry is to be made to whom, and by whom, and since when.'
'Concerning wardships which belong to the lord king.'
'Concerning churches to which the crown has the right of presentation, and who has them, and through whom, and what is their value.'
'Concerning purprestures [encroachments] on the king's lands and obstructions of his highways.'
'Concerning those who were accused [by the juries of presentment] and who fled but have now returned.'
'Concerning deceased usurers and their chattels' [for these were forfeit to the crown.]

(3) *The promulgation and enforcement of regulations*
For example:
'Wines sold contrary to the assize shall be seized on behalf of the lord king, and the owner of the wine as well as the seller shall be at the king's mercy [i.e., would have to pay an 'amercement assessed by the justices.]

(4) *Malfeasance by local officials*
For example:
'Of keepers of seaports, if they have received anything which they have not paid over, and if they have taken bribes for witholding the king's rights.'
'Of prises [i.e., things requisitioned for the king's use] by sheriffs or constables [of castles] or other bailiffs against the will of those whose chattels were taken.'

(5) *Special tasks of a non-recurring nature*
For example, in 1176 the justices were to enquire into the aftermath of the great war and were to check 'that the castles which have been destroyed are utterly demolished and that those due for destruction are utterly razed to the ground.' In 1194 they enquired into the aftermath of Count John's rebellion; and in the same year

into the anti-Jewish riots which had disfigured the start of the Third Crusade.

The articles of the eyre, wide-ranging though they were, do not indicate to the full the penetration of the eyre into what had been happening in the hundreds. The hearing of the pleas of the crown not infrequently brought to light irregularities, laxity, and maladministration by local people and were the occasion for sharp reminders of the law and their duties. Those at fault would be 'in mercy' and have to pay an amercement arbitrarily fixed by the justices. The records of the eyre in Lincolnshire in 1202 (which are among the earliest to survive) tell of hundred serjeants amerced for failing to summon the wapentake to a dead body, for omitting to call for an inquest, for putting a man known to be a villein on a jury of *novel disseisin*, for failing to attach (i.e., to put under surety) persons required to attend a trial.[32] One serjeant had omitted to attach the finder of a child drowned in a marsh; he explained that the person in question lived outside his jurisdiction; but the justices amerced him for not having informed the sheriff or the coroners 'who have power to make attachments throughout the county.'[33] Juries of presentment were amerced for failing to present cases which the justices learned of in other ways, or for presenting as pleas of the crown cases which were nothing of the kind.[34] One jury presented an appeal of wounding which came to nothing because the appellor failed to pursue the matter and was amerced; but the testimony of the coroners was that the original appeal had including an allegation of robbery, so the presenting jury was amerced also for having omitted it.[35] The jury of presentment of the town of Stamford wasted the justices' time by 'presenting foolishly' a case which had previously been heard and omitting another which they should have presented; but they were poor men who should not have been saddled with the task so the justices fined the whole township for not having appointed a proper jury.[36] A man died as the result of an accident in a quarry at Canwick, but the body had not been officially viewed before being buried, so the whole neighbourhood was 'in mercy'.[37] The amercements levied for minor defaults and technical infringements were not usually large – the villagers of Canwick had to pay half a mark (6s 8d) – but they were a reminder that there were rules to be observed and that the searchlight of the king's government swept into small corners. The sheriff of

[32.] *Earliest Lincolnshire Assize Rolls*, nos. 708, 820, 166, 543.
[33.] *Ibid.*, no. 701.
[34.] *Ibid.*, nos. 583, 604, 618, 880, 893a.
[35.] *Ibid.*, no. 882.
[36.] *Ibid.*, nos. 531, 532, 534.
[37.] *Ibid.*, nos. 805, 1051.

Lincolnshire at the time was Gerald de Camville, one of the greatest landholders in the county and a friend of the king, but even he did not escape rebuke for having failed to deliver a writ which his clerk revealed had been received.[38]

Peace-keeping

The eyres did not trespass upon the sheriffs' jurisdiction over petty crime nor inquire into local arrangements for enforcing the law and keeping the peace which the sheriffs supervised. How the arrangements worked in practice was nevertheless brought to light in the presentation of pleas of the crown as the justices heard evidence about the raising of the hue and cry, about the arrest or escape of suspects, and about the 'attachment' of persons required to attend before the justices on the security of pledges. The assize rolls generally recorded such matters only when there was a fault to be punished, but occasionally some of the customary procedures are revealed to us, as in this grim tale:

> Thomas son of Lefwin appealed Alan the reaper in that against the peace of the lord king he assaulted him as he was going along the road and carried him into his house and broke his arm and robbed him of his cap and his knife and held him down while Emma his wife cut off one of his testicles and Ralph Pilate the other. And after he had been castrated the aforesaid Alan threw him out onto the street. As soon as he could he raised the hue and cry and neighbours came at the cry and saw what had been done to him. Immediately afterwards he sent to the king's serjeant who came and found evidence of the robbery in Alan's house. And afterwards, as soon as possible, he reported the matter to the wapentake and shire courts. The serjeant being questioned testified that he went to Alan's house and found there the knife and the testicles in a small bowl but not the cap. The whole shire however testified that he had never previously accused Alan of breaking a bone in his arm.[39]

No one contested the main charge, but surprisingly the justices dismissed it; having heard what Alan had to say they seem to have concluded that the castration was a well-deserved act of vengeance. A story which follows is of admirable police-work recorded in detail because it provided evidence of a serious obstruction of justice.

> Thomas of Hainton the king's serjeant arrested Ralf of Ashby at Bardney fair because he was suspected of burglary at the house of Ranulf of Stainton and of binding Ranulf and his wife. And when he

---

[38]. *Ibid.*, no. 1146
[39]. *Earliest Lincolnshire Assize Rolls*, nos. 773, 773a, 773b, slightly abbreviated and paraphrased.

arrested him he advised him that it would go well with him if he indicted his confederates, and by his indictment Thomas arrested three others. But when he was leading them to a boat to convey them to Lincoln and was passing the gate of Bardney abbey the monks took the four robbers from him and put them in their almonry; and for this he produces witnesses namely Helto of Snelland and Robert of Alford and Ralf of Barkwith and Richard Malbersun. Ralf, however, escaped from the almonry but the servants of Thomas the serjeant were laying in wait for him and captured him. And he was brought before the justices; before whom the knights of the hundred testified that when he was captured he confessed to the robbery. And so he was sentenced to be hanged. The abbot was summoned to be at London at Michaelmas to answer for the monks.[40]

Unfortunately the outcome is not known; it must be assumed either that the monks were trying to protect their men or, more likely, that they were asserting a right to make arrests locally and to exclude the sheriff's men. The assize of Clarendon had forbidden this in respect of suspects indicted by the juries of presentment, but that applied only to Ralf in this case, not to his confederates.

The records speak more usually of defaults in the administration of the law: of failures to arrest, of escapes from gaol, of pledges who could not produce in court the man they had pledged. They were recorded because the defaulters were in mercy. For example:

William FitzRobert fled for the death of Andrew his brother; and he was in the frankpledge of Witherne, so it is in mercy. And his chattels amounted to 13s 8d and were handed over to Ralf the reeve of Brattleby and he does not have them before the justices, so he is in mercy. And Englishry was not satisfactorily presented, so it is a case of *murdrum*. The sheriff shall answer for the chattels.[41]

Often there was nothing that could be done about indictments made by the juries of presentment. For example:

Robert of Orleans was indicted of burglary at the house of Wolnet; he fled to sanctuary and has abjured the realm. And he has no chattels to be seized. Herman of Enderby, indicted for the same, has fled, and he was in the frankpledge of which William de Keinet of Enderby is the headman, and hence is in mercy. And there are no chattels.[42]

It was no doubt the impressions gained by the visiting justices of the state of the realm that prompted the king's government to make some attempts at overhauling the traditional methods for keeping the peace.

40. *Ibid.*, no. 1476.
41. *Ibid.*, no. 557.
42. *Ibid.*, nos. 588, 588a

In 1181 King Henry II made an Assize of Arms.[43] It required all freemen to take an oath that they would possess and bear arms in the king's service. They were to be divided into categories according to their wealth reckoned in terms of the value of their rents and chattels, and the weapons and armour for each category were specified. Those, for example, with chattels or rent worth 10 marks were to have at least a short coat of mail, a headpiece of iron and a lance. This measure may be seen as a revival or at least a reformulation of the old obligation on a freeman to *fyrd* service, with the substitution for the old hidage assessment to liability of a new principle of liability according to the wealth of individuals as assessed by juries of local knights. The assize was at first applied by the justices itinerant who were to proclaim it, take the oaths, arrange for the juries to make assessments, and have the names enrolled of those who were liable; but this did not become a regular function of the eyre. In the thirteenth century the rules were applied by the sheriff and two knights specially appointed for the purpose in the shire.[44] It was an obvious convenience to have armed men available to constitute a shire militia for local defence, and they were mobilized in 1193 to suppress the rebellion of Count John and in 1205 as a precaution against invasion; but local defence was not a pressing consideration in 1181 and there can be little doubt that the measure was intended also to ensure that there were everywhere well-armed men who could be called out for the pursuit and arrest of malefactors. Whenever the assize was subsequently renewed it was closely linked with arrangements for peace-keeping, and the Statute of Winchester of 1285, which provided comprehensively for local policing, referred to Henry II's measure as 'the ancient assize for keeping the peace'.[45]

In 1195, according to the chronicler Roger of Howden, Hubert Walter as justiciar had an edict applied throughout the realm which began as follows:

> That all men of the kingdom of England shall to the best of their ability keep the peace of their lord the king; and they shall not be thieves nor robbers nor harbourers of them; and that whenever they may know of such malefactors they are to endeavour to the best of their ability to take them and deliver them to the sheriffs, and they are on no account to be set at liberty except by the lord king or his justiciar; and if they are unable to capture them they shall report them whosoever they may be to the bailiffs of our lord the king. When a hue and cry is raised for the pursuit of outlaws, robbers, thieves, or the harbourers of them, all shall

---

[43] *EHD* ii. 416–17, C. Warren Hollister, *The Military Organization of Norman England* (Oxford, 1965), pp. 158–9.
[44] *EHD* iii. 357.
[45] *Ibid.*, iii. 357–8, and 461, clause VI.

join in the pursuit to the best of their ability; and if they shall see anyone who has manifestly not joined in the pursuit, or that he has withdrawn himself without permission from it, they shall take the same as though they were the offenders and deliver them to the sheriffs. Also, the knights who are appointed for the purpose shall require all persons of their respective districts of the age of 15 and upwards to appear before them to take an oath that they will keep the peace of our lord the king in the manner aforesaid.[46]

This edict is strikingly modelled both in form and wording on similar provisions in the laws of King Cnut, differing only in the appointment of knights to take the oaths and that the age for the swearing-in of boys was raised from 12 to 15.[47] It may be assumed that there was a continuous history since pre-Conquest times of the reception of boys by the hundred courts when they were old enough to take the oath to keep the peace and be recognized as law-worthy; but it may also reasonably be assumed that traditional practices were being slackly observed for Roger of Howden reports that the edict was immediately followed by the arrest of many malefactors and the flight of many more.

In 1205 the government of King John required the appointment in each shire of a 'chief constable' (*capitalis constabularius*), who should himself appoint constables in the hundreds and vills who should answer to him 'for the protection of the kingdom and the preservation of the peace against aliens or against any other disturbers of the peace.'[48] This was undoubtedly an emergency measure under the threat of invasion after the loss of Normandy: the 'aliens' were those who held lands on both sides of the Channel who had opted for allegiance to the king of France, and the term 'constable' had always hitherto had a military connotation. Nevertheless the constables merged with the other peace-keeping arrangements, though when they can next be seen they were no longer under the orders of a chief constable of the shire. In the peace-keeping legislation of 1242 the sheriffs and two knights appointed for the purpose were to have all men, including villeins, assessed and sworn to arms. Head-constables were to be appointed in the hundreds, with under-constables in the vills, 'on whose orders all in his hundred who are sworn to arms shall assemble and obey him in doing what concerns the keeping of our peace', including the pursuit and arrest of malefactors after the raising of the hue and cry. The constables were to be at the command of the sheriffs and the two knights, in whom may be seen the

[46.] Howden, iii. 299.
[47.] II Cnut 20–1, *EHD* i. 457.
[48.] Gervase of Canterbury, *Opera Historica*, ed. W. Stubbs (Rolls Series, 1879–80), ii. 96–7.

origin of the later 'keepers of the peace'.[49]

This co-ordination of peace-keeping arrangements in 1242 contrasts with the earlier piecemeal measures which did little more than bolster traditional practices; but it should be observed that there was a consistent policy to insist on the responsibility of local communities for policing and peace-keeping instead of a reinforcement of the sheriff's authority or (with the possible exception of the emergency measure of 1205) the appointment of royal peace-officers. This was of course wholly in line with Anglo-Saxon practice, with the knights of the shire taking over the role of the earlier thegns as influential members of the local communities. They did so as a function of their status rather than of their lordship. It is indeed striking that none of the measures for the government of the shires assigned a role to landlords: the units of local government remained the vills and the hundreds not the manors and fiefs. In point of fact many landlords had acquired rights to control local policing and the adminstration of justice through their own servants and to the exclusion of the sheriff and his servants; but the workings of these 'liberties' as indeed of local government generally in the shires in very ill-documented before the thirteenth century and must be reserved for consideration in a later chapter. It should however be observed that from the first penetration of the king's government into the shires, the rights of landlords to a share in government were regarded merely as complications in the operation of normal processes and not as exceptions to the law of the realm.

Revenue and Taxation

The methods used under Henry II and his sons to raise ever-increasing sums of money for the crown's use were both highly successful and fundamentally unsatisfactory. They were successful in that the king's most pressing needs were met, but unsatisfactory in that a problem remained, demand frequently threatened to outrun the supply, and the king's ministers were constantly having to improvise *ad hoc* expedients instead of consolidating the better solutions. No one accused these kings of profligacy in the expenditure of the realms's wealth, but there were frequent and mounting complaints of unbearable demands and dubious methods which persisted until Magna Carta.

It is impossible to draw up a balance sheet: there are no records of expenditure, and the surviving Pipe Rolls record only the ordinary revenues, or rather the outstanding balance of them. Extraordinary income, such as from newly devised taxes, was gathered into special

49. 'Form for keeping the peace, 1242', *Close Rolls 1237–42*, pp. 482–5, *EHD* iii. 357–9, A. Harding, 'The origins and early history of the keepers of the peace', *TRHS* 10 (1960), 85–109.

treasuries and accounted for in *ad hoc* 'exchequers', by-passing the regular exchequer and leaving few surviving records. If they leave any trace at all on the Pipe Rolls it was only because the arrears were transferred to the normal debt-collecting process after the special arrangements were closed down. The frequency of special arrangements and separate accounting is symptomatic of improvisation; the regular exchequer was operating at full stretch and had to be protected from overloading, but what was really needed was a thorough overhaul of the financial system. The patchy information available to us about financial expedients and special taxes comes mainly from chroniclers and a few royal writs; the gaps in the evidence are unbridgeable. The *Dialogus de Scaccario*, written about 1178, has no sequel. What can be attempted here therefore is a review of the methods but not an analysis of financial administration or a reckoning of the revenue.

The sources of royal revenue referred to by Henry II's treasurer in the *Dialogus de Scaccario* do not differ from those which may be detected in the one surviving Pipe Roll of Henry I's reign. They were broadly of three kinds: *domainal*, the revenues from royal estates and royal boroughs, *feudal*, the exploitable rights over the king's vassals, and *jurisdictional*, such as the profits of offering and doing justice. In addition kings of England had a special source of revenue in the geld levy. There was nothing comparable in other European realms. There was no recognized principle in the early Middle Ages by which a ruler could levy a general tax from his subjects; its absence is a reflection of the lack of any real conception of 'the state'. The geld itself of course was not a levy on each and everyone of the king's subjects, for it bore unevenly upon those who dwelt on 'geldable' estates; but it did have a 'national' character in being levied throughout the realm at a standard rate as a public duty. In the twelfth century it was known as 'danegeld', from which it may be inferred that the Normans recognized it as a unique tax levied for a unique purpose. This indeed is how the author of the *Dialogus de Scaccario* saw it: 'because this tax was instituted mainly on account of the Danes it was called danegeld.' He recognized that its purpose abated in the reign of William the Conqueror and believed, mistakenly, that it was thereafter levied less frequently than before the Conquest, being retained only 'in case of unforeseen attacks'.[50] In fact under Henry I it became a regular tax levied almost annually; but the mistake of Henry II's treasurer is understandable for in his personal experience it had been levied only two, or at the most three times. Its value had diminished. What had sufficed to meet the emergency of Danish attacks was not adequate for the continental wars and expensive alliances of post-Conquest kings. The geld had

[50.] *Dialogus*, pp. 55–6.

been designed to yield a specified sum of money and could not be made to tap the real resources of the realm without a major revision of its artificial assessment system. The Domesday survey had revealed what there was to be exploited and the limitations of the geld system, but no reassessment had followed. The reason is probably that the Norman barons were never reconciled to geld levies and resisted revision which would have drained even more money from their tenants. Their co-operation would have been necessary for a thorough reassessment. It was necessary also for a levy under the traditional system for although the assessment was on the hidage the collection of the amount due was through the agency of estate-holders. Henry I had compensated for the inadequacy of the return by levying it more often, but had to pay a price for doing so by excusing his barons from payments in respect of their demesne lands: in effect they divided the proceeds between them. Henry I insisted that remission was an act of grace conceded to individuals so that he could treat it as a form of patronage; but in fact remissions were so numerous that although a levy at the standard rate of two shillings on the hide should theoretically have yield about £5000 the actual return to the treasury was little more than £3000.[51]

The Pipe Rolls of the Henry II's reign show that he levied danegeld in 1155 and 1161 but record no subsequent payments. It has been assumed that Henry II abandoned it, either because it was no longer worth the trouble of collecting, or because of 'an unrecorded baronial victory over the Crown.'[52] The assumptions are questionable. It was certainly never formally abolished. There are indications that it may have been levied in 1173–4 but that collection had been overtaken by the great rebellion; the author of the *Dialogus de Scaccario* assumed that it was still operative though 'rare'; and a levy was taken on the old assessments as one of the methods for raising money rapidly to secure the release of King Richard I from captivity in 1193. Moreover, it should not be overlooked that Henry II may have introduced a substitute for the old form of danegeld: this at least is a plausible explanation of what *Dialogus de Scaccario* calls 'common assessments', and says were 'made from time to time in the counties by the justices in eyre. . .and apportioned in common at so much a hide by those who have lands in the county.'[53] How the sum was determined for the county and how the money was collected is not revealed; indeed the *Dialogus* treats 'common assessments' as too well-known to need much explanation, and mentions them chiefly to observe that

51. J.A. Green, 'The last century of danegeld', *EHR* 96 (1981), 243–58 and *Government under Henry I*, pp. 69–75.
52. Painter, *English Feudal Barony*, p. 78
53. *Dialogus*, pp. 47–8, see also pp. 57, 105, 108.

barons of the exchequer were exempt from such payments, as they were from danegeld. It is possible that by fixing the sum for each county instead of setting a rate per hide throughout the realm some of the disparities between counties in the old hidage assessments were adjusted; and further that the complications of individual remissions and the pursuit of arrears were avoided. It may thus be that 'common assessments' yielded more than danegeld; but until there was a better method of reckoning liability to pay than the antiquated and incomplete hidage there could be no hope of spreading the levy more evenly and drawing more payers into the net.

In 1198 under the justiciarship of Hubert Walter a determined effort was made to establish a new basis of assessment. The unit was to be the 'carucate' of 100 acres of ploughland. There was an elaborate procedure for assessing liability. A commission was appointed for each shire consisting of two nominees by the crown and two by the shire court. Each hundred was to nominate two knights before whom a delegation of the reeve and four men from each vill testified. Landlords or their stewards could challenge or confirm the testimony of the villagers. When the knights of the hundred were satisfied they reported to the county commissioners, who when they were satisfied had the details enrolled with copies for the sheriff, the hundred and the estate stewards. A levy on the carucates was known as a 'carucage' and estate holders were held responsible for the payments due from their lands in each vill; the money was to be tendered to the headman of the hundred and the two knights who had conducted the assessment; they paid it over to the sheriff who accounted for it at a special exchequer of receipt.[54] Despite the careful thought behind the arrangements for assessing and collecting the carucage of 1198 there were suspicions of malpractice. The justices who set out on eyre that year were instructed to inquire how the assessors and collectors had conducted themselves, whether everyone had paid what was due, and whether there had been any concealments.[55] The government's suspicions seem to have been justified for the Pipe Rolls reveal that no fewer than 23 counties subsequently offered lump sums 'for quittance of the carucage' or 'to be quit of an inquiry into the carucage.'[56] A second carucage was taken in 1200, but not again in John's reign despite his financial difficulties, which suggests that the attempt to bring the danegeld up to date was not adjudged a success. A later carucage in 1220, levied by the simpler expedient of counting ploughteams, is known to have brought in about £5500. The earlier carucages, being levied at a higher rate on a more meticulous assessment, must have

---

[54] Howden, iv. 46, Mitchell, *Taxation*, p. 97.
[55] Howden, iv. 62.
[56] Mitchell, *Studies*, p. 8 and n. 26, *Taxation*, pp. 91, 97, 108, 129–30.

brought in considerably more but probably not more than half the 20,000 marks which King John promised in 1200 to pay his overlord the king of France as a succession duty (the feudal relief) for his continental inheritance.[57]

For the kind of effort put into levying a carucage a vastly greater return could be had if the basis of assessment was income and personal property rather than units of productive land. This was well known in the later twelfth century from the levies to raise money for the Holy Land, promoted by the Church and based on the principle of the ecclesiastical tithe. In the first of these in 1166 all laymen and clergy were required to swear to contribute sixpence in the pound of their annual income and of the value of their chattels. A more rigorous procedure was used in England in 1188 in response to a papal appeal to rescue Jerusalem from Saladin. The money raised was collected by the crown as a direct contribution to the mounting of the Third Crusade. All laymen and clergy who had not personally taken the Cross were commanded by the king to 'give in alms' a tenth of their annual income and of the value of their movable property. The Church provided the sanction of excommunication and the clergy were prominent in the arrangements for collection; but the method of ensuring that no one cheated was typical of Angevin government: the king's ordinance required that if anyone was suspected of giving less than he ought 'four or six lawful men shall be chosen from the parish who shall declare upon oath what amount he should have declared, and this sum shall then be added to the smaller amount he tendered.'[58] Five years later as part of the prodigious efforts to raise the money for King Richard's ransom a tax of a fourth was levied on revenues, and according to one chronicler on movable property also; but information on how it was assessed and collected is scanty, and it seems likely that in the haste to gather money quickly lump sum payments were accepted in lieu of careful assessments.[59]

The levies for the Holy Land and the ransom were of course in every way exceptional; they stemmed from personal appeals by the pope or king; and they rested on a sense of obligation which could not be gainsaid even by those (and the chroniclers report that there were many) who complained about their disturbing novelty.[60] Nevertheless in 1207 King John succeeded in raising a tax from his subjects on incomes and personal property in preparation for a great campaign to recover the

[57]. Mitchell, *Studies*, pp. 32–4, 129–36.
[58]. 'Ordinance of the Saladin Tithe', *EHD* ii. 420. The writ for the collection of the levy of 1166 is given by Gervase of Canterbury, *Opera Historica*, i. 198–9, and that for 1188 in *Gesta Regis Henrici Secundi*, ii. 31.
[59]. Mitchell, *Taxation*, pp. 124–6.
[60]. Eg., William of Newburgh in *Chronicles and Memorials of the Reigns of Stephen, Henry II, and Richard I*, ed. R. Howlett (Roll Series, 1884–9), i. 282.

lands taken from him by the king of France. He persuaded a council of his barons, though not it is said without 'much murmuring', to agree to the levy of what was termed a 'Thirteenth', though it was actually slightly less at the rate of 12 pence in the mark of annual income and of the value of chattels possessed on the day that the council meeting concluded. The writs for collection declared that it had been authorized 'by the common counsel and assent of our council at Oxford for the defence of our realm and the recovery of our rights.' The need for justification seems to have been recognized. The method of assessment was relatively simple: the steward of every baron was to swear before the king's justices as to the value of his lord's income and chattels, and every other layman to swear personally. Teams of as many as 14 justices were appointed for every county to divide the work between them. The penalty for fraud or refusing to swear was the forfeiture of chattels and imprisonment at the king's pleasure. Some suffered it. Despite the simplicity and indeed crudity of the method the yield was over £60,000.[61]

King John was not able to take such a levy again: when he next needed large sums of money he was so much at odds with his barons that neither assent in council nor co-operation in the shires would have been forthcoming. The Thirteenth of 1207 has however been seen as the first example of the kind of national taxation which was to become normal and which replaced feudal and customary dues by public obligations. It exhibits already the characteristics of the later 'subsidies' in being a universal levy at a standard rate justified on a plea of necessity and legitimized by the acceptance of that plea by a body which was taken as speaking for the community.[62] But although it set a precedent it was not without roots. Some historians have seen the origins of it in the feudal principle of a 'gracious aid' by which a lord in financial difficulties could appeal for the help of his vassals and tenants.[63] It is not a subject about which much is known, but the returns to the so-called Inquest of Sheriffs in 1170 reveal, for instance, that the earl of Arundel not only received help from his vassals to defray his expenses on campaigns in Wales but also contributions from his tenants 'of their own free will' to discharge 'his debts to the Jews'.[64] Kings did indeed ask for 'aids' and 'gifts' from those subject to their lordship on the royal estates and in the towns; but there was no way in which the principle could be extended from the crown's tenants to all its subjects. Other historians have seen in the acceptance of

---

[61.] Mitchell, *Studies*, pp. 84–92, *Taxation*, p. 91 and n. 31, Painter, *King John*, pp. 131–5; the writ is in *Rot. Lit. Pat.*, p. 72.
[62.] Harriss, *Public Finance*, pp. 3, 27ff.
[63.] *Ibid.*, pp. 17–21.
[64.] *EHD* ii. 441–3; cf. Mitchell, *Taxation*, pp. 267–9.

'national taxation' the influence of ideas deriving from the revived study of Roman law in the twelfth century which reintroduced to western Europe the notion of the state and gave currency to long-obscured principles of political obligations and public duties. One aspect of this undoubtedly was to justify the superior right of a legitimate ruler to impose burdens for the common good when manifest necessity required it.[65] The higher clergy may be assumed to have been exposed to such ideas in the Schools; and at the Third Lateran Council in 1179 the papacy allowed that the clergy's duty to safeguard ecclesiastical property was not a bar to contributing to taxation by lay rulers for reasons of urgent necessity.[66] Nevertheless it has to be observed that in England it was the ecclesiastical tenants-in-chief who offered most resistance to taxation for secular purposes. In 1207, for example, King John first proposed that the prelates should help by granting him a percentage of the revenues of every beneficed clergyman, and only after their refusal subjected them to the levy of the Thirteenth to which the barons as a whole had agreed. John's half-brother, Geoffrey archbishop of York, staunchly denied the king's right to tax the tenants of lands held by the church and excommunicated the justices who entered upon his estates to take the sworn assessments; his lands were seized into the king's hands and the levy enforced.[67] For both Richard's ransom and the Thirteenth many, perhaps most, of the ecclesiastical tenants-in-chief salved their consciences, aligned themselves with the myth of the martyred Archbishop Becket, but also kept the king's goodwill by proffering large sums in lieu of having assessments made on their demesne lands.[68] Nor should we suppose that the lay tenants-in-chief were moved by theoretical justifications for national taxation: for both the release of King Richard from captivity and the recovery of Normandy their interests as well as their instincts were engaged. Baronial acceptance of new forms of taxation on incomes and personal property is less remarkable than that no more was required of them for assessment and collection than their forbearance, and that the procedures prescribed by the crown were effectively applied. This we should see as an outcome of forty years of royal government in the shires. The obligations of all subjects to the king as sovereign had become as accustomed as their obligations to their landlords. For the majority of the crown's subjects the alternatives to the levy of danegeld must have seemed a change of method not a change of principle.

[65] Eg. G. Post, *'Plena potestas* and consent in medieval assemblies', *Traditio* 1 (1943), 335–408, *Studies in Medieval Legal Thought* (Princeton, 1964), especially chapter iii.
[66] Post, *Medieval Legal Thought*, pp. 258, 81, 440 n. 18, Harriss, *Public Finance*, pp. 22ff.
[67] Painter, *King John*, pp. 134–5.
[68] Mitchell, *Studies*, pp. 87–9.

The inescapable fact, however, was that for the whole of the twelfth century danegeld and its substitutes were an inadequate supplement to normal revenues to sustain the king's defence budget. For specific campaigns 'aids' and 'gifts' and 'scutage' might be taken; but specific campaigns were infrequent. The more constant drain was for defensive operations and for disciplining disorderly vassals on the continent, for the payment and the maintenance of mercenaries, for ever more elaborate castle-works and the upkeep of garrisons, for siege engines, armaments and the transport of supplies. The revenue system of the continental dominions beyond Normandy was relatively primitive, so it was England and Normandy which had to pay for it. The costs mounted steeply from the last years of Henry II's reign as the French king became more challenging and better able to sustain threats, and as some of the continental vassals wavered in their allegiance, and, from the end of the century as inflation devalued the currency. The consequence was that all customary sources of revenue had to be made to yield more, eventually to the point at which and beyond which custom was strained and abused.

A resource which had been under-exploited by the Norman kings was what Domesday Book calls *terra regis* – the king's land. Although this greatly exceeded the royal estates in the reign of Edward the Confessor, it would be a mistake to think of it as intended to be a permanent landed endowment for the crown from which it expected to finance the operations of government.[69] It would be better to paraphrase *terra regis* as 'land in the king's hand'. There were of course manors especially regarded as 'royal' – the property of the royal family – which had been organized anciently to provide for the upkeep of the royal Household; but at least by the time that Bishop Roger of Salisbury was running the exchequer the victualling duties of these manors had been commuted into rents. By and large the *terra regis* was a pool of resources from which the king could make grants to his barons, reward his sheriffs and patronize the Church. The distribution of manors to Norman incomers was far from complete at the time of the Domesday survey, and under the Conqueror's sons there were lavish grants to buy support, set up followers, and reward service, which were to only a small extent counterbalanced by fiefs falling in again for default of heirs or forfeit for rebellion.

The *terra regis* was farmed by the sheriffs, that is to say each sheriff on taking office agreed to pay a lump sum in respect of the revenues from the relevant lands in the shire, and himself collected the rents or let the manors out to farm. The difference was his profit. So although

69. B.P. Wolffe, *The Royal Demesne in English History* (London, 1971), chapter 1 discussing the arguments of R.S. Hoyt, *The Royal Demesne in English Constitutional History* (Ithaca, New York, 1950).

the crown received a substantial sum from the *terra regis* via the sheriffs' farms – amounting in 1130 to over £9000 – it was much less than direct estate management – if that had been practicable – could have brought in. For the convenience of the exchequer the farms chargeable to the sheriffs became fixed in amount in Henry I's reign, with allowances made at the time of account for subsequent grants. In Henry II's reign ways were sought of increasing the yield which incidentally led to the emergence of a definable concept of 'the royal demesne', though the term itself did not become generally current until after 1194.[70] The royal demesne should not be thought of simply as land under cultivation for it included not only manors but also the boroughs and those towns which were not under baronial control. So the royal demesne may be most conveniently defined as comprising those communities rural and urban which had no lord but the king.

After the upheavals and confusion of Stephen's reign pertinacious inquiries were made as to what lands ought to be in the king's hands. Unauthorized encroachments, once identified, were usually neither confiscated nor restored to the sheriffs' control, but assigned a rental which was separately accounted for at the exchequer – in effect a diminution of the lands for which the sheriff farmed to the crown's benefit. Estates falling in, if not sold to a bidder, were put to farm separately or entrusted to a custodian who accounted for the revenues. The amount of separate farms could be increased from time to time to keep pace with rising prosperity. The manorial economy generally flourished in the twelfth century, in part because of an increasing population, and in part because of climatic changes which favoured the growing of cereal crops. It was not however easy to evaluate the many hundreds of manors under the sheriffs' control; the information supplied by Domesday Book became outdated, and the shire farms remained fixed. Ways were nevertheless found of siphoning off some of the sheriffs' increasing profits. Richard I notoriously auctioned the sheriffdoms at the beginning of his reign. The more usual method, introduced under Henry II, was to charge the sheriff an 'increment' in addition to the farm. The problem was to determine what a reasonable increment should be, but presumably the sheriff had himself to estimate the profitability of the royal demesne in his care and bargain with the king's ministers. Under Hubert Walter's management the exchequer better equipped itself to know the profitability of the royal demesne by commissioning itinerant justices in 1194 to make inquiries.

> Most diligent inquiry shall be made as to what is the fixed rent for every
> single manor in the demesne, and the value of all other assessments in

70. Wolffe, p. 21.

the said manors, and how many ploughlands there are and how much they are worth, evaluating them not at a standard rate of 20 shillings but according to whether the land is better or worse than that . . . Inquiry shall also be made as to how many draught animals should be supplied for the ploughlands, and how much stock the manors can support. And the answers shall be set down clearly and distinctly in writing. The value set upon a bull shall be four shillings, and a cow the same, and a plough-horse the same; and upon curly-fleeced sheep 10 pence, and upon a sheep with coarser wool six pence; and upon a sow 12 pence, and upon a boar 12 pence . . .[71]

Increment, however, was disliked by the men of the shires, especially at the very high rates charged in John's reign, for it induced the sheriffs to recoup themselves by extortion. Its renunciation was one of the concessions made in Magna Carta (clause 25).[72]

Much more satisfactory, but much more difficult to accomplish was to change the financial rôle of the sheriff from farmer to custodian, that is to say from paying a lump sum to accounting directly to the exchequer for all the issues from the royal demesne.[73] It required not only much more work at the exchequer but also a detailed knowledge of what the issues should be. Nevertheless, the experiment was tried in 16 shires in 1204 and the revenue increased by a third. By 1208, however, the experiment had foundered in all but a few shires. The reason was only partly the difficulty of getting proper accounts out of the custodian sheriffs (some of whom made proffers to be excused); it was also that political considerations cut across financial advantage. The profitability of the sheriff's office made it a convenient form of royal patronage: *familiares*, ministers and favoured barons held sheriff-doms, sometimes several, taking the profits but leaving the routine work to professional undersheriffs. The success of the experiment depended on the appointment of efficient administrators whose chief concern was a lasting career in the royal service; this was undoubtedly appreciated when the experiment was tried, for several such men were appointed to vacancies, often the very men who had been employed as undersheriffs; moreover, since professional administrators might be less effective at another of the sheriff's duties, that of managing the shire militia, the cognate experiment was tried in 1205 of appointing chief constables. It seems, however, that in pursuing this policy the justiciar and the exchequer found themselves at odds with the king and the court; and the worsening relations between the king and his barons

---

[71.] *EHD* iii. 304–5.

[72.] This concession was omitted from the reissues of Magna Carta and increment again became a bone of contention under Henry III, see J.R. Maddicott, 'Magna Carta and the local community', *Past and Present* 102 (1984), 28–30, 44–6.

[73.] On this topic see B.E. Harris 'King John and the sheriffs' farms', *EHR* 79 (1964), 532–42, and D.A. Carpenter, 'The decline of the curial sheriff in England, 1194–1258', *EHR* 91 (1976), 1–32.

made it imperative to have in control of the shires, their castles and their militia, political appointees whom he could trust. Some of them were notorious for extortion: in 1210, for example, the men of Dorset and Somerset proffered a large sum to be quit of William Brewer;[74] some of them were the king's foreign military captains, and Magna Carta was to concede that sheriffs should be men who 'know the law of the land and mean to keep it well' (clause 45).

Another way of increasing the yield from the royal demesne was to tax it, and this proved to be the most productive. In parallel with a lord's right in custom to seek a 'gracious aid' from his vassals and free tenants was his right to impose a levy known as 'tallage' upon his unfree tenants. In principle tallage was arbitrary, in practice it was regulated by custom to fixed amounts at regular times. Although tallage was a normal feature of the manorial economy after the Norman Conquest it was not levied by the Norman kings on their manorial tenants because they had a substitute in the geld which bore on their tenants as well as their other subjects. But with the ending of the traditional geld levy under Henry II some way had to be found of taxing the king's manorial tenants to complement the other substitutes for the geld in the 'aids' and 'gifts' taken from the king's towns and the 'common assessments' from his other subjects who were not his tenants. The tax which took shape from 1168 as a manorial levy was at first kept distinct from the aids of cities and boroughs on the Pipe Rolls, but it soon came to embrace all the tenants of the royal demesne, urban and rural, and to acquire the name of tallage.[75] Royal tallage, however, differed markedly from seigneurial tallage: it was not servile, it was not fixed in amount, it was not small and regular, it was large and occasional; and something too of the character of an 'aid' clung to it. It was taken only when the king had urgent need of additional money, and although it was imposed at the king's will and could not be refused, the amount to be paid was not determined arbitrarily but was open to negotiation. The method was characteristically ingenious. The agents in the negotiations were the itinerant justices (either as part of a normal visitation of the shires or specially commissioned); they required each urban or manorial community to make the king an offer; if an acceptable offer was forthcoming the community itself was allowed to apportion and collect it; but if the offer was unacceptable the justices assessed contributions from individuals which were collected by the sheriffs, with distraint, if necessary, upon defaulters. Collective offers were common, but in 1168 and from time to time thereafter the justices seem deliberately to have

[74.] *Pipe Roll 12 John*, p. 75, *Calendar of Charter Rolls*, i. 281–2.
[75.] On royal tallage see Mitchell, *Taxation*, Harriss, *Public Finance*, pp. 12–16; Wolffe, *Royal Demesne*, pp. 22–4.

made individual (*per capita*) assessments, no doubt to provide a yard-stick by which subsequent collective offers could be judged.[76]

The Pipe Rolls show that collective offers were usually paid promptly, and the exchequer was spared the trouble of pursuing individual debts. As much could be collected in a tallage from the royal demesne in Henry II's day as a danegeld without any remissions would have yielded from the realm as a whole. The return increased with rising prosperity and the tenants' capacity to pay. Care was taken to foster the prosperity. Justices in eyre had to check on the proper stocking of manors; tenants on the royal demesne were exempt from burdens, such as jury service, which fell on other men in the shires; the towns were allowed an increasing measure of self-government which freed them from the sheriffs' jurisdiction. The payment of royal tallage and its concomitant privileges not only gave the royal demesne an identity but also a special character. It is significant that in 1237 the tenants on the royal demesne said they would prefer to be tallaged rather than contribute to the subsidy of a thirtieth like the rest of the king's subjects.[77] A serious disadvantage, however, was that tallage on the royal demesne was at the king's will, and in John's reign that meant a crushing burden of frequent levies with collective offers spurned in favour of *per capita* assessments.

In parallel with the development of a tax on the tenants of the royal demesne, Henry II attempted to tax his feudal tenants – those who held fiefs from him by knight-service, including of course the greatest of barons.[78] In the early years of his reign Henry II raised money from his tenants-in-chief as his predecessors had done by 'aids' and 'gifts' and 'scutage'. This last – literally 'shield money' – was a payment in lieu of knight service. The provision of knights was an obligation on fief-holders, and the acceptance instead of scutage was a concession by the crown, granted to individuals, most commonly ecclesiastical tenants-in-chief. There could have been no objection in principle if the crown had at its convenience required the payment of scutage instead of knight-service in order to hire mercenaries, though whether it ever had been so levied is not clear; indeed the early history of scutage is very obscure. Although his intentions were not revealed, Henry II seems to have attempted to turn scutage into a general tax on his feudal tenants, on occasions other than military campaigns, and levied not on the amount of knight-service owed as an obligation (the *servitium debitum*) but on the amount of knight-service which was actually owed to the barons from the sub-fiefs which they had created on their honors. Exact figures cannot be determined, but the most

[76] *Dialogus*, pp. 108–9, Mitchell, *Taxation*, pp. 252–3, 258, 315–16.
[77] Mitchell, *op.cit.*, p. 239.
[78] On this topic see Keefe, *Feudal Assessments*.

trustworthy estimates put the *servitium debitum* at about 5300 knights, and the actual amount of knight-service at about 7500.[79] The latter figure was not known to the crown, but in 1166 the king required his barons to inform him by letters bearing their seals of all their tenants by knight-service. In 1168 he demanded contributions to the expense of marrying his eldest daughter, Matilda, to the duke of Saxony, though in fact it was levied after the event and much of the money went to finance military operations. It was the kind of aid which feudal custom allowed as of right to a lord, not a gracious aid requiring assent. It was to be assessed on the barons according to the actual amount of knight-service from their sub-fiefs. This was the occasion also for the first of the levies on the royal demesne: all the king's tenants, domainal and feudal were to be taxed at the same time for the same purpose.

The barons dutifully subscribed on their *servitia debita* but withheld additional payments. The exchequer persisted in trying to collect and year after year marked down their debts on the Pipe Rolls.[80] In 1187 Henry II made a deal and wiped the slate clean: he withdrew from having the barons assessed on the actual amount of knight-service but chivied out of them individual increases over their *servita debita* which brought the total knights' fees under assessment to over 6400.[81] Some adjustments in later years brought the total to nearer 6500 and so it remained for the rest of the history of scutage. Scutage was taken in the traditional way from those who did not serve or send their knights to the expeditions to Ireland in 1172 and to Galloway in 1187; but the next occasion for the taking of a general obligatory aid was for King Richard's ransom and it was levied on the agreed assessments. Henry II's sons pressed harder on scutage and tried to make it yield more. It was levied more often (four times in the first seven years of John's reign), sometimes without the option of supplying knights, sometimes even for proposed campaigns which did not take place, and at increased rates. Scutage could be productive: John financed his well-organized and well-paid expedition to Ireland in 1210 largely from a relentless tallage and a high-rate scutage. The barons demanded in 1215 that scutage be made subject to consent by 'common counsel'; but the acceptable compromise in the 1225 version of Magna Carta which became enshrined in law was 'that scutage shall be taken as it used to be taken in the time of King Henry II'.[82]

It has been said that 'the obtaining of consent was never any real

[79]. *Ibid.*, pp. 82–8.
[80]. Warren, *Henry II*, pp. 278–81.
[81]. Keefe, *Feudal Assessments*, p. 52.
[82]. Magna Carta 1215 clause 12, 1225 clause 37.

difficulty for the Angevin kings';[83] but while there is much truth in this statement, it has to be qualified. It is indeed remarkable that the assent of those with a duty to give counsel and a right to be consulted was obtained for all the changes in custom and law which produced so marked an extension of the king's government into the shires; but what we do not know is how much bargaining, and what persuasions and concessions went into the securing of assent. It may reasonably be suspected that a withdrawal from interference in lords' relations with their manorial tenants, as was threatened in the inquiries of 1170, was traded by Henry II for consent to the offer of royal justice to all freemen. And it may be that he backed away from developing a tax on feudal tenants in return for a free hand in taxing all freemen as subjects of the crown. It may be observed that in the better-documented history of his relations with the Church, and despite the bitterness of his quarrel with Archbishop Becket, Henry II obtained what he most needed but by no means all that he had demanded; he conceded that clergy should be exempted from trial in secular courts, except (as he adroitly secured from the pope) for offences against his forest law; and he never renounced the Constitutions of Clarendon, but released the bishops from their oaths to obey them, and achieved a *modus vivendi* with the Church which securely protected the royal interests.[84] King John knew how to bully or to buy to get his own way, but he conceded only when he had no option, and did not cultivate that bargaining skill which, we may believe, secured for his father a remarkable degree of baronial assent.

Much of the favour and patronage dispensed to individual tenants-in-chief must have been directed to securing their support, including their support in council. Unlike the Norman kings the Angevins had no large pool of *terra regis* from which to make grants of estates; but they could let manors at farm, grant wardships, the marriages of heiresses and well-dowered widows, profitable offices, the custody of castles, hunting privileges. The later twelfth century saw a marked extension of franchisal powers of lords, though usually of a minor kind and at the expense of the sheriffs' jurisdiction. The exercise of the crown's feudal rights could be moderated or withheld by the acceptance of proffers for assigning a wardship to kinsmen, for example, for having a free choice of marriage partner, for not being obliged to marry, for release from personal service on a campaign. Proffers swelled the Pipe Rolls, but the exchequer did not always press for payment even though it carefully recorded the debts; debts were themselves a source of patronage: when a baron sought a favour, the

[83.] J.C. Holt, *The Northerners* (Oxford, 1961), pp. 191–2.
[84.] Warren, *Henry II*, chapter 14. On the dispensing of patronage to individuals see J.E. Lally, 'Secular patronage at the court of King Henry II', *BIHR* 49 (1976), 159–84, and Keefe, *Feudal Assessments*.

king's ministers would drive a hard bargain, but the king might have the baron's payments on his proffer remitted, reduced or postponed. It is noticeable that the more influential barons were let off lightly in the revision of assessments of knights' service, and that their scutage payments were often in arrears. But dependence on the king's favour could be perilous; large debts could keep a baron in leading strings, and the withdrawal of the king's goodwill could lead to ruin. In 1158 William de Briouze, a prominent baron in Wales, secured from Henry II half the honor of Barnstaple for a proffer of 1000 marks. He made no payment for 20 years, and thereafter only small instalments. In 1201 King John cancelled the debt, which then stood at 640 marks, for William de Briouze the younger, who had helped John secure the throne and was high in his favour. At the same time King John accepted his proffer of 5000 marks for the vast lordship of Limerick in Ireland. Instalments were set by the exchequer, but William had good reason to think that he would not be pressed for payment. The loss of Normandy, however, soured John's relations with erstwhile friends, and William de Briouze, who knew too many of the king's secrets for comfort, in particular fell under his malevolent suspicion. John set about ruining him, advertising as his justification that William had defaulted on his debt payments for Limerick, ordering distraint for the debt on his Welsh estates, and sending in one of his mercenary captains, who held office as sheriff of Gloucestershire, with a force of 500 infantry and 25 mounted serjeants.[85] Making a proffer for an expensive favour was not the only way of becoming in debt to the crown; it was difficult to avoid it, for tenants-in-chief were obliged to pay relief for their inheritances. They too of course expected to take reliefs from those who held sub-fiefs from them; but inheritance dues were always a sensitive issue. Henry I had acknowledged that they should be 'reasonable'. Henry II, who had to fight for what he regarded as his inheritance and did much in his legal reforms to safeguard the rights of heirs, decreed that a reasonable relief for undertenants to have to pay to their lords was £5 per knight's fee; but the payment of relief by tenants-in-chief was too convenient a way for kings to dispense or withhold favour for the crown to forgo it by fixing a rate. As *Glanvill* states: 'for baronies there is no certain figure laid down; the tenants-in-chief in making satisfaction to the lord king for their reliefs are at his mercy and pleasure.'[86] Richard and John sometimes even took proffers for allowing themselves to be satisfied with a 'reasonable' relief.[87] Magna Carta (clause 2) decreed a standard rate of £100 for a barony.

85. Keefe, pp. 119, 121, Painter, *King John*, pp. 242–6.
86. *Glanvill* IX. 4, cf. *Dialogus*, pp. 96, 121.
87. J.C. Holt, *Magna Carta* (Cambridge, 1965), pp. 45, 207–8.

Although the Angevin kings had less scope than their Norman predecessors for granting lands they had more for dispensing favours; the expansion of royal government widened the market. Their subjects made proffers not only for the confirmation of charters and the consolidation of treasured rights, but also for having royal justice opened to them, for having a plea heard before the king's justices, or before the king himself, for having a plea transferred from the shire to Westminster, or from Westminster to the shire, for not being impleaded before anyone but the king himself, for hastening a hearing, or for having a plea postponed, for having a point in dispute put to a jury, or for being excused jury service.

The exercise of jurisdiction was highly profitable. Though the writs which initiated the new legal processes had to be paid for, this was probably not in itself a major source of profit to the crown for many of them (the writs 'of course' which could be issued without the necessity of the king's permission) were cheap and the charges could barely have covered the costs of the greatly enlarged judicial bureaucracy; but the visitations of the justices for the hearing of pleas swelled the river of judicial revenue. Quite apart from the sale of felons' chattels there were the amercements. Defendants in civil actions were amerced if the action succeeded, plaintiffs if the action failed. Appellors in criminal pleas were amerced if they withdrew their appeal or if the case was dismissed. Participants in whatever capacity, jurors, pledges, local officials, were amerced for every conceivable kind of mistake, misdemeanour or default. Amercements were generally small in amount, but so numerous that by the end of the century the exchequer had to abandon listing them: the sheriffs had the names of individuals from whom they had to collect and accounted at the exchequer only for the total. Amercements were determined arbitrarily by the justices, and what might seem small to them might not seem so to those who had to pay. It was the oppressive side of royal government. Magna Carta provided a welcome remedy. It then became the law of the realm that: 'A freeman shall not be amerced for a trivial offence except in accordance with the degree of offence and for a grave offence in accordance with its gravity, but not so that he is ruined; and a merchant in the same way, saving his stock-in-trade; and a villein . . . shall be amerced in the same way saving his livelihood (clause 20).'[88] The method of assessing an appropriate amercement was to be the method that had become the cornerstone of Angevin government: 'by the oath of good and law-worthy men of the neighbourhood'. The exercise of Angevin government whether in the exploitation of the king's rights or in the administration of the law was

[88.] Magna Carta 1225 clause 14.

most open to criticism not for harshness but for arbitrariness; but there was one respect in which it could be, and was, criticized for both, and that was in the application of forest law.

The Forest

Hunting rights have always been a mark of lordship. The laws of King Cnut declared, 'It is my will that every man be entitled to his hunting in wood and field on his own land; and everyone is to avoid trespassing upon my hunting wherever I wish to have it preserved.'[89] From long before Cnut's time there had been something special about the royal hunt. By ancient tradition which still left traces in parts of Domesday England, a ruler periodically traversed his territories to show himself to his people and at customary places held a great hunt at which his subject did him service, erecting, furnishing and victualling a hunting lodge, digging ditches and erecting fences to limit the chase, and beating game for their lord's sport.[90] There was something special too, but in a very different way, about royal hunting after the Norman Conquest. The Norman kings imported continental practice which derived not from Dark Age lordship but from Carolingian royal prerogative.[91] Districts suitable for hunting were designated as preserves, known as 'forests' and collectively as 'the forest', in which the beasts of the chase and their habitat were protected for the king's benefit. The boundaries of forests were widely drawn and embraced not only heath and woodland but also cultivated land, homesteads, villages and even towns. Some of it was the king's own land, but the lands of other lords fell within the bounds of designated forests and the rights which they would normally have exercised over their estates were circumscribed by the provisions of forest law administered by royal officers. To live under forest law was not to be excluded from the normal law as administered in the shires but to be subjected to an additional law of a harshly restrictive and punitive kind administered in special courts. Parts of many shires, and the whole of Essex, were under forest law.

There are no surviving forest records from any date earlier than the thirteenth century, and its boundaries and organization in the twelfth century are indistinct. Once there was a forest law there must of course have been ways of enforcing it. It is possible that in early days local

89. *EHD* i. 430.
90. W. Rees, 'Survivals of ancient Celtic custom in medieval England', in *Angles and Britons*, ed. H. Lewis (Cardiff, 1963), pp. 162–4, *VCH Lancashire*, i. 275–6, *VCH Durham*, i. 217, 286, 299, 301.
91. C. Higounet, Les forêts de l'Europe occidentale du Vᵉ au XIᵉ siècle', in *Agricoltura e Mondo Rurale in Occidente nell L'Alto Medioevo* (Seltimane di Studio del Centro Italiano di Studi sull' Alto Medioevo, 13, Spoleto, 1966).

royal foresters were answerable to the sheriff; but from Henry I's day it seems likely that there was more central control at least in the form of periodic visitations by royal justices with a roving commission.[92] From Henry II's day the administration of the forest seems to have developed in parallel with the rest of the king's government, with a chief forester corresponding in administrative duties to the justiciar, and with forest justices and forest eyres. What can be a little better known in the twelfth century is what forest law involved, from the accounts of chroniclers (invariably hostile) who included the texts of forest assizes, and from forest offences recorded on the Pipe Rolls.

In the districts designated forest the beasts of the chase – the red deer, the fallow deer, the roe, and the wild boar – could be taken only by the king and his men or those who had his warrant; anyone else, even on their own land, was restricted to hares and coneys, foxes and wolves, badgers and wildcats, and could hunt at all only after notifying a royal forester. More vexatious even than the restrictions on hunting, however, were those for the protection of the habitat (the *vert* of forest law). The cutting of timber, even the gathering of firewood were subject to restrictive rules; clearings to extend cultivation were severely limited. Pigs could be sent into the woods to forage acorns only under supervision and in specified weeks. To take a cart off the highway in a forest, to carry bows and arrows, to lead dogs without a couple, even to own a dog which had not been 'lawed' by having its forefeet clipped, were serious offences.

After the disorder of Stephen's reign when forest law was widely flouted, searching inquiries were made, the king's rights established, and the organization overhauled. A periodic inspection of the forest in each county (known as the *regard*) was made by the sheriff and 12 knights to answer a list of questions about the state of the woods and herbage, as to who were properly licensed, as to whether there were charcoal burners, miners and iron forgers at work, as to licensed clearing (*assarts*) both old and new, and as to unauthorized encroachment (*purprestures*). The crops on assarts had to be noted, for a rent was charged according to the crop grown even though the assart was not on land belonging to the king; purprestures for which penalties were levied could include extending a hedge, erecting a mill or digging a fishpond. A regard was held on the king's instructions whenever forest justices were about to visit. Forest eyres seem to have been held regularly at intervals of a few years from 1166. It was probably in 1166, that remarkable year for innovative measures, that Henry II made his first assize of the forest which clarified the rules and warned

92. H.A. Cronne, 'The royal forests in the reign of Henry I', in *Essays in British and Irish History*, ed. H.A. Cronne, T.W. Moody and D.B. Quinn (London, 1949), pp. 1-23.

that they were to be strictly enforced in future.[93]

The area under forest law was greatly expanded in the second half of the twelfth century, and, though it is difficult to be precise, may have covered as much as a third of the realm. When inquiries were made in the thirteenth century as to afforestation under Henry II it was said to have included the whole of Huntingdonshire; in Oxfordshire it was said that all the woods of knights and freemen had been brought under forest law whereas previously it had applied only to the king's demesne woods in the county.[94] The only reason which contemporaries offer for the expansion is the king's passion for hunting; but there were forests in parts of England which the king never visited: Pickering in north Yorkshire for example, Allerdale in Cumberland, Exmoor in Devon. The reason must be economic advantage. The forest produced a useful revenue. There was a regular income from rents for the agisting of pigs, for pasturage on cattle meadows, for assarts, and for the harvesting of timber; and a much larger casual income from fines and amercements and from the sale of privileges and exemptions. A forest eyre brought in on average about £2000. A particularly savage eyre in 1212 put debts totalling nearly £5000 on the Pipe Roll; but even that pales in comparison with the forest eyre of 1175. Forest law had been relaxed during the civil war of 1173–4 by the justiciar with the assent of the king; but after his victory Henry II revoked the concession and a searching forest eyre netted over £12,000.[95] It is a measure of what the royal foresters and the law they applied normally held in check. The forest was also useful to the crown for its produce. Venison, fresh or salted, was supplied to the king's Household wherever he was, and was sent at his order to friends and garrisons. Timber was cut for building works at royal residences and castles; and the difficulty and high cost of transporting timber made local supplies desirable. Forest industry produced large quantities of hides, peat, roofing shingles, arrows, iron arrow heads and quarrels. It may also be that behind the restrictive forest law was some thought of conservation: there can be little doubt that the swelling demands for disafforestation reflect an expanding population and increasing pressure on available land; and there can equally be little doubt that without the restrictions there would have been indiscriminate and imprudent destruction of woodland. The extension of cultivation was not altogether prohibited: the bounds of the forest expanded but so too did assarting within it; it was however controlled and a price in rentals exacted. The crown was as it were taking a toll on

93. J.C. Holt, 'The assizes of Henry II: the texts', in *The Study of Medieval Records*, ed. D.A. Bullough and R.L. Storey (Oxford, 1971), pp. 97–8, Young, *Royal Forests*, p. 34.

94. Young, pp. 19–20.

95. *Ibid.*, pp. 37–9, 55.

land development. The build-up of resentment was however such that the government under Richard I and John sought first to appease it and take a quick profit by accepting proffers for disafforestment, and then in the crisis of 1215 conceded the demand for reduction of the forest to its bounds at the coronation of Henry II.[96]

Contemporary chroniclers tell lurid tales of harassment by royal foresters and imply that widespread peculation, bribery and extortion were inseparable from the enforcement of forest law. Something of the profitability of the office of forester can be gauged from proffers: 900 marks and five palfreys were offered for custody of the forest of Cumberland, and 200 marks for permission to marry a forester's daughter with the reversion of his office after his death.[97] John's chief forester loaned the king 3350 marks from his personal fortune against future forest revenues. Angevin government was not oblivious to abuses nor insensitive to criticism. The author of the *Dialogus de Scaccario*, although he was the royal treasurer, disapproved of forest law because it rested 'not on the common law of the realm but on the will of the ruler.'[99] A few years after he wrote, Henry II, in 1184, countered the criticism by having the forest law reformulated and modified in an Assize of the Forest made, we are told, 'with the advice and assent of the archbishops, bishops, barons, earls, and magnates of England.'[100] But he was not prepared to bend to the criticism that a forest eyre troubled a whole county and not just those who dwelt within or near a forest, insisting that all including the greatest of barons and even the bishops must attend a forest eyre at the summons of the chief forester 'if they would avoid falling into the mercy of the lord king.' In 1215 Magna Carta (clause 44) allowed that 'Men who live outside the forest need not henceforth come before the justices of the forest upon a general summons unless they are impleaded or are sureties for any person or persons who are attached for forest offences.'[101] On the other hand the most important reform in the administration of the forest law must have preceded Magna Carta in the appointment from the end of the twelfth century of new officials known as 'verderers' who were similar in function and purpose to coroners. They were men of knightly status, usually four in number for each forest, elected in the shire court and receiving no emoluments or perquisites. They inspected the evidence for a forest offence having been committed, and supervised the attachment by pledge or imprisonment while awaiting trial of those alleged to have committed

96. Holt, *Magna Carta*, pp. 52–3, 235–6.
97. *Pipe Roll 6 John*, pp. 143–4, *Pipe Roll 9 John*, p. 149, Young, *Royal Forests*, p. 52.
98. Young, pp. 50 and 182 n. 103, Painter, *King John*, pp. 68–9.
99. *Dialogus*, pp. 59–60.
100. *EHD* ii. 418–19.
101. Reissued as the Charter of the Forest, 1217, clause 2, *EHD* iii. 338.

offences.[102] Without their supporting testimony no case could be effectively prosecuted before a forest eyre. Nevertheless the reason why forest law was held to be oppressive as well as restrictive can be appreciated from a case on the earliest surviving record of a forest eyre. The Assize of 1184 had allowed that a lord who had a wood on his land within a forest might appoint his own forester but had to stand surety for the redress of any transgressions by his forester against the king's rights. On the eyre of 1209 in Northamptonshire the justices heard that the head of a hart recently dead had been found by royal foresters in a wood belonging to Henry Dawney at Maidford; but the forester of Henry Dawney could not testify about it because he was dead. The verdict of the justices was that 'because nothing can be ascertained of that hart, it is ordered that the whole of the aforesaid town of Maidford shall be seized into the king's hand with the wood belonging to it, on the ground that the aforesaid Henry can certify nothing of that hart.'[103]

In 1215 King John promised to have 'evil customs' of the forest investigated and abolished. The Charter of the Forest of 1217 provided for a drastic curtailment of the extent of the forest, eased the restrictions on a man improving his own land within a forest 'without fear of prosecution', abolished the old law that a man taken for offences against the king's venison might suffer mutilation or death, and released from outlawry all those who had been outlawed for forest offences alone.[104] Something of the fear as well as the vexation of forest law must then have been lifted. For a century and a half the forest law and its enforcement must have been for all ranks of society the most persistent and alarming expression of the wilful authority of post-Conquest kings; and it was the strongest justification for having that authority 'lawed'.

Magna Carta as a Critique of Angevin Government

We should not suppose that Magna Carta was a set of demands imposed on a reluctant king made helpless in 1215 by the united opposition of an overwhelming majority of his barons. It was an attempt to find a formula for peace between the king and those of his subjects who had taken up arms against him made by those barons who wished to avert a civil war. Nor should we suppose that grievances about the operations of royal government were the mainspring of the rebellion against King John. The grievances of the rebels were multifarious and often personal. The leading rebels, who had shown their

102. Turner, *Pleas of the Forest*, pp. xix–xx.
103. *Ibid.*, p. 4.
104. Magna Carta 1215 clause 48, Charter of the Forest 1217, *EHD* iii. 337–40.

hand as early as 1212, were those excluded from royal patronage and unable to recoup the losses they had suffered in Normandy. They hit upon the exploitation of grievances as a means of recruiting support, the main issues at first being military service overseas, the crown's exploitation of its feudal rights, and the restrictions and savagery of forest law. That grievances about royal government were his Achilles' heel was belatedly recognized by King John and from 1213 he tried not only to placate individuals and the Church, but also, for example, reined in forest officials. The bidding and counter-bidding for support had by the spring of 1215 produced a stalemate with neither side quite sure of winning in an open conflict. That was the opportunity for those who wished to avoid civil war but were also keen to pin the king down to concrete concessions. The Charter of Liberties of 1215 was expressly intended both for 'the restoration of peace' (*ad pacem reformatum*) and 'the rectification of the realm' (*ad emendationem regni*). It was a test of the sincerity of both the rebels in alleging the redress of grievances as their justifiable purpose and of the king in offering concessions 'for the better allaying of discord'; but neither the king's determination to crush rebellion, nor the extremist rebels' determination to be rid of King John could stand the test, and the Charter failed as a formula for peace. It was nevertheless instrumental in isolating the extremist rebels and eventually putting an end to the civil war. King John died in October 1216 while taking the offensive against the rebels, leaving as his successor a nine-year-old son in the care of a regency council. The middle ground was won for the young king by the reissue of the Charter in his name as a royalist manifesto, though it was shorn of those concessions which were least acceptable to the crown. It was, however, a principle of the regency council that grants made while the king was a minor could only be provisional. It was therefore the version of Magna Carta (with an accompanying Charter of the Forest) which was issued in 1225 by the king's 'own spontaneous goodwill' which became the law of the land. It may then be argued that Magna Carta, so far from being the radical demands of rebels, reflects what reasonable men thought was amiss with Angevin government. The objections may be summarized as the arbitrary exercise of royal rights, discrimination against individuals, and the overriding of acknowledged principles for administrative convenience. This is not the place for an analysis of Magna Carta nor a commentary upon its clauses, but we may rest a critique of Angevin government upon aspects of it.

In the forefront of the charter are clauses limiting the crown's exploitation of its feudal lordship in respect of the payment of relief by heirs (clauses 2 and 3), wardship (clauses 4 and 5), the marriage of heiresses (clause 6), and the widows of tenants-in-chief (clauses 7 and

8). The crown had, through the practice of its courts, fixed rules on what was reasonable for lords to exact from their vassals but had preserved its own freedom to make arbitrary demands upon tenants-in-chief and their families. As *Glanvill* says on the levying of reliefs: 'for baronies there is no certain figure laid down: the tenants-in-chief in making satisfaction to the lord king for their reliefs are at his mercy and pleasure.'[105] It was generally acknowledged that a lord who had the wardship of an heir who was a minor and drew the revenues from the estate could not reasonably demand a relief when the heir came of age; both *Glanvill* and the *Dialogus de Scaccario* say so; but Angevin kings exempted themselves.[106] For example, the inheritance of Eustace de Vesci was in the hands of the crown for eight years yielding to the exchequer an annual income of at least £400; but when he came of age in 1190 he was charged a relief of 1300 marks (£867).[107] The king's courts administered to other men the strictest rules for the protection of widows, their dower and their re-marriage; but the crown itself was not so punctilious.[108] The widows of tenants-in-chief were usually allowed to remain unmarried if they wished, but a stiff price was exacted. For example, Henry II took £50 from the widow of William de Heriz that she should not be obliged to marry against her will.[109] The widow of the earl of Warwick offered 700 marks 'to have the land of her father and her dower, and that she should not be married except to someone of her choice'.[110] Similarly in John's reign the widow of Ralf of Cornhill offered 200 marks and three palfreys that she should not be married to Geoffrey of Louvain but could marry whomsoever she wished.[111] The crown could exploit its feudal lordship not only for financial but also for political reasons when it had heirs at its mercy. For example, King John demanded the huge relief of 7000 marks from John de Lacy, whom he distrusted, and required him to surrender his castles of Donington and Pontefract until the debt should be discharged, and to contribute £40 a year to their upkeep.[112] Similarly, in demanding from Nicholas de Stuteville the exorbitant relief of 10,000 marks King John was not expecting him to be able to pay, and did not in fact press for payment, but took from him two manors and the castle of Knaresborough as security for the debt.[113]

Discrimination against individuals lies behind another important

---

105. *Glanvill* IX. 4, p. 108, cf. *Dialogus*, p. 96.
106. *Glanvill* IX. 4, p. 107, *Dialogus*, pp. 96–7.
107. Holt, *Magna Carta*, p. 210.
108. *Glanvill*, book VII.
109. *Pipe Roll 28 Henry II*, p. 17.
110. *Pipe Roll 31 Henry II*, p. 76.
111. *Rot. de Ob. et Fin.*, p. 37; for other examples see Holt, *Magna Carta*, p. 46.
112. *Rot. de Ob. et Fin.*, pp. 494–5, Holt, *The Northerners*, p. 182.
113. *Rot. de Ob. et Fin.*, p. 305, Holt, *Magna Carta*, pp. 208–9, 257–8.

concession in Magna Carta: 'To no one will we sell, to no one will we deny or delay right or justice' (1215 clause 40, 1225 clause 29). Henry II was accused of being a seller and delayer of justice. The author of the *Dialogus de Scaccario* came to his defence, arguing that the crown does not sell *judgements*, but might accept proffers to open the door to speedier justice, adding that 'the king has ordained that applicants shall not be required to tender their offerings until justice has been done, whether judgement is for them or against them.'[114] But the defence is not altogether reassuring, and there is evidence to tell against it. Large proffers were accepted simply for allowing a man to have a hearing. William Mowbray offered King John 2000 marks for justice in his case when William de Stuteville claimed his barony.[115] Here is an item recorded on the Memoranda Roll of the exchequer in 1208: 'The earl of Clare owes £100 for having a writ of *mort d'ancestor*';[116] but an ordinary man could have a writ of *mort d'ancestor* for half a mark as a matter of course. The crown could close its courts altogether against the disfavoured. The same Memoranda Roll notes: 'The king is to be consulted about the 20 marks which Robert de Crec was required to pay for having right about a certain manor; the sheriff says the lord king has prohibited him from pleading.'[117] In 1206 Alexander of Caldbeck had a plea about an estate in Cumberland postponed indefinitely 'because it was not pleasing to the king that he should have a jury.'[118] But surely, said John, 'it is only reasonable that we should do better by those who are for us than those who are against us.'[119]

That the crown considered itself exempt from the rules it applied to its subjects is illustrated, if somewhat obscurely, in clause 38 (1225 clause 28): 'Henceforth no official shall oblige anyone to stand trial without bringing credible witnesses to the charge.' There was nothing novel about this: it was the principle which Henry II had insisted in the Constitution of Clarendon should be observed by the church courts, and it was the principle which lay behind the substitution in 1166 of juries of presentment for prosecution by official accusers. But although a principle it did not become a law applicable to the crown until Magna Carta made it so. An even more striking example of 'executive privilege' claimed by the crown is illustrated in the most famous clause of Magna Carta (1215 clause 39, 1225 clause 29): 'No free man shall be arrested or imprisoned or disseised of his freehold

114. *Dialogus*, p. 120.
115. *Pipe Roll 3 John*, p. 157.
116. *Memoranda Roll 10 John*, ed. R.A. Brown (Pipe Roll Society, 1957), p. 58.
117. *Ibid.*
118. *Curia Regis Rolls 1205-6*, p. 99.
119. *Rot. Lit. Claus.*, i. 87; see also R.V. Turner, *The King and his Courts*, pp. 60-4.

. . . nor in any way ruined . . . except by the lawful judgement of his peers or by the law of the land.' Again, the principle was not new; it had achieved concrete expression in Henry II's edict that disseisin was wrong and punishable as a plea of the crown if it did not follow from the judgement of a court. But there was no sanction to apply to the crown itself if it resorted to disseisin without judgement, as it frequently did. Disseisin 'at the king's will', or 'by the king's order' was used, with some justification, as a means of disciplining royal officials: King John, for example, disseised Theobald Walter, sheriff of Lancashire (who in the previous reign had enjoyed the protection of his brother, Hubert Walter, the justiciar) 'for his many transgressions'; but it was also used as a political weapon or against someone who had fallen foul of the king.[120] Adam of Hales and his brothers petitioned King John 'to have seisin of the lands of their father in Shoreham from which their father was disseised, and was imprisoned by the will of King Henry, for no other reason that that he was with the Blessed Thomas [Becket] in his persecution.'[121]

It was a valid criticism of Angevin government that it allowed its servants to act arbitrarily in the crown's interests. There is a clutch of clauses in the charter to control the requisitioning of corn, timber, and horses and carts for the king's service (1215 clauses 28, 30, 31, 1225 clauses 19 and 21). And clause 9 (1225 clause 8) prohibits the seizure of land in payment for debt 'so long as the chattels of the debtor are sufficient to repay the debt; nor shall the sureties of the debtor be distrained so long as the debtor himself is capable of paying the debt.' Such debt-collecting practices were contrary to an ordinance of Henry II described in the *Dialogus de Scaccario*, but King John had overturned that in 1201.[122]

On the other hand it should be observed that Magna Carta tacitly accepts the transformation of royal government since 1166. It did not seek to overturn any of the judicial or administrative developments which had made the crown a compelling force throughout the realm. On the contrary it asked for more accessible royal justice. Clause 17 (1225 clause 11) provided that 'common pleas . . . shall be held in some fixed place', instead of being heard in the court which followed the king, as they had been since King John closed the bench at Westminster in 1209. And clause 18 (1225 clause 12) required visitations of the shires as often as four times a year by justices commissioned to determine cases brought by writs of *novel disseisin* or *mort d'ancestor*.

120. *Calendar of Inquisitions Post Mortem*, i, (Public Record Office, 1904) no. 264. For the weapon of disseisin as used by the Angevin kings see Jolliffe, *Angevin Kingship*, chapter iii.
121. *Pipe Roll 5 John*, p. 103.
122. *Dialogus*, pp. 110–12, Howden, iv. 152.

Angevin government, directed by the will of imperious kings, could be arbitrary, unreasonable, unjust and harsh; but Magna Carta's acceptance of it, with royal wilfulness curbed, should remind us that there was much to be said in its favour. Let us take three examples of royal government in action. The first is from a Pipe Roll of Henry II's reign: 'The village of Malden accounts for three marks for hanging a thief without the view of a royal official.'[123] The headman of the village was separately fined five marks. This may have been a technical breach of a rule; but the implication of the rule was important: the crown will not tolerate lynch law. The next example is from the record of an eyre in Lincolnshire in 1202: 'Eustace of Thoulebi, the serjeant of the wapentake, is in mercy because he said that with the counsel of the wapentake he took charge of the chattels of a certain man who hanged himself, and the wapentake failed to corroborate him.'[124] A local official has been pilfering in the course of his duties; the crown will not tolerate it. The third example is from the same eyre. In the city of Lincoln the bedells 'took a certain stranger and put him in the pillory because he could not find pledges.' Unfortunately the staging collapsed under the pillory, the stranger 'let his feet drop' and before anyone could get to him he died. The reeves of the city come before the king's justices and say that they were in London at the time delivering 'the farm of the city' and ask for the testimony of a jury that they were not responsible. The coroners come before the king's justices and say that they were not there at the time, that they had never seen the man and did not know who he was. The entry concludes: 'Let those responsible be held in custody.'[125] A man has died; it was an accident but it should not have happened; there was no justification for putting him in the pillory; and example must be made of those responsible; the matter cannot be hushed up. These are small cases; the people out of whom the cases arose were nameless nobodies – a thief, a suicide, a vagrant; but it is their insignificance which makes these cases important. It is astonishing that the crown bothered; it is astonishing that the king's justices with a mass of business requiring attention took the time to uncover little local tyrannies and stamp on them. This was better government than in other places and at other times. The crown imposed discipline; but it required disciplining itself.

---

123. *Pipe Roll 31 Henry II*, p. 17.
124. *The Earliest Lincolnshire Assize Rolls, 1202–9*, ed. D.M. Stenton (Lincoln Record Society, 1926), no. 918.
125. *Ibid.*, no. 1012.

Bibliographical Note

The Politics of Kingship

The most detailed study of the reign is F.M. Powicke, *King Henry III and the Lord Edward. The Community of the Realm in the Thirteenth Century* (Oxford, 1947). A useful short survey is E.F. Jacob, 'England: Henry III' in *The Cambridge Medieval History*, vi (Cambridge, 1929). For a revisionist interpretation see M.T. Clanchy, *England and its Rulers 1066–1272* (London, 1983), part 3, and 'Did Henry III have a policy', *History* 53 (1968), 203–16. On the nature of the sources see G.R. Elton, *The Sources of History: England 1200–1640* (London, 1969).

Central Administration, Finance, and the Sheriffs

The seminal work is T.F. Tout, *Chapters in the Administrative History of Mediaeval England*, i (Manchester, 1920), but it should be observed that the sub-title of the work is *The Wardrobe, the Chamber, and the Small Seals*. A shorter but broader review of the administrative history of the reign is the first chapter of R.F. Treharne, *The Baronial Plan of Reform 1258–63* (Manchester, 1932, reprinted 1971). There are major contributions to administrative history in F.M. Powicke, *Henry III and the Lord Edward*, and E.F. Jacob's chapter in *The Cambridge Medieval History*, vi, cited above, and in B. Wilkinson, *Studies in the Constitutional History of the Thirteenth and Fourteenth Centuries* (Manchester, 1937). A convenient digest of earlier work is supplied by S.B. Chrimes, *An Introduction to the Administrative History of Medieval England* (Oxford, 1952). Finance is most conveniently approached through G.L. Harriss, *King, Parliament, and Public Finance in Medieval England to 1369* (Oxford, 1975), chapters II, VI and VIII. For the policy of the crown towards the sheriffs see D.A. Carpenter, 'The decline of the curial sheriff in England 1194–1258', *EHR* 91 (1976), 1–32.

Government in the Localities

Shires and hundreds

For an introductory survey see H.M. Jewell, *English Local Administration in the Middle Ages* (Newton Abbot, 1972). Of major importance are A.B. White, *Self-Government at the King's Command* (Minnesota, 1933, reprinted 1974), and H.M. Cam, *The Hundred and the Hundred Rolls. An Outline of Local Government in Medieval England* (London, 1930). There is much useful information in W.A. Morris, *The Medieval English Sheriff to 1300* (Manchester, 1927, reprinted 1968), and *The Early English County Court* (Berkeley and London, 1926). See also M.T. Clanchy, 'Law, government and society in medieval England', *History* 59 (1974), 73–8; T.F.T. Plucknett, *The Medieval Bailiff* (Creighton Lecture, London, 1953).

Franchises and liberties

There is as yet no adequate study of this topic. General introductions are provided by F. Pollock and F.W. Maitland, *The History of English Law before the time of Edward I* (2nd ed., Cambridge, 1898), i.571ff, S. Painter, *Studies in the History of the English Feudal Barony* (Baltimore, 1943), chapter IV, and most usefully by H.M. Cam, 'The evolution of the medieval English franchise', *Speculum* 32 (1957), 427–42, reprinted in *Law-Finders and Law-Makers in Medieval England* (London, 1962), pp. 22–43. See also: H.M. Cam, *The Hundred and the Hundred Rolls* (London, 1930), pp. 202–20; N. Denholm-Young, *Seignorial Administration in England* (Oxford, 1937), chapter III; D.W. Sutherland, *Quo Warranto Proceedings in the Reign of Edward I* (Oxford, 1963), chapter I. The following more specialized studies are particularly illuminating: G. Barraclough, *The Earldom and County Palatine of Chester*, reprinted as a

7
Government under Henry III, 1216–1272

The Politics of Kingship

King John died in October 1216 in the midst of a civil war, and was replaced on the throne by his eldest son Henry, then a boy of nine years. Although the succession of a minor was unprecedented it did not create unprecedented problems for the governance of the realm, for in practice the situation was not unlike that of King Richard's prolonged absence on crusade and in captivity. The overriding problem in 1216 was the civil war, which was not ended by the death of King John for his opponents had their own candidate for the throne in Louis, son and heir of the king of France, who was at large in the realm with a formidable force of French troops. The young Henry III

---

pamphlet (Oxford, 1953) from *Transactions of the Historic Society of Lancashire and Cheshire*, 103 (1951); H.M. Cam, 'The king's government as administered by the greater abbots of East Anglia' in her *Liberties and Communities in Medieval England* (London, 1963), pp. 183–204; M.T. Clanchy, 'The franchise of return of writs', *TRHS* 17 (1967), 57–79, and his introduction to *The Roll and Writ File of the Berkshire Eyre of 1248* (Selden Society, 1973), pp. xxviii–xxxiii; F.R.H DuBoulay, *The Lordship of Canterbury* (London, 1966), chapter 7; R.R. Davies, 'Kings, lords, and liberties in the March of Wales, 1066–1272', *TRHS* 29 (1979), 41–61; N.D. Hurnard, 'The Anglo-Norman franchises', part II, *EHR* 64 (1949), 433–60; E. Miller, *The Abbey and Bishopric of Ely* (Cambridge, 1951), chapter VII; J. Scammell, 'The origins and limitations of the liberty of Durham', *EHR* 81 (1966), 449–73; E. Searle, *Lordship and Community: Battle Abbey and its Banlieu* (Toronto, 1974).

The eyres, justice, and the law

For introductory surveys see A. Harding, *A Social History of English Law* (London, 1966), and *The Law Courts of Medieval England* (London, 1973). For a more specialized study of legal history see S.F.C. Milsom, *Historical Foundations of the Common Law* (London, 1969). There is more legal history than the title indicates in N.D. Hurnard, *The King's Pardon for Homicide* (Oxford, 1969). On the eyres see C.A.F. Meekings, introduction to *Crown Pleas of the Wiltshire Eyre, 1249* (Wiltshire Archaeological and Natural History Society, Records Branch, Devizes, 1961); D. Crook, *Records of the General Eyre* (London, 1982), and 'The later eyres', *EHR* 97 (1982), 241–68. The principal sources utilized in this section are *Crown Pleas of the Wiltshire Eyre, 1249*, ed. C.A.F Meekings (see above), *The Roll and Writ File of the Berkshire Eyre of 1248*, ed. M.T. Clanchy (Selden Society, 1973), and *The Roll of the Shropshire Eyre of 1256*, ed. A. Harding (Selden Society, 1981).

was a ward of the pope, for King John had made his realm a fief of the papacy, and the pope was represented in England by a legate; but the cause of the young king needed a standard bearer who could rally support and that rôle was filled by the staunch loyalist and paradigm of chivalry William Marshal, earl of Pembroke and lord of Leinster. He was styled *rector regis et regni* 'guardian of the king and the kingdom'. The management of the machinery of government, however, rested with the justiciar, Hubert de Burgh, who had been appointed by King John to replace Peter des Roches at the height of the political crisis in June 1215. William Marshal died in May 1219, having won the civil war, ejected the French, and restored the kingdom to its allegiance. It is significant that no one replaced him as *rector*: the customary management of the realm by a justiciar was sufficient even with the king a minor, though it did mean that no grant by charter in perpetuity could be made until the king was of full age.

The critical question, however, was whether the rôle of the justiciar as director of the realm in the king's place could survive the ending of the minority, for then the analogy would be not with the situation of a king's absence but with the situation as it had been after the loss of Normandy had made King John resident in his realm for most of the remainder of his reign. Then the management of the realm had been brought much more directly under the control of the king's *curia*, the 'bench' had been suspended, the exchequer overseen by *familiares*, and the rôle of the justiciar diminished. When the minority of Henry III ended in 1227 Hubert de Burgh sought to preserve his pre-eminence by making himself indispensable to the young king; but he behaved more like a shogun than the chief minister of a king who naturally expected to take over the reins of government himself. An open breach occurred in 1230 when the impulsive young king accused the justiciar, not without reason, of being lukewarm towards his military expedition to Brittany and Poitou. The venture was a dismal failure. In 1232 Hubert de Burgh was not merely dismissed but humiliated by being accused of a shoal of malpractices, including the use of witchcraft, in which it is hard to distinguish the half-true from the fantastical. He was replaced by Stephen of Segrave. Hitherto Stephen's service to the crown, assiduous though undistinguished, had been principally

---

Crown and Community

Of fundamental importance is J.R. Maddicott, 'Magna Carta and the local community', *Past and Present* 102 (1984), 25-65. For the boroughs, dealt with here cursorily, see: G.H. Martin, 'The English borough in the thirteenth century', *TRHS* 13 (1963), 123-44; S. Reynolds, *An Introduction to the History of English Medieval Towns* (Oxford, 1977), especially chapters 3 to 6; C.R. Young, *The English Borough and Royal Administration*, 1130-1307 (Durham, North Carolina, 1961).

judicial. It continued to be so. He was in effect 'chief justice'.[1] Two years later the office of justiciar lapsed altogether.

The fall of Hubert de Burgh marked the end of an era in the history of English government. The man who engineered it and advised the young Henry III on how he might be more truly king was Peter des Roches, bishop of Winchester. It had been he who, as a *familiaris* of King John had sought to bring the administration more firmly and directly under royal control after the death of Geoffrey FitzPeter in 1213; but his tenure of the justiciarship had then been short-lived, overtaken by the political crisis which required the appointment of a man who could command the respect of the barons. That man was Hubert de Burgh, an experienced administrator but a considerable landowner too, and the hero of a resolute defence of Chinon in 1205 against the king of France when all had seemed lost. Peter des Roches was one of the executors of King John's will, and had been personal guardian of the young Henry III and his tutor until Hubert de Burgh had elbowed aside all competitors to his influence. Peter had then gone abroad for several years and had become a respected visitor at the courts of Emperor Frederick II, Pope Gregory IX, and King Louis IX of France. He returned to England in 1231 to find the king chafing at the restraints of the justiciar, and instructed him how to become in effect his own justiciar, controlling the administration through his Household.

Peter des Roches did not take up office again himself. The agent for the reconstruction of the king's government was his kinsman Peter des Rivaux, who was appointed to an extraordinary collection of offices simultaneously: to custody of the Wardrobe, the Chamber, the treasury of the Household, the keepership of the king's personal seal, to the post of king's chamberlain of London and his buyer in all markets and fairs, to the custody of several royal castles, to be chief justice of forests in England, keeper of all escheats and wardships, to similar offices in Ireland, to control of the Mint and the Jews, and to the sheriffdoms of 21 counties. Finally in January 1233 he became treasurer of the exchequer. The intention seems to have been to facilitate a review and overhaul of the administration particularly in respect of all sources of revenue. At the same time nine more counties were held by four other members of the king's *curia*.[2]

There were to be two major changes in the structure of the administration. First the justiciarship was to lapse and its co-ordinating functions drawn into a reconstituted king's Council – or rather, to

[1.] F.J. West, *The Justiciarship in England* (Cambridge, 1966), pp. 265–71.
[2.] S.B. Chrimes, *An Introduction to the Administrative History of Medieval England* (Oxford, 1952), pp. 92–3 and 93 n. 1, G.L. Harriss, *King, Parliament and Public Finance in England to 1369* (Oxford, 1975), p. 196.

speak more precisely since the Council was not formally an institution, a body of king's counsellors. They were, however, more clearly
identifiable as king's counsellors than the shifting group of *familiares*
of old, for they took a special oath, the terms of which are elusive
before 1258. It was a group of mixed composition but always with a
core of senior administrators. It was a group similar to the 'barons of
the exchequer' who had hitherto, under the justiciar's chairmanship,
performed the co-ordinating function; and whereas household
officers, administrative officials and royal advisers had hitherto met
in 'the king's court at the exchequer' they now met in the Household.
The second major change was that the king's business which until the
end of John's reign had been serviced by the Chamber was now taken
over by the Wardrobe, which hitherto had been a sub-department of
the Chamber. In origin the Wardrobe was a depository, safeguarding
the king's robes and valuables, looking after documents which the
king wished to have at hand, and holding sufficient ready cash from
which to pay the king's personal expenses. Its officials were therefore
very close to the king and frequently his trusted intimates. Some
historians have suggested that the development of the Wardrobe to
overshadow its parent Chamber was an historical accident, a consequence both of the minority and Rivaux's apprenticeship in the Wardrobe. During the minority of Henry III the Chamber had diminished
because a boy king had little business for chamberlains to conduct; but
even a boy king had need of personal services, and the royal Household had expenses, so the Wardrobe was still needed; its treasurer was
Peter des Rivaux. It may, however, be suggested that there was good
reason not to restore the Chamber to its former eminence when Henry
III came of age: the unspecialized Chamber of old with chamberlains
turning their hand to whatever task needed attention was outdated; a
resident king could more readily call upon the specialists of a resident
administration. The Chamber had been characteristic of a separate,
peripatetic Household, the new Wardrobe was characteristic of a
Household more closely linked with the administrative structure of
the realm.

Peter des Rivaux inaugurated a period of reform in the structure of
administration and in its financial operations of enduring importance,
but his direction of it was short-lived. In 1234 the king was obliged to
dispense with his services and to distance himself from Peter des
Roches in response to a baronial opposition which trembled on the
edge of violence. It was an opposition which Henry III was to placate,
parry, contain or circumvent for over 20 years, but which he never
stilled and which was to overwhelm him in 1258. It should not be
equated with the opposition which had wrung Magna Carta from King
John in 1215; the opponents of Henry III saw themselves as the

successors of those who had rescued the throne for John's heir, and strengthened it by converting Magna Carta into a compact between the crown and the community of the realm. It was for 'the community of the realm' that the opposition to Henry III was to claim to speak, though its leaders were often so close to the king personally that they might have been expected to speak for the crown. It is characteristic of the opposition to Henry III that its first leader from 1234 until he was done to death in Ireland in 1236 was Richard Marshal, the heir of William Marshal. At other times the lead was taken by the king's brother, Richard of Cornwall, or his brother-in-law, Simon de Montfort. It was the 'loyalism' of the king's most prominent critics which for long limited the effectiveness of the opposition. The basic reason for the outbreak of criticism was that those who expected to play a leading part in the formation of royal policy found themselves, in the words of Sir Maurice Powicke, 'cold shouldered at court'.[3] The opposition was directed not at the reform and restructuring of the administration itself but at some of its consequences, and in particular at the opportunity it offered to the king, for whom many of his critics had little respect, to rule unfettered by baronial counsel.

Historians have often commented that this baronial attitude was a legacy of the minority of Henry III, for then frequent consultation between the regents and the barons had been indispensable for holding the realm together; but in this respect we should see the minority as the culmination of a long period of government without the king, stretching back at least to King Richard's crusade and captivity, and interrupted only by King John's prolonged residence in England in the latter part of his reign. Longchamp's vice-gerency at the beginning of this period had failed because he disdained baronial counsel; by contrast the comparatively smooth management of the realm by Hubert Walter and Geoffrey FitzPeter, despite the inordinate pressure to raise more revenue, must be attributed to the skill with which they were able to carry the leading barons with them. It may be an exaggeration to speak of baronial participation in the government of the realm at that time, but at least the barons were sufficiently consulted and their interests sufficiently respected for them to feel that their influence counted.

It is significant that the opposition to Henry III's moves towards personal government manifested itself first in a wave of sympathy for Hubert de Burgh which secured his release from demeaning captivity, reversed the sentence of outlawry upon him, and let him end his days with dignity. It is all the more significant in that Hubert de Burgh in the later years of his justiciarship had few friends; he was as autocratic

---

[3.] Powicke, *Henry III and the Lord Edward*, pp. 123, 296ff.

as ever Ranulf de Glanville had been, and more greedily self-seeking than any of his predecessors. Nevertheless he represented the kind of government which the barons knew and understood and had learned to live with. Though the opportunities which justiciars had taken to build their family fortunes may have caused some resentment, the consequence had been to put them in the ranks of the baronage; they themselves were substantial landholders, they knew what it was to be a baron. They were not set apart. Geoffrey FitzPeter became earl of Essex, Hubert de Burgh earl of Kent. They had family connections with political ramifications: the brothers of Hubert Walter and Hubert de Burgh had a major stake in Ireland. Nor were their contacts only with leading barons, for they were out and about in the realm on the eyres. They knew the realm far better than any king. They were accessible. They were the mediators of a patronage system which oiled the wheels of government, and were no doubt frequently its dispensers. They wielded an authority which could moderate the workings of an administrative system and the exigencies of government policy. We can read of the exchequer accepting instructions from Hubert de Burgh by word of mouth 'without writ' as sufficient warrant for letting a man off an amercement or quitting another of a forest offence.[4] This was not the kind of government which could earn a commendation for impartiality, but it was government with a human face. The elimination of the justiciarship depersonalized the bureaucracy. It made the motor of government more remote.

The second reason for baronial disquiet was that Peter des Roches and Peter des Rivaux hailed originally from Poitou. They represented an interest which was dear to Henry III but not to his barons.[5] The loss of Normandy had terminated the barons' continental interests but not the king's. He was still styled 'duke of Normandy and of Aquitaine and count of Anjou', and although most of the former Angevin 'empire' was now directly ruled by the king of France there still remained to Henry III the southern part of Aquitaine; and he cherished hopes of recovering the rest of what he regarded as his rightful inheritance. It was ironic that the Aquitanians who had for so long resisted what they regarded as Henry II's 'curtailment of their liberties' should have turned to Henry III to save them from the menace of the king of France. In Henry's eyes they were equally his subjects as were Englishmen, and he expected to recruit men into his service from any of his dominions. To the barons the intimate counsel of 'foreigners' threatened to deflect the king from English interests, especially if they themselves were excluded from counsel.

4. West, *Justiciarship*, p. 262.
5. For Henry III's foreign policy and English attitudes towards it see Clanchy, *England and its Rulers*, chapters 9 and 10.

Although the barons tried to distance themselves from the king's ambitious policy abroad it had repercussions on the government of England. It raised the problem of how it was to be paid for when the barons limited or denied the levying of subsidies, and it raised in an acute form the question of liability to military service. Above all it impelled the king to rely for counsel on those whose views he was glad to hear, which meant in practice royal servants and foreign friends, and impelled the barons to demands for consultation as his 'natural' (that is to say, native born) counsellors, and to have watchdogs on his Council. The alienation of king and barons, moreover, had unfortunate effects on legislation, for changes in the law required both royal authority and baronial assent. Between the definitive version of Magna Carta in 1225 and the baronial proposals for legal reforms in 1259, which did not achieve settled form until the Statute of Marlborough in 1267, there was only one major attempt at reform of the law in the so-called 'statute' of Merton in 1236. Significantly that came from the period when Henry III was trying to placate the baronial opposition provoked by the Poitevin take-over.

Henry III was not a man to inspire respect. He did not have Henry II's dominating personality, nor Richard I's self-confidence, nor even his father's energetic imperiousness. He tended, like his father, to quail in moments of crisis; but he was resilient, dogged and persistent, and he inherited in full measure the Angevin characteristic of wilfulness. He had been taken aback by the force of baronial reaction to his first moves in changing the style and forms of central government but he was not blown off course. Administrative reform was pressed forward, and for a period of about 20 years until 1258 Henry III ruled England in the way he chose to do despite recurrent baronial protests. He was fortified in his resolve by his marriage in 1236 to Eleanor of Provence which gave him not only a supportive and resolute wife but also the counsel of three of her uncles of Savoy, who were notable for their belligerence and thrusting ability. They introduced other Savoyards to the king's service. His foreign companions and dependents were after 1247 reinforced (it would be wrong to say strengthened) by more Poitevins who followed to England his half-brothers of the family of Lusignan, for Henry's mother, Isabella of Angoulême, had after King's John's death married her first love, Hugh of Lusignan.

More fundamentally, however, Henry III was sustained by his ideology of kingship.[6] There was nothing particularly striking or original about it, but in the circumstances of the political traditions of

6. Clanchy, 'Did Henry III have a policy?', pp. 203–16, *England and its Rulers*, pp. 222–30, 280–3.

England it did seem an exotic plant. In much of the rest of Europe it would not have seemed remarkable, for the thirteenth century saw a widespread attempt to reassert monarchical authority and give it an ideological basis. It revived the terminology of Carolingian conceptions of Christian kingship which from the later years of the eleventh century had been challenged and shaken by clerical claims to the supremacy of ecclesiastical authority; but now the concepts were supported not as of old by biblical quotations but by the precepts of Roman civil law, the recovery of which had been one of the major achievements of the twelfth-century 'renaissance'. Moreover, the aspirations of rulers were given practical expression by another major consequence of the twelfth-century renaissance – the men educated in the universities who entered government service and developed bureaucratic methods of administration. As Michael Clanchy writes: 'Decisions no longer had to be made orally at large meetings of counsellors. Instead, little conclaves of experts executed their orders by written instructions to sheriffs and bailiffs in the localities. The key officials therefore became the keepers of privy seals and the accountants of the king's household. Traditional offices like that of steward, justiciar and even chancellor began to wane in importance not only in England but in France, Sicily, Aragon and Castile.'[7] Henry III was no intellectual; and the principles of Magna Carta denied him the opportunity to expound monarchical authority in a law code such as the *Liber Augustalis* of Emperor Frederick II, the *Libro de las Leyes* of King Alphonso 'the Learned' of Castile, or the *Establissements* of King Louis IX of France; but he behaved as if his authority were God-given and his wishes beyond reproach. He thought of himself as the Vicar of Christ and as the father of his people to whom all his subjects of whatever degree could look for protection. And these were not simply pious sentiments: he insisted that the barons should apply the principles of Magna Carta to their own men; he admonished his officials to inquire diligently and 'righteously' into oppressions by landlords; and in 1252 he ruled against the introduction of the Inquisition into England for it harassed the poor and compelled good Christians to give evidence upon oath about the private sins of others; it was too beyond the control of royal jurisdiction and therefore offensive to the dignity of the crown.[8] Henry, though personally pious, would not countenance clerical claims to an autonomous authority; he even persuaded the pope to confirm explicitly the old rule of the Constitutions of Clarendon that bishops could not excommunicate royal servants without the king's

[7]. Clanchy, *England and its Rulers*, p. 215.
[8]. Clanchy, 'Did Henry III have a policy?', Appendix, pp. 215–16, *Close Rolls 1251–3*, p. 225.

permission.[9] Henry's exalted conception of kingship, presumably fostered by the cosmopolitan Peter des Roches, was expressed in the iconography of his splendidly reconstructed Westminster Abbey, adjacent to the royal palace of Westminster, by his promotion of the cult of Edward the Confessor, a royal saint who had founded the abbey and had his tomb there, and in the elaboration of royal cere-monial: in 1233 for example, just as he was launching his new-style government, he increased the frequency of the ceremonial chanting of the *Laudes Regiae*. As Clanchy has written: 'Henry III created the impressive theatricality of the monarchy which has lasted to the present day.'[10]

Henry, it may be suspected, succeeded in impressing himself more than his subjects. There is an interesting example of this from Michaelmas 1247, when Henry proposed to have one of his grand ceremonies. His magnates were invited individually to come to Westminster to celebrate the feast of the translation of St Edward, when the king would confer on his brother-in-law, William of Valence, the dignity of knighthood, and when he would also impart 'most agreeable news of a holy benefit recently conferred by heaven upon the English'. When the magnates assembled and asked what this 'good news' was they were told that a brother of the Knights Templar was bringing some of Christ's blood from the Holy Land in a beautiful crystal container, fully authenticated under the seals of the patriarch of Jerusalem and the other archbishops, bishops, abbots and magnates of the Holy Land. The king kept the vigil of St Edward in devout prayer and fasting. On the morrow he assembled with all the clergy of London at St Pauls. By the king's order the clergy were vested in festive robes but the king himself was humbly clad in a simple cloak without a hood. They then walked in procession the mile or so to Westminster Abbey, the king bearing the precious relic aloft in both hands, 'his eyes fixed always either on heaven or on the container itself', so Matthew Paris relates, even though the road was sometimes rough and uneven. The magnates were not impressed. Some doubted the authenticity of the alleged relic and said so openly when sitting around after the ceremony. The prior of the Knights Hospitaller at Jerusalem challenged them to say what motive there could be for duplicity by those who had affixed their seals, and called the king to testify that no payment had been sought. But the doubters persisted; how could it be, they said, that some of Christ's blood had been left

[9.] Paris, v. 109–10, translated in R. Vaughan, *Chronicles of Matthew Paris* (Gloucester, 1984), p. 211.
[10.] Clanchy, *England and its Rulers*, p. 282; on the *laudes* see E. Kantorowicz, *Laudes Regiae* (Berkeley, California, 1946), pp. 175–7.

lying around the Holy land when He had risen from the dead whole and entire.[11]

It is more than likely that a similar scepticism extended to the king's belief in his God-given authority. Henry would no doubt have claimed, as Frederick II did, that to contradict the royal wishes was tantamount to blasphemy; but his orders were sometimes challenged even by his servants. In 1240 the chancellor and the keeper of the Wardrobe formally washed their hands of the king's grant of a heavy toll on wool exports to the queen's uncle. On the Patent Roll there is a note of protest against one of the king's instructions, that it had been done 'without the counsel and consent of any clerk of Chancery'.[12] A sworn councillor, Simon 'the Norman', jeopardized his career by refusing to apply the king's seal, of which he was the keeper, to a charter of grant to the count of Flanders because it was contrary to the best interests of the crown; though Matthew Paris, who tells the story, adds with his characteristic prejudice against men of 'alien' origin, that it was the one decent act that redeemed a malign career.[13]

In 1258 the barons told the pope that the king's Poitevin half-brothers 'damnably whispered to him that a prince is not subject to law thus putting the prince outside the law, and so justice itself is banished out of the realm.'[14] This reflects a common argument of those who rested a ruler's authority on Roman Law, but it was not one shared by the English jurist Henry de Bracton, royal justice and king's councillor, and author of an influential treatise on 'The Laws and Customs of the Realm of England'. He had no quarrel with the precept of Roman Law that 'the princes's will is law', but did not see it as a justification for authoritarianism.[15] English practice conformed to the principle in the sense that there could be no law which did not have the king's approval; it was royal authority which made law; but the king of England could not make law simply at his own pleasure: custom could be changed or new laws framed only with the concurrence of the king and his barons. The king of England was as Roman texts said 'loosed from the law', but this did not mean that he was above the law or could disregard it with impunity; what it meant was that there were no sanctions which could by process of law be applied against him. The 'sanctions clause' of Magna Carta of 1215 had been expunged from the reissues. Clearly he was 'loosed from the law' in the sense that 'no writ runs against the king'; and since there

11. Paris, iv. 640–4, translated Vaughan, pp.18–19.
12. *Calendar of Patent Rolls 1258–66*, p. 317.
13. Paris, iv. 63, v. 91, Powicke, *Henry III and the Lord Edward*, pp. 295–6 and Appendix E.
14. *Annales Monastici*, i. 463–4.
15. Discussions of Bracton's views on kingship are reviewed in B. Tierney, 'Bracton on government', *Speculum* 38 (1963), 295–317.

was no person in the realm who was the equal let alone the superior of the king there was no one who could judge him except God. But the fact that no sanction could be applied did not absolve a man, especially a king, from respecting the law; indeed a ruler who dis- regarded the law undermined his own authority for 'law makes the king'; a king who acts on will without respect for law could not expect to remain for long an effective ruler, for disregard for the law is the path to anarchy and 'where there is no law there is no king'.[16] Although the processes of the king's law could not be used against him, there was a remedy by petition, and a king should heed a just complaint for not to do so would be to condone injustice, and to do that undermines kingship which is instituted to uphold justice. Although there was no person in the realm who was the equal or superior of the king, there was an authority that was superior to that of the king and that was the authority of the king and magnates jointly. This last argument derives from an analogy with the canon lawyers' conclusions about episcopal authority: a bishop had no equal or superior in his diocese; he was superior to the canons of his cathedral church; nevertheless a bishop and canons acting jointly had more authority than the bishop alone: they could do things that the bishop himself could not do, such as alienate church property.[17] Similarly, Bracton pointed out, king and magnates acting together could change old laws and make new ones, which the king alone could not do. Some canon lawyers applied a similar reasoning to the author- ity of the pope, arguing that a decision of a general council carried greater weight than a decision of the pope alone; but this did not make a general council itself superior to the pope for the pope was himself part of the council; his authority was, as it were, fortified by that of the other bishops. But what if a pope and the rest of a general council were odds; which side should prevail? Contemporary canon lawyers gave differing answers to this question: some that the judgement of the bishops in council outweighed that of the pope alone, others that in the last resort the judgement of the pope must prevail. Bracton does not specifically consider this point in relation to a dispute between king and magnates; but if he were entirely consistent in his views he would have to concede that in an irreconcilable difference of view the king's will should carry the day. An addition to the text of his treatise, however, for which Bracton himself may not have been responsible, suggests that the magnates might 'bridle' a king who was heedless of justice.

Herein lay the dilemma for Henry III's magnates. Their behaviour

16. *Ibid.*, p. 305.
17. *Ibid.*, p. 315.

implies that Bracton accurately reflected their views about kingship. Within the terms of Magna Carta they did not impugn royal authority; there were no sanctions they could apply by legal process; they could not bring themselves to impose a bridle; they could protest and petition, but they were dependent on his goodwill for remedy; if they were to effect a change in the way the realm was governed they could do so only with his co-operation. To their petition that he set aside his alien counsellors, appoint his chief ministers with their advice, and admit their nominees to his Council, he replied that he would be as free in the management of the estate of the realm as they were in the management of their estates: did they allow anyone to choose their servants for them? In 1248 he rounded on his assembled barons, telling them, according to Matthew Paris, 'You are trying to bend your king to your will, and force him into subjection, and denying to him what is allowed to any of you: any head of a family can appoint anyone from his household to this or that office, or suspend or dismiss them, something which you presume to deny to your king, and rashly so since servants should by no means impose conditions on their master, nor vassals their prince. On the contrary, whoever is thought of as inferior should rather be guided and ruled by the pleasure and will of the lord.'[18] If the realm were to be conceived as a feudal lordship in which the king was supreme lord it was difficult to counter this argument except by dodging it, which the barons did by talking instead of the realm as a community.

In 1258, however, the king himself presented the barons with the one lawful solution to their dilemma: he offered to cooperate with them in 'reforming the state of the realm'. He had no option: his ambitious foreign policy had undone him. Competing in the stakes to be regarded as a ruler of European stature Henry was consistently outplayed by King Louis IX of France; but in 1250 Emperor Frederick II died, and Henry was tempted to intervene in what appeared to be a disintegrating Holy Roman Empire. Henry's connections with Savoy, which commanded the Alpine passes, offered a link between the lands which still remained to him in southern France and northern Italy; his brother, Richard, was offered the crown of Germany and elected King of the Romans (as an emperor-designate was styled); and in 1254 he accepted for his younger son Edmund an offer from the papacy of the crown of the kingdom of Sicily (which included all of Italy south of the papal states). There was a price: Henry was to repay the costs incurred by the pope in attempting, unsuccessfully, to eject a German claimant. The price was stiff – nearly as much as King Richard's ransom. By 1258 Frederick II's bastard son, Manfred, had taken control of the

18. Paris, v. 20, translated Vaughan, p. 143.

kingdom of Sicily, and Henry was left with nothing but a vast debt to the pope which he could not repay, and was under threat of excommunication and an interdict on England. He begged his barons for help. Their conditions were that 'the state of the realm be ordered rectified and reformed', and that he abide by the proposals to be drawn up by a committee appointed for the purpose.

When king and barons met again at Oxford in June 1258 there were two main items on the agenda about the government of the realm. One was a set of petitions about matters requiring changes in the law – the neglected business of the period of the king's personal government.[19] The other was a set of proposals by the committee for rectifying the government of the realm. The decisions taken on the latter were embodied in a document known as the Provisions of Oxford.[20] Much of it consisted of memoranda on matters to be looked into; the concrete proposals to be implemented immediately were along the lines which the baronial opposition had been advocating for many years. The king's personally chosen Council was replaced by a Council of Fifteen, selected by an elaborate procedure to ensure that the king's interests and the barons' interests were fairly represented. This Council was to report frequently to a conference of barons (for which the colloquial term 'parliament' was employed); but to save the barons the inconvenience of having to meet regularly as a body they appointed a Committee of Twelve (a kind of Standing Committee) to meet with the Council of Fifteen. The post of justiciar was resurrected, and its holder was to be a kind of 'head of the civil service' with power 'to amend the wrongs done by all other justices and bailiffs'.[21] The justiciar, the chancellor and the treasurer were to be appointed to serve for one year at a time and were annually to render account of their stewardship to the Council of Fifteen. The sheriffs also were to be subject to annual appointment and were to be chosen from substantial landholders in the shire. The effective centre of government after June 1258 was the Council of Fifteen; it was still being called the king's government but his power over it had in effect been put into commission.

These measures did not in themselves constitute a radical reconstruction of government: they were rather the means by which the barons cut into the king's government to take control of it, as a prelude to review and reform. The review was put in hand, and included a special eyre (distinguished from a normal eyre 'for all

---

19. *Documents 1258–67*, no. 3.
20. *Ibid.*, no. 5, *EHD* iii. 361–6.
21. On the revived justiciarship see C.H. Knowles, 'The justiciarship in England, 1258–65', in *British Government and Administration*, ed. H. Hearder and H.R. Loyn (Cardiff, 1974), pp. 16–26.

pleas') to be conducted by the justiciar – a kind of royal commission into the state of the realm. At the same time inquiries were to be made by a panel of four knights in each county into 'all excesses, trespasses, and acts of injustice' committed by 'justices, sheriffs, and other bailiffs, and all other persons whatsoever'.[22] Some reforms followed swiftly: in October 1258 there was an Ordinance of Sheriffs laying down rules on the conduct of business by sheriffs.[23] No fundamental changes, however, were introduced into the central administrative system. It may be that the period of baronial reform was in the event too short for radical restructuring; but the striking fact is that no proposals were ever advanced. The reforms of the 1230s had created an efficient machine which needed no more than to be purged of abuses. The outstanding problems lay in the sphere of local government.

Central Administration, Finance and the Sheriffs

The overhaul of the administrative system which began after the dismissal of Hubert de Burgh was slowed but not interrupted by the onset of baronial opposition. Whether there was a grand design for a fundamental change in the structure of government, or whether the intention was simply to make necessary adjustments to meet changed circumstances is debatable; but there can be little doubt that the outcome was more a revision of traditional practices than the creation of a new system of government. It may be as T.F. Tout hinted in his pioneering work on administrative history that Peter des Roches had in mind 'a logical system of despotism' with firm control by courtiers of all aspects of finance and administration such as was to be established in France before the end of the thirteenth century; but if there was such an aspiration it foundered in the political crisis of 1234 for which Peter des Rivaux and his mentor, Peter des Roches, were made the scapegoats. Tout went on to argue that the residual consequence of the brief ascendancy of the two Peters was to leave Henry III with the household department of the Wardrobe as a kind of central administrative service in miniature which enable him at will to by-pass the established routines of chancery and exchequer;[24] but the notion of 'household government' distinct from 'offices of state' cannot be squared with the facts. The alternative argument of R.F. Treharne that Henry III, after the anomalous circumstances of the minority, was doing no more than restoring a traditional concept of government by the king, and that 'in bringing all offices of state and

22. *Documents 1258–67*, no. 6.
23. *Ibid.*, no. 8, *EHD* iii. 368–70.
24. Tout, *Chapters*, i. 227.

all departments of government under the crown's immediate control' he was 'simply perfecting the Angevin system of government' has more generally commended itself to historians, but does not adequately recognize that a major shift in the way that government was organized did take place.[25] For all the elements of continuity with the past, Henry III's reign is a transitional phase between Angevin government and the institutional structure of later medieval government.

An overhaul of the administrative system was overdue by 1230. Henry III's desire to be rid of great officials who controlled the levers of power and could obstruct his wishes provided the occasion and impetus for it, but the justification went deeper. It was two-fold. First, a structure of government designed specifically for a ruler who had several dominions and was frequently absent for prolonged periods was inappropriate for a ruler who was normally resident in England and could expect to exercise direct control. Secondly, the very success of Angevin government, the vast expansion in the amount of business transacted, the proliferation of subordinates, the increase in specialization, and the developing complexity of government threatened not only to make the traditional system unmanageable but to undermine the presuppositions on which it rested. To appreciate this let us remind ourselves of the essential features of the system of government as established under Henry II. There were two distinct elements: there was the 'household' element travelling with the king throughout his dominions, operating principally through departments known from Henry II's time as the Chamber and the chancery, and there was the element which remained in England under the direction of the justiciar, including the treasury, and controlling the sheriffs and the justices. But although readily distinguishable these two elements were not intended to be wholly separate with distinct spheres of activity: they were interrelated and interdependent. The principle of the unity of the king's government received more than lip-service. There were in particular two institutional arrangements which exemplified that unity. One was the existence, in principle, of only one secretariat for all the king's business under the chancellor who controlled the issue of documents under royal seal. In the German empire there were separate chancellors for Germany, Burgundy and Italy; in the Angevin empire there was only one chancellor. The second was the exchequer, for its twice-yearly sessions were joint meetings of treasury officials with senior officials from the peripatetic royal Household and others of the king's counsellors who were appointed to be 'barons of the exchequer' under the chairmanship of

25. Treharne, *Baronial Plan of Reform*, p. 23.

the justiciar to oversee the conduct of the king's government. As described by the *Dialogus de Scaccario* the exchequer had three elements: there was the 'lower exchequer' which received payments, assayed coin and issued receipts, there was the 'upper exchequer' where sheriffs were examined upon their accounts, and there was the *thalamus secretorum*, the private room into which the 'barons' retired for their confidential discussions 'all others being excluded unless they are summoned by their masters for the expedition of the king's business.'[26] In the work of the upper exchequer, treasury officials and chancery officials were equal partners; the treasurer and the chancellor's clerk divided the interrogation of the sheriffs between them, and two copies of the Pipe Roll were simultaneously drawn up, one for the use of the treasury the other for the chancery. The treasurer dictated, but the chancellor's clerk was equally responsible with him for the wording. A detachment of chancery clerks drew up the exchequer summonses and writs. When these arrangements were devised in Henry I's reign the king was never further away than Normandy and it was not usually difficult for members of his Household to attend exchequer sessions at Winchester; Henry II's much wider dominions and his greatly prolonged absences put the system under some strain, and the chief officials of his Household had more often to be represented at exchequer sessions by deputy, but the principles were maintained. Since the royal seal could not for long be separated from the king himself it became necessary to have another seal readily available for exchequer use, but significantly the decision was that it should not be a distinct 'departmental' seal but should be a duplicate of the seal which travelled with the king and should remain under the control of the chancellor. The *Dialogus* makes this clear in describing the rôle of the chancellor at exchequer sessions: 'In the exchequer as in *curia* the chancellor is so great a man that nothing important is or should be done without his consent and advice. He is the official custodian of the king's seal which is in the treasury but which is only taken out when, by order of the justiciar, it is brought from the lower to the upper exchequer, and then only for exchequer business. When this is completed, it is put in a purse which is sealed by the chancellor and handed to the treasurer to keep. When it is required again it is handed to the chancellor still under seal in view of everyone, and no one may take it out of the treasury on any occasion.'[27]

Clearly these arrangements were intended to oblige the two wings of the king's government to work together and to maintain regular personal contact, but in practice the exigencies of expanding business weakened the links. The *Dialogus* says that the chancellor's clerk

26. *Dialogus*, p. 44.
27. *Ibid.*, pp. 18–19.

'though only a deputy, is occupied with important and multifarious duties, so much so that he cannot leave his post from the beginning to the end of the accounts.'[28] In the earlier years of Henry II's reign his exchequer duties would have occupied him for a few weeks twice a year; but by the end of the century exchequer sessions took up nine months of the year and in those circumstances the chancellor's clerk must have become more of an exchequer official than the chancellor's agent. Already by the end of Henry II's reign the detachment of chancery clerks which serviced exchequer business had been replaced by clerks permanently on the treasurer's staff and with no connection with the chancery. The much less regular attendance at exchequer sessions of senior officials meant that the 'doubtful or troublesome questions' which as the *Dialogus* says 'continually arise' could with less frequency be settled on the spot and notes had to be kept of matters to be referred to them.[29] From the first year of John's reign a Memoranda Roll of such notes survives and the frequency of the heading 'Speak with the justiciar' testifies to how often he was unavailable, occupied as he was on the eyres and on the 'bench'.[30] The exchequer's functions did not change but its methods of discharging them did, and it must be doubted whether regular conferences of the king's officials and close advisers at Easter and Michaelmas were any longer fixed point in the calendar. We are much less well-informed about the development of chancery, but there can be no doubt that it too increased greatly in size with the expanding volume of its business, and that as it did so its relationships changed with other branches of the king's government.[31] No longer could it be thought of as staffed by the king's chaplains who wrote his letters when they were not ministering to his religious needs. A major change must have followed the expansion of procedures by writ. Many humble clerks were employed solely in drawing up writs of course (and hence were known as 'cursitors'). It may be suspected that by the later years of the twelfth century a major part of the chancery was quartered at Westminster, and although we may suppose that a portion remained in attendance upon the king, there are signs of a developing separation of Household and chancery from the middle years of John's reign. The evidence for this is that many of the documents enrolled in chancery bear a note that they were issued on written instructions from the king authenticated with his

28. *Ibid.*, p. 33.
29. *Ibid.*, p. 15.
30. *Memoranda Roll I John* (Pipe Roll Society, 1943).
31. There is no adequate study of the chancery in this period; helpful are the first chapter of B. Wilkinson, *The Chancery under Edward III* (Manchester, 1929), P. Chaplais, *English Royal Documents: King John – Henry VI* (Oxford, 1971), L.B. Dibben, 'Chancellor and keeper of the seal under Henry III', *EHR* 27 (1912), 39–51, Tout, *Chapters*, i. 127–39, 284–9.

personal or 'small' seal. Significantly it is from this time that the seal under the care of the chancellor comes to be called the 'great seal'; hitherto it had been referred to as the 'royal seal' or the 'king's seal.'[32] Sometimes an impatient King John by-passed the chancery: in May 1208 he despatched a letter from Tewkesbury sealed with his personal seal and bearing the note that he used his 'privy' seal because 'we do not have the great seal with us.'[33] The note implies that such use of the king's personal seal was then unusual, but it was to become more common, and in the last years of the reign even letters patent were issued under the privy seal.

The king's personal seal was kept in his Chamber. This household department was always particularly intimate with the king since it ministered to his bodily needs and managed his 'privy purse'. But its functions had been at least since Henry II's day much more than merely domestic.[34] It readily responded to the demands of impetuous Angevin kings to have their wishes carried out promptly, unchallenged by the kind of routine procedures which they imposed on the justiciar's subordinates. The Chamber conducted the king's confidential business. It could act as his intermediary with officials and agents throughout his dominions. It negotiated deals with those who sought favours and set in motion the procedures for giving effect to them. It was the department which expended the king's revenue or authorized its expenditure not only for his domestic needs but also for diplomacy and war. It pledged his credit and arranged for ready cash to be available as the king required. It had not only a treasury for cash in hand (the Wardrobe) but also a secretariat staffed by increasingly important chamber clerks. In John's reign the Chamber became 'the principal centre of administrative activity around the king'.[35] Its financial operations were so prodigious that they outran supply from the treasury at Westminster, which was supplemented by deposits of cash in castles around the country to service the king's relentless progresses. The expansion of the Chamber's activity was probably in part because King John preferred to conduct his business through confidants, but also because it offered a convenient way of supplementing the methods by which a resident king sought to take personal

32. Tout, *Chapters*, i. 151.
33. *Rot.Lit.Claus.*, i. 114, cf. H.C. Maxwell-Lyte, *Historical Notes on the Use of the Great Seal* (London, 1926), p. 21, S. Painter, *The Reign of King John* (Baltimore, 1949), pp. 106–7.
34. On the chamber see Harriss, *Public Finance*, chapter VIII, Chrimes, *Administrative History*, pp. 78–81, Tout, *Chapters*, i, chapters III and IV, J.E.A. Jolliffe, 'The *Camera Regis* under Henry II', *EHR* 68 (1953), 1–21, 337–62, and *Angevin Kingship* (London, 1955), chapters XI and XII, H.G. Richardson, 'The chamber under Henry II', *EHR* 69 (1954), 596–611, H.G. Richardson and G.O. Sayles, *The Governance of Mediaeval England* (Edinburgh, 1963), chapter XII.
35. Chrimes, *Administrative History*, p. 78.

control of the government of England. The operations of the 'bench' at Westminster were suspended and its business drawn into the court with the king; not only the chancellor and the justiciar but also the treasurer were required to be in frequent attendance upon him personally.[36] But in addition John used chamber clerks to monitor or intervene in other branches of government. William of Cornhill, for example, was employed in a wide variety of tasks: he is to be found on occasion in the chancery or the exchequer, he handled special business arising from the interdict, he served on the commission to assess the tax of the thirteenth of movables, he negotiated with the Londoners at the onset of the civil war.[37] More significantly two of the leading chamber clerks, Peter des Roches and Richard Marsh, together with another of John's intimates, William Brewer, were 'associated' with the justiciar, Geoffrey FitzPeter, in exchequer and judicial business.[38] At crucial periods Richard Marsh briefly combined the functions of chamberlain, chancellor and treasurer. He was keeper of the great seal from June 1209 to October 1213, and was appointed to the chancellorship itself in October 1214.[39] Peter des Roches was appointed justiciar in February 1214, and was succeeded in June 1215 by another former chamberlain, Hubert de Burgh.

King John's methods for taking control of the by then sprawling central administration were methods appropriate to his paranoiac suspicion that he was constantly being cheated and betrayed and his wishes flouted or circumvented. They were not the methods adopted in his son's reign. The Chamber, which had shrunk to insignificance during the minority, was not revived; an enlarged Wardrobe sufficed for the king's domestic needs. The central administration was brought more firmly under royal control by reorganizing and rationalizing it. The overhaul had several facets. First the separation of departments and their specialization in function was recognized. The chancellor's clerk at the exchequer became the 'chancellor of the exchequer'.[40] The chancery clerks were distinguished from the king's chaplains and assigned quarters at Westminster. Secondly, the roles of the justiciar and the chancellor were drastically altered. The holders of these offices had acquired great influence and a quasi-independent status, with an intermediary role between the king and the administrative service. That was now to cease. The justiciarship was abolished, its functions in financial administration taken over by the treasurer and in judicial administration by a chief-justice. The office of chancellor,

36. West, *Justiciarship*, chapter V.
37. Painter, *King John*, pp. 106, 174, 178, 194, 283.
38. West, pp. 169–71, 176–7.
39. Painter, pp. 205–6.
40. Tout, *Chapters*, i. 146.

held since 1226 by Ralph Neville, bishop of Chichester, had been granted to him for life and he did not die until 1244; but after 1238 he was a titular chancellor entitled to receive the profits of the office but without having custody of the great seal. After his death there was no formal appointment to the chancellorship, the seal being in the custody of a succession of keepers whose appointments were of short duration.[41] There were more keepers of the great seal in the middle years of Henry III's reign than there had been chancellors since the beginning of Henry II's. The barons in 1258 insisted on having a chancellor personally responsible for the use of the great seal, but they accepted the man who had been discharging the duties of the office for the past three years, and accepted too the major change in chancery practice introduced after chancellor Neville's death. Hitherto the profits of the fees for drawing up and sealing documents were the perquisite of the chancellor; but after 1244 the fees were collected by the 'keeper of the hanaper' who paid the operating costs of the chancery and presented accounts for scrutiny by the Wardrobe.[42] Even when the chancellorship was revived its holder was a paid official. Thirdly, and most importantly for the future shape of central government, the old function of the exchequer as the forum for meetings of the major officials from both wings of the king's government was abandoned (the 'barons of the exchequer' becoming exclusively finance officers) and replaced by meetings of a king's Council embracing senior administrators. The old dual structure of government, with peripatetic and resident elements, disappeared, and with it the old methods of co-ordination. It was replaced by a single structure of government with methods of co-ordination which led directly to the king. It is customary to speak of the 'personal rule' of Henry III in the years between the downfall of Hubert de Burgh and the baronial take-over in 1258, but what distinguished his personal rule from that of his predecessors was that there was now a well ordered bureaucracy of government of which the king could if he wished take direct control. It is significant that Henry III did not find it necessary to use his privy seal to authorize administrative action or as a substitute for it: the administrative machine was more readily at his bidding through the Council.

It is difficult to be sure of the composition and functions of the Council under Henry III because it kept no records. The evidence for it is sparse and comes mainly from chronicles. It seems unlikely that it had a fixed membership or defined functions, though its members

---

[41]. Dibben, 'Chancellor and keeper of the seal under Henry III', pp. 39–51, Wilkinson, *The Chancery under Edward III*, Appendix II.
[42]. Tout, *Chapters*, i. 286.

were identifiable in that they took a 'councillor's oath'.[43] The form of the oath is not known, though it may be assumed that at the heart of it lay a promise to preserve the confidentiality of the king's business. The absence of instructions from the Council in administrative records suggests that its function was advisory rather than executive. The possibility cannot be excluded that decisions reached in Council were conveyed to departments by word of mouth, but that is not to say that the Council as a body took decisions and authorized their implementation. In the later years of the reign when references to the Council begin to appear in letters patent the kind of phraseology used was that 'after treating of this matter diligently with his Council the king commands. . .'. It was only during the king's final illness that such phrases were used as 'as ordained by the Council'.[44] So far as can be seen the Council was from its inception a small and mainly ministerial body which brought administrative expertise to bear on decision making at the highest level, or at least that professional advice was available to the king if he chose to take it. The king of course, as always in the past, could take counsel from whom he would, and it is likely that Henry III's most influential advisers were his intimates rather than professional administrators; but it was not unusual for administrators to become intimates. Some of those who did were members of the household staff, such as Peter des Rivaux and John Mansel; but others, such as Walter Ralegh, Henry of Bath, Robert Passelew, Henry Wengham, or Philip Lovel, were senior officials of the judiciary, chancery or treasury who because of administrative functions were brought into personal contact with the king and gained his confidence, rather than intimates who were appointed to high office.[45] Beside them, however, were intimates who performed no administrative function but were simply the king's friends, and most notably were, as Henry III's critics constantly complained, his foreign relatives who did not know the realm nor have its welfare at heart. It is tempting to distinguish between coun*cillors* and coun*sellors*, and to regard the former as a professional core within a looser group; but it is unlikely that any such distinction was either conceived in theory or discernible in practice at a time when informal methods of government still prevailed at the top. There were simply the king's personally chosen counsellors who were sworn 'to be of his Council'. Nevertheless it is significant that the chronicler Matthew Paris, who was remarkably well-informed about what went on at

43. On the Council in this period J.F. Baldwin, *The King's Council in the Middles Ages* (Oxford, 1913) is largely outdated; more helpful is Wilkinson, *Studies in Constitutional History*, chapter V.
44. Wilkinson, *Studies*, p. 121 and n. 2.
45. *Ibid.*, pp. 146–6, Powicke, *Henry III and the Lord Edward*, chapter VIII.

court, never numbered the king's foreign friends among those he identifies as 'counsellors'.[46] If he is right, it may be said that there had emerged or was emerging from the old undifferentiated and amorphous *curia regis* a body charged with a particular responsibility in the business of government. What is difficult to determine is whether we should see the Council as simply advisory to the king who was the sole executive (which was undoubtedly the theory) or whether in practice the Council, as it were, occupied the bridge of the ship of state and directed its course subject to the wishes of the king as master of the vessel. Perhaps the Council's function fluctuated between the two as the king chose. What is unmistakable is that the barons regarded the Council as the means to control of government and demanded to have their nominees on it. The Council, it seems, had become the focal point of the government of the realm.

The overhaul of the administration in the 1230s introduced major changes in exchequer practice and the management of the king's revenues.[47] In 1236 the royal demesne was taken out of the hands of the sheriffs. The condition and value of its constituent manors were meticulously assessed and they were then leased piecemeal. The administration of wardships, custodies and escheats, which had commonly been entrusted to sheriffs, was transferred to new officials known as 'escheators' who accounted for the revenues at the exchequer. For what remained of the old farm of the shire the sheriff had to render strict account instead of tendering an agreed lump sum, and details of what was due to the treasury was entered on a series of special rolls. So although the sheriff remained the crown's debt collector he ceased to be its land agent. The sheriff became only one of many officials who accounted at the exchequer – the accounts of escheators, of the custodians of castles, forests, vacant bishoprics and abbeys, of the Wardrobe, of Ireland, Wales and Gascony, and of the collectors of tallages and taxes were separately audited.

Efficient revenue collecting was the more necessary to Henry III because the proceeds of taxation were severely restricted.[48] Clauses 12 and 14 of Magna Carta of 1215 requiring consent to extraordinary taxation and specifying how consent 'by common counsel of the realm' was to be obtained, were both omitted from the Charter of 1225. They had however determined how taxes had been levied during the minority, and Henry III found himself obliged as a practical necessity to seek the consent of the magnates for extraordinary financial assistance. 'Urgent necessity' was accepted as a legitimate

46. Wilkinson, *Studies*, pp. 142–6.
47. M.H. Mills, 'The reforms at the exchequer (1232–42)', *TRHS*, 4th series, 10 (1927), 111–33, Carpenter, 'The decline of the curial sheriff', pp. 19ff.
48. On taxation see Harriss, *Public Finance*, chapter II.

reason for requesting aid, but the barons made themselves the judges of the validity of the plea in relation to the welfare of the realm. There were in the reign of Henry III few necessities which did not arise from the king's foreign policy, so consideration of the requests was the occasion for criticism of the policy. Consent in the form of approval by the major tenants-in-chief of the crown reinforced and indeed gave expression to the barons' assumption that they could speak for 'the community of the realm'. Their grant of taxes assessed on movable property in 1232 and 1237 was held to imply not only the assent of the archbishops, bishops, abbots, earls and barons who actually gave it, but also of all the others required to pay: 'clergy holding land other than benefices, knights, freemen, and the villeins'.[49] Consent was used as a bargaining counter: in 1237, for example, it was linked to a demand for confirmation of the Charters and for three magnates to be included on the king's Council. Thereafter, until the crisis of 1258, requests for financial aid were refused as not being in the interests of the realm. The king was told that there would be no necessity if he had not been prodigal in his expenditure, if he had not embarked at his own will on ambitious, expensive and foolish foreign schemes which were no concern of the realm. The defence of his rights of lordship in Gascony was, however, regarded as a legitimate ground for requesting aid. The king tried to claim that the interests of England were engaged in his defence of his continental dominion; the barons would have none of that, but they accepted that as his vassals they had a personal obligation to assist him as their feudal lord; this, however, they clamed to discharge by military service or by paying scutage.[50] The distinction became clearer between taxes on grounds of 'necessity' for which consent was required on the one hand, and on the other the king's prerogative rights to dues which arose from his feudal lordship and to the levy of tallage on those subject to his seigneurial lordship. There were four taxes on movables in the reign but 14 tallages. When taxes were withheld the efficient exploitation of prerogative rights became a priority with king's government. Improvements in the methods of managing the shires were an essential part of it.

The major reform of 1236 had two aspects: the royal demesne ceased to contribute to the sheriff's profit, and for the remaining proceeds of shire administration he was held strictly accountable to the exchequer and was assigned allowances for his expenses. The sheriff was henceforth a 'custodian' not a 'farmer' of the shire.[51] The experiment of custodian sheriffs in John's reign had been short-lived.

---

[49]. *Ibid.*, p. 30.
[50]. *Ibid.*, pp. 33ff.
[51]. Carpenter, 'The decline of the curial sheriff', pp. 16ff.

In the last years of his reign and in the early years of the minority security had been a prime consideration, and patronage for the crown's supporters politically vital, so the shires had been held mainly by military captains, members of the king's entourage, prominent servants and trustworthy friends. Custodians had fitfully reappeared in the later 1220s, but it was only after 1236 that the policy was applied consistently. There had long been a tension between the competing claims of the sheriffdoms as a source of royal patronage and the siphoning off of sheriffs' profits for the benefit of the treasury. From the standpoint of the exchequer the holding of sheriffdoms by courtiers (*curiales*) was inconvenient as well as expensive. As D.A. Carpenter writes: 'There were several reasons why the *curialis* was an unsuitable sheriff from the exchequer's point of view. He was more troublesome in general to control than a man of less influence and favour; he frequently consigned the administration of the county to a deputy which created difficulties over the division of responsibility; . . . and, above all, he was reluctant to hold office on terms which deprived him of private gain'.[52]

After 1236 *curiales* were no longer interested in holding sheriffdoms, and the way was open for the exchequer to select sheriffs from members of the knightly class in the shires without interference from the court. This was a popular development; even Matthew Paris welcomed it. Curial farmers of the counties had employed as undersheriffs men who may have been competent administrators but whose delegated authority was often resented and whose private interest in extracting their own margin of profit conflicted with the interests of the men of the shires. Local men of substance had less need to peculate and had a reputation to lose. Unfortunately, after 1241 the political advantage of this popular reform was discarded because of the king's desperate need for money. He was frequently in debt and a truculent baronage was refusing subsidies to support his foreign policy. The screws were turned on shire revenues. The charging of increments was reintroduced in steadily escalating amounts. The financial gain to the exchequer was considerable but at the cost of exacerbating 'the endemic corruption of local government'.[53] Sheriffs were impelled to recoup themselves by exacting fees, gifts and bribes, by leasing some of their rights at enhanced rates, and by abusing their customary perquisites to hospitality for themselves and their servants. It is significant that the kind of substantial local men who had taken on the sheriffdoms in 1236–41 were no longer willing to serve and so incur the hostility of county society; instead those appointed had been, as the

52. *Ibid.*, p. 4.
53. *Ibid.*, p. 22.

baronial reformers were to complain, 'men coming from far away and utter strangers in the counties'.[54]

In the Provisions of Oxford the barons prescribed what was, in effect, a return to the practice of 1236–41, with the added safeguard of annual appointments: 'Sheriffs shall be appointed who are loyal men and sound landholders. . . . And let him take no payment, and let him not be sheriff for more than one year at a time. And during that year let him render his accounts at the exchequer. . . . And let the king pay him out of his own revenues sufficient to enable him to administer the county justly. And let him take no bribes neither himself nor his officials. And if they be found guilty, let them be punished.'[55] It was one of the first reforms to be implemented. In October 1258 the Ordinance of Sheriffs took the form of proclamation 'to all the people' of each county. The king informed them that 'we wish and will that speedy justice be done throughout our realm, no less to the poor than to the rich', and 'that the wrongs which had been done in your county, no matter who had done them, be reported to the four knights we have appointed for the purpose'. They were reminded that as the sheriffs were to be appointed for no more than one year, they could reveal wrongdoing without fear of reprisal. They were told in detail of the requirements of an oath which was to be taken by the sheriffs: 'that he would do justice in common to all people', and specifying from whom he could exact hospitality, with what frequency, and with how many horses and men, and that he 'shall not take from any man . . . lamb, sheaf, corn, wool, nor any other kind of goods, nor money, nor anything that has money value, as many have been accustomed to do in times past'.[56]

The baronial reformers were assuring the men of the shires that they meant business and were recruiting support. The shortcomings in local government were a powerful reinforcement of the baronial cause in two respects: they demonstrated the incompetence of the king's personal government and justified the baronial take-over, and secondly the widespread support in the shires for reform effectively disarmed the king.

Government in the Localities

Shires and hundreds

Writing of the reign of King John, Sidney Painter described the sheriff as 'the errand boy for the central administration'.[57] This is a graphic

54. *Documents 1258–67*, no. 37C, pp. 276–7, Carpenter, p. 29.
55. *Documents 1258–67*, no. 5, p. 109
56. *Ibid.*, no. 8, *EHD* iii. 368–70.
57. S. Painter, *The Reign of King John* (Baltimore, 1949), p. 90.

phrase which other commentators have picked up. R.C. Van Caenegem has said that a major consequence of Henry II's judicial reforms was to define the sheriff's functions within a limited range of duties 'which gave him the air of the errand boy of the royal courts, with few important or responsible tasks'.[58] The transformation in the powers and functions of the sheriff in the course of the twelfth century is indeed remarkable. He had ceased to be the governor of a shire with a wide authority to act at his own discretion. He no longer normally had jurisdiction over pleas of the crown. His conduct of the king's business had been subjected to close scrutiny at the exchequer. His management of the shire was overseen from time to time by itinerant royal justices on general eyres. His discretionary authority had been curtailed and many of his powers could be exercised only on explicit instructions conveyed by royal writ. It is true too that by the later twelfth century many of the tasks which the sheriff and his officers had to perform could be described as fetching and carrying on behalf of the central administration. But to describe the sheriff as an errand boy is seriously misleading. It ignores the authority he still exercised without the necessity of a royal writ, and it belittles his rôle as the indispensable executant of royal writs both judicial and administrative. The importance of the sheriff as an agent and not simply an errand boy is demonstrated during the years from 1258 to 1265 when the barons and the king vied for control of the central government: as each side achieved a temporary ascendancy its first move was to change the sheriffs. Some shires had four changes.[59] Furthermore, it should not be overlooked that the sheriff had several rôles only one of which was to be the king's representative in the shire As Lapsley wrote: 'the thirteenth-century sheriff stood in various relations to the community and court of the county and exercised an authority drawn from more than one quarter.'[60] He was the presiding officer of the shire court and acted sometimes as a member of it and sometimes as its agent. The distinction is manifest in penalties laid upon a shire by the king's court for having acted wrongly: the sheriff too would be penalized if he had participated in a decision of the shire court, but he would escape liability if he were acting under its instructions. He could not, for example, participate in the judgements of the shire court on judicial pleas which lay within its competence but had the duty of implementing those judgements.

We are much less well informed about government in the localities than about central government because records of the former were not

---

[58.] R.C. Van Caenegem, *Royal Writs in England* (Selden Society, 1959), p. 204.
[59.] Morris, *Medieval Sheriff*, pp. 171–5.
[60.] G.T. Lapsley, 'The court, record, and roll of the county court in the thirteenth century', *Law Quarterly Review* 51 (1935), p. 300.

so carefully preserved. That there once were records of shire business is attested both by contemporary references and by surviving fragments, but it seems that they were of limited scope: notes made for the sheriff as *aides-mémoire*, coroners' records of crown pleas, and the enrolment of such decisions and judgements of which it was necessary to keep a record, but nothing in the nature of minutes of meetings which might reveal the full range of shire business. Such information as there is comes mainly from royal records, for the decisions and actions of the shire court could be challenged in the royal court. Representatives of the shire – usually the sheriff and four or six knights – would be required to 'bear the record of the county' and testify to what had been done before the royal justices. In this way something more than a mere record of decisions came to be entered on the *Curia Regis* Rolls, but of course only in relation to judicial pleas. Nevertheless it usefully supplements information to be derived from the Eyre Rolls and from contemporary legal treatises and enables us to get closer to the actual operations of government in the localities in the reign of Henry III than hitherto and to form some impression of the shire court at work.

Magna Carta of 1225 (clause 35) prescribed that shire courts should not be held more often than once a month and at longer intervals where that had been customary. In practice 'monthly' meant at intervals of 28 days with thirteen sessions in the year. In Lincolnshire and probably also in Yorkshire, Lancashire and Northumberland the customary minimum interval was 40 days with meetings usually every six weeks.[61] The ruling of Magna Carta, however, applied only to regular meetings. Extraordinary meetings could be convened by the king's order. Forty days notice was given for the shire to assemble before the justice in eyre. In 1220 and 1225 the sheriffs were instructed to convene special sessions to arrange for the levy of taxes.[62]

Although pleas of the crown had to be reserved for the itinerant justices, criminal business could come before the shire court by way of preliminary hearings whether on the procedure of indictment by juries of presentment or on appeal by private accusers. Confessions and the showing of wounds, for example, might be made in the shire court and recorded on the coroners' rolls as witnessed by the shire. Appeals which did not involve accusations of felony would be judged in the shire court according to customary procedures. Even in appeals which were reserved for hearing by the king's justices the first steps had to be taken at a session of the shire court with a full recital of the details of the accusation, and sometimes cases were remitted by the justices back to the shire. 'Presentment of Englishry' in murder cases was usually

61. Morris, *County Court*, p. 90.
62. *Ibid.*, p. 96.

made in the shire court, and proclamations of outlawry could only be made there. Some crimes which in seriousness fell between pleas of the crown and misdemeanours were 'pleas of the sheriff'. Many of them, such as causing an affray or brawling, were no doubt settled in the hundred courts, but some of them, especially theft, came up from the hundreds to the shire.

Similarly with civil litigation, the development of writ process did not remove all cases from the shire court, and such cases as were sent for judgement before the justices often involved the shire in some way or another. Land cases between the vassals of two different lords had by Henry I's ordinance to be brought there, and if lords' courts defaulted in doing justice the shire took cognizance. If the defendant did not 'put himself upon the king's assize' such cases were determined in the shire court. Actions before the king's courts might be considered by the justices to be better settled locally and transferred to the shire by writ of *justicies* to the sheriff. This commonly happened in cases of nuisance, such as impeding a pathway or watercourse, or encroaching upon the common. Actions heard and determined in the king's courts came to the attention of the shire in various ways. Pending a hearing in the royal court the sheriff was instructed to have the property put in the king's peace and the plaintiff would commonly have the writ read out in the shire court. The preliminaries to a hearing in the royal court and the application of its decisions involved several instructions to the sheriff which he could most conveniently discharge at a meeting of the shire: the appointment of summoners of the parties, the testing of the validity of excuses for non-appearance, for example, or the designation of the four knights who were to select the jury for a grand assize, or of those who were to apportion reasonable dower to a widow, or to settle the boundaries in a division of property decreed by the justices. So although the drawing of litigation before the royal courts deprived the shire courts and the feudal courts of much judgement giving, it involved the sheriff and leading men of the shire in much business connected with cases which hitherto would have been private to the courts of lords.

Civil actions which did not involve questions of right in land were still commonly initiated not by writ but by plaint in the shire court and settled there. Many of them were pleas of debt or trespass. Most common of all in the thirteenth century seem to have been complaints arising from distraint or, in legal parlance, 'distress'. The seizure of chattels, usually beasts of the field or farm implements, was the normal method of enforcing judgements or obligations by sheriffs and their deputies, by manorial officials and by private individuals. It was an everyday occurrence and frequently abused, so that numerous pleas arose of beasts seized for no just cause, or wrongfully detained after satisfaction had been made. Abuse of distress was regarded as a serious matter in the thirteenth century and treated as an offence against the king's peace but remitted to the sheriffs because of the need for speedy remedy.[63] Manorial business could thus come before the shire courts, and some landlords took the precaution of securing a judgement of the shire in their favour before levying distress for overdue rents. Fugitive villeins were claimed in the shire courts; but if the alleged fugitive denied his villeinage the case would be removed to the royal court for although the shire could restore to a lord his rights it could not pronounce upon status.

The shire could make bye-laws and regulations, such as fixing a close-season for salmon fishing, but could do so in the thirteenth century only with the approval of justices in eyre. It was the duty of the eyre to uphold custom and punish its infractions, so the practice was for the 12 knights of the shire who were chosen to answer to the articles of the eyre to seek the justices' assent to changes in custom. W.A. Morris commented on this that the influence of the justices in eyre 'checked the earlier trend toward a diversity in county usage which might have grown into a local legislative power'.[64] It must, however, be doubtful if this was considered policy; it is just as likely to have been an incidental consequence of the eyre system. Nevertheless it reminded the shires that they were now in leading strings. Another and more constant reminder was the amount of business before the shire which was authorized or commanded by royal writ. No longer were the shires the self-contained, insulated compartments of the realm which they had been at the time of the Norman Conquest. On the other hand it should be observed that shire courts had not waned with the expansion of royal government: they did not stand alongside it, they had been integrated into it. Indeed they occupied centre-stage in the governance of the realm, overlapping in one direction with the royal courts, and in the other with manorial and feudal courts.

When, however, we speak of shire courts what do we mean; who constituted them? This is not an easy question to answer. Although it is clear that the notion popularized in the seventeenth century of a general assembly of the freemen of the shire is mistaken, the available evidence is not easy to interpret. When the community of the shire was to assemble before the justices in eyre summonses went out to all bishops, abbots, priors, earls, barons, knights and freemen holding land in the shire, and requiring each vill to be represented by its reeve and four law-worthy men, and each borough by 12 law-worthy burgesses. These of course were extra-special sessions; but there was

---

63. On distress see P & M, ii. 577ff.
64. Morris, *County Court*, p. 135.

still a tradition in the thirteenth century of twice-yearly 'great' or 'general' sessions of the shire – a lingering memorial it may be, of the old rule of King Edgar in the tenth century requiring the shires to assemble twice a year, and reflecting a time when all but the weightiest business was disposed of at monthly hundred courts. In the days of King Cnut twice-yearly meetings of the shiremoot were still regarded as normal though provision was made for more frequent meetings if need be. In the early years of the twelfth century the author of the *Leges Henrici* writes as if the same was true of his day, though he may simply be repeating the provisions of Cnut's law.[65] The same author has some puzzling words on attendance at the twice-yearly meetings which seem to imply that they should be attended by all fief-holders in the shire (who might, however, be represented by their stewards) and by office holders – the bishop, the earl, hundredmen (*prefecti*) and village reeves (*tungrevii*).[66] It is not inconceivable that estate holders and representatives of communities were similarly the twin constituents of 'great' sessions of the shire in the thirteenth century, as they were of assemblies before the justices in eyre, but the available evidence is too thin for certainty. What is abundantly clear, however, is that attendance at sessions in the intervening months had become narrowed to a group of 'suitors' – those who bore the duty of attending, and were said to 'owe suit of court'.[67] When this came about is wholly obscure, though it is reasonable to assume that it was a consequence of more frequent meetings becoming normal, and a product of arrangements agreed between sheriffs, who had to ensure that there was sufficient attendance to discharge the business, and lords who wished to be relieved of the burden of frequent meetings. That private arrangements were reached has to be assumed from the absence of any law or customary rule on the matter. The most common arrangement was to saddle the holders of specified lands on each estate with the duty of suit. They were usually men of the knightly class or substantial freeholders who could bear the burden of the penalties for defaults which not infrequently fell upon the suitors, but not exclusively so for there are references to *minuti homines* owing suit and even villeins. Some lords preferred to have their stewards attend, and in Yorkshire the shire court is said to have consisted primarily of stewards of tenants-in-chief. A few holders of baronies seem never to have deputed the duty of suit but to have attended regularly in person.[68] But

[65] *Leges Henrici*, 7.4, II Cnut 18, *The Laws of the Kings of England from Edmund to Henry I*, ed. A.J. Robertson (Cambridge, 1925), p. 183.
[66] *Leges Henrici*, 7.2, 7.7.
[67] On suit see P & M, i. 540ff., F.W. Maitland, 'The suitors of the county court', *EHR* 3 (1888), 417–21, reprinted in *Collected Papers*, ed. H.A.L. Fisher (Cambridge, 1911), i. 458–66, Morris, *County Court*, 100–5, Cam, *The Hundred*, pp. 109–12.
[68] Morris, *County Court*, pp. 104–5.

whatever the arrangements made and whatever differences there were between shires, the situation for each sheriff was clear: he had a list of suitors and could compel attendance by distraint or amercement.

The restricted duty of suit did not of course imply that others were excluded: the shire court was a public assembly and anyone who chose to attend might do so, but judgement-giving and decision-making fell to the regular suitors. Nor should it be forgotten that there was a more numerous attendance from those who had business before the court or were summoned for particular purposes. Acquaintance with the shire court must have been widespread; but there was a core of regular attenders whose lifetime experience of shire business outran that of the sheriff, whose understanding of the workings of government in the localities and the implications of royal commands was sharper than that of the king or his chief ministers or the barons, and without whose co-operation government could barely function at all.

The hundred of the eleventh century could be described as 'the shire in little'. That could not be said of the hundred of the thirteenth century. By then it was closer to being a subdivision of the shire for administrative purposes. In discharging the king's business the sheriff passed instructions to bailiffs in the hundreds. The importance of the hundreds in the government of the realm should not however be underestimated. They were the units through which the public duties of all subjects were exacted, the assessment of taxes, the swearing-in to keep the king's peace and bear arms in his service, the reporting of crime and the indictment of suspects. The juries of presentment were hundred juries. The business of the hundred court, however, was contracting, some of it siphoned off into the shire court and some into the courts under the jurisdiction of landlords.

It may be a sign of the declining importance of hundred courts that kings more readily granted the right to hold them to magnates. In Wiltshire in 1066 no more than six hundreds were in the hands of lords; by 1194 the number had doubled; by 1275 it had risen to 27, leaving only 11 administered by royal bailiffs. In the country as a whole by the later thirteenth century 358 hundreds were in the hands of lords out of a total of 628. The distribution, however, was uneven: in Sussex all the hundreds were in the hands of lords, in Buckinghamshire none, nor in Warwickshire, very few in eastern England, but many in the south-west.[69]

It is another sign of the wilting of hundred courts that less frequent meetings were thought necessary. Fortnightly meetings had been usual in Henry II's day, but in 1234 Henry III decreed, 'by the common

69. *VCH Wiltshire*, v. 44–51, Cam, *The Hundred and the Hundred Rolls*, p. 137 and Appendix IV.

counsel' of his barons, that the interval between meetings should henceforth be three weeks.[70] This was, however, in response to views emanating from the shires that two meetings a year would suffice.[71] It may be suspected that requiring meetings every three weeks was more for the advantage and profit of the court-holders than for the discharge of urgent business.

Hundred courts can nevertheless be seen to be performing a useful function for the local community. A thirteenth century lawbook defines the jurisdiction of hundred courts as pleas of battery and brawls which do not amount to felony, of the wounding and maiming of beasts, and of debts which could be collected without a royal writ.[72] Surviving evidence, however, suggests that the common business of the court was more aptly described in the twelfth-century *Leges Edwardi Confessoris* as dealing with cases 'between vills and neighbours . . . about pastures, measures, harvests, disputes between neighbours and many things of this kind which frequently arise'.[73] Typical cases were the turning loose of horses on private pasture, the pilfering of garden produce and flowers, allowing dogs to worry beasts, cheating by tradesmen, breaches of verbal agreements and slander. Very common were minor debts such as arrears of rent and non-payment for goods delivered.[74] Such business is barely distinguishable from that which came before manorial courts, but whereas the latter could deal only with the pleas of tenants of the manor the hundred court could settle disputes between tenants of different lords. Judgements in the hundred court were given by the suitors, and as with the shire courts the duty of suit had become restricted to the tenants of specified land-holdings.

Hundred courts which had not been handed over to lords were presided over by bailiffs appointed by the sheriffs.[75] As the sheriff's local deputy the other duties of the hundred bailiff lay in the serving of royal writs and sheriff's mandates, the collection of debts owed to the exchequer, executing judgements of the shire court, levying fines and amercements, arresting and attaching accused persons, seizing and holding beasts and chattels by way of distraint and empanelling juries. Examples can be found of bailiffs holding hereditary office – they were common in Cornwall, Somerset and Lancashire – but more usually the sheriff appointed a man for a fixed term. There is evidence

---

70. *EHD* iii. 350.
71. J.R. Maddicott, 'Magna Carta and the local community', *Past and Present* 102 (1984), pp. 34ff, 50.
72. *Bracton's Notebook*, ed. F.W. Maitland (London, 1887), case no. 1110.
73. Leges Edwardi, c. 28, *Gesetze*, i. 652.
74. Cam, *Hundred*, pp. 181–3.
75. On the hundred bailiff see *ibid.*, chapter X.

of bailiffs being regularly reappointed under a succession of sheriffs, though frequently moved from one hundred to another, so it seems that there were men who made a profession of local government service. Lords who had been granted hundreds made their own appointments, but their bailiffs were answerable to the sheriff for the discharge of the king's business. Bailiffs usually farmed their hundreds, that is to say they paid the sheriff or the lord who appointed them a lump sum for the privilege of office and expected to make a profit out of fees and perquisities levied on the men of the hundred. These were supposed to be regulated by custom, but it was difficult to control the taking of 'commission' on distraints, the levying of debts and the delivery of writs, or the acceptance of *douceurs* and tips for favours rendered. The opportunities for abuse were infinite. A prevalent practice which the king's government tried to repress through the justices in eyre was the 'scotale': bailiffs took as a customary perquisite sheaves of barley at harvest, and from these they brewed ale which villagers were obliged to purchase, often at a compulsory junketings, at prices above those charged in the ale-houses which were regulated by the assize of ale.[76]

Twice a year the sheriff made a visitation of the hundreds which was known as 'taking his tourn'.[77] The sheriffs' tourns were the equivalent on a lesser scale of the visitations of the shires by the justices in eyre, but more frequent. The tourn was the occasion for 'great' or 'general' meeting of the hundred: not only the regular suitors but all estate owners in the hundred and all males over the age of 12 were expected to attend upon the sheriff and would be fined if they did not. It was particularly burdensome to estate owners who held lands in several hundreds. Penalizing non-attendance was one of many sources of profit to the sheriffs on their tourns. At the tourn the headmen of the tithings were interrogated about infractions of the law. Unlike the 'articles of the eyre' there was no prescribed list of questions, but surviving examples show that a more or less standard form had developed by the thirteenth century. It was remarkably comprehensive. In addition to inquiries about pleas of the crown, lesser crimes and breaches of the king's assizes, there were questions about 'usurers, sorcerers and heretics', about 'boundaries broken down or removed, about 'waters diverted from their courses or stopped', about 'dikes, walls, causeys, ponds and the like, which are set up or taken down to the nuisance of others', about 'roads and pathways wrongfully stopped or narrowed', about the keeping of watch and ward, and even

76. *Ibid.*, pp. 150–1.
77. On the sheriff's tourn see *ibid.*, pp. 118–28, 185–7, P & M, i. 530, 558–60, 570–1, W.A. Morris, *The Frankpledge System* (New York, 1910), pp. 123–9, D.A. Crowley, 'The later history of frankpledge', *BIHR* 48 (1975), 1–15.

the selling of second-hand clothes.[78] The answers of the headmen of the tithings, who were usually villeins, were then put to a jury of 12 freemen who were required to state on oath whether they believed the accusations to be well-founded and whether anything had been concealed. The coroners took note of pleas of the crown which had to be reserved for judgement before the king's justices, but the sheriff gave summary judgement on those lesser and probably more numerous matters which fell within his jurisdiction. The tourn was also the occasion for inquiring into the operations of the frankpledge system 'so that peace should be kept and the tithings made up'. In the twelfth century this had been done at both tourns, but Magna Carta in its revised versions limited it to the second tourn of the year (1217 clause 42, 1225 clause 35). Breeches of the rules were amerced, and 'head-money' of a penny from each tithing member collected. The 'view of frankpledge', as it was known, entailed much preliminary work by the hundred bailiff. At each village he checked the old lists of tithing members, crossing off the names of those who had died or left the district, adding the names of boys over 12 who had to be sworn before the sheriff to keep the king's peace. He inquired if there were incomers and vagrants who could not be vouched for, and noted the names of those who claimed to be exempt from frankpledge since the sheriff would wish to check if the claims were valid. So the 'view', besides ensuring that the pledging and surety system was properly organized, constituted a census of the male population of the countryside.

The work of the sheriff and his subordinates was frequently hampered by the franchisal privileges of landlords. Probably the most common of all franchises in the thirteenth century was 'view of frankpledge'. Those who had it were entitled to withdraw their manorial tenants from the sheriff's view, hold a private view and collect the headmoney and fines for irregularities. But since the view was the occasion for reporting crimes there had to be some way of safeguarding the king's jurisdiction. It seems that some lords claimed that their franchises gave them the right to take presentments and forward pleas of the crown to the coroners, and it is likely that this usually happened when the lord held the hundred as a whole. Other lords baulked at that responsibility and came to some arrangement with the sheriff. Some held the view on their manors but sent their unfree tenants, or representatives, to attend the sheriff's tourn and answer to the rest of the articles. Some admitted the hundred bailiff as an observer to take notes and report to the sheriff.[79] The details of the arrangements varied widely, which suggests that each

---

78. *Fleta*, ed. H.G. Richardson and G.O. Sayles, ii (Selden Society, 1953), 175–6.
79. Cam, *The Hundred*, p. 186.

lord with view of frankpledge negotiated an arrangement with the sheriff. The implication, however, is clear: private rights could not obstruct the king's government however much they complicated its workings.

Another way in which franchises hampered the sheriffs was in the execution of royal writs, both common law writs and the exchequer writs for the collection of debts owed to the king.[80] It is not clear how this was done in earlier days, but it appears from *Glanvill* that the necessary arrangements involved in common law writs would be done publicly at meetings of the shire court; there sureties could be taken, summoners nominated and juries empanelled. But with the vast expansion in the number of writs issuing from chancery, sheriffs had by the early years of the thirteenth century developed a bureaucracy of clerks for handling them and used the hundred bailiffs for executing them. But what of those lords who claimed the right to exclude the sheriff and his subordinates from entering upon their lands, a right originally intended to protect private jurisdiction? The practical difficulty could have been met by having writs redirected to the holders of liberties instead of to the sheriff, or by the sheriffs simply transmitting the writs to the liberty holders. Significantly neither of these methods was adopted. Instead the chancery continued to address writs to the sheriff, but if a liberty excluding the sheriff was involved the sheriff issued an instruction under his own seal to the officials of the liberty transcribing the royal writ and concluding with the sentence 'And so I command you to execute the king's command'. If the officials of the liberty failed to comply the sheriff reported to the chancery which reissued the royal writ to him with the addition of a command that he was not to omit (*non omittas*) to have the writ executed regardless of the liberty. If there was still no proper response the sheriff could execute the writ in person by force of arms if necessary. The right to receive and execute transcripts of royal writs came to be known as 'return of writs', from the Latin *returnum* meaning a transcript. The emergence of the franchise of 'return of writs' in the early thirteenth century may be seen as a triumph for lords in protecting their liberties; but significantly it took the form of a concession withdrawable if abused: the sheriff deferred to privileged lords by having transcripts made, but his authority when acting as the king's agent could not be gainsaid.

[80.] On this topic see M.T. Clanchy, introduction to *The Roll and Writ File of the Berkshire Eyre of 1248* (Selden Society, 1973), pp. xlv–xlvii, and Appendix 7, and 'The franchise of return of writs', *TRHS* 17 (1967), 59–79.

Franchises and liberties*

The history of franchises and liberties is beset with many uncertainties and difficulties of interpretation. The existence and nature of them becomes clearer only with the extensive inquiries conducted into them by the crown in the later thirteenth century. Before then it is possible to know of them mainly from charters, but that tends to limit our information to ecclesiastical estates for until the later twelfth century it was usually churchmen who sought charters and carefully preserved them; lay lords were more likely to rely on 'prescription' – the continued enjoyment of a right from time immemorial, which might only come to light in the records if disputed or infringed. So it is hard to generalize about the earlier history of franchises and liberties.

There were two principal reasons for the creation of those liberties which went back to pre-Conquest times. Many of them were ancient chieftainries, mainly but not exclusively in eastern England and in the north, which were consigned to trustworthy men close to the king – abbots, bishops and royal kinsmen, who ruled them as 'areas of special jurisdiction'. Secondly, at a time when kings were making laws for the better ordering of the realm but had no direct means of law enforcement it was sensible to enlist the co-operation of the greater lords, acknowledging the traditional association of lordship with jurisdiction, and by the grant of franchises reducing the likelihood of friction with the king's representatives in the shire, who were then the earl and the bishop. Those reasons were augmented when, after the Conquest, the rôle of the earl and the bishop in the administration of the shire disappeared and sheriffs took over their functions. The prestige of great lords was offended by men of inferior status meddling in the affairs of their tenants, so it was politic to grant them exemption from the sheriff and to allow their servants to do his work in a privileged area. Such exemptions usually applied, however, only to manors which tenants-in-chief retained in their own hands and not to the rest of their estates which had been granted as fiefs to sub-tenants.

A critical period in the history of franchises and liberties came in the second half of the twelfth century when royal government moved into the shires, taking over the hearing of pleas of the crown, disciplining local administrators, extending the reach of royal justice in civil litigation and over a widening area of lesser offences construed as breaches of the king's peace, and applying new regulations which

---

*These two words are commonly used interchangeably, but for the sake of clarity 'franchise' will here be used to denote a privilege allowed to a subject of exercising a function which normally belonged to the crown, and 'liberty' to denote the conjunction of several such privileges and the area within which they were exercised.

encompassed even the brewing of ale and the baking of bread. The development of royal government undermined the old justifications for the exercise of franchisal powers and devalued existing privileges. Fences erected against the sheriff's jurisdiction were no protection against the jurisdiction of royal justices nor against the sheriff himself when acting on the instructions of a royal mandate. Moreover, the changes wrought by Angevin government tended to consign some franchisal rights to the scrapheap of worthless anachronisms. The right to share in the proceeds of a levy of danegeld ceased to be worth anything with the lapse of the levy. The right 'to plead whatever the sheriff pleads in the shire court' was diminished when the sheriffs' jurisdiction was reduced. The right to take the monetary penalties levied under the old customary law on the tenants of a privileged estate who were convicted of crime became an anachronism unless it could be converted into the right to receive amercements imposed by the king's justices and 'felons' chattels'. Whether old rights could be effectively updated depended on the indulgence of the crown.

It might be expected that dissension between king and lords over franchisal powers would have erupted in the reign of Henry II. Even before the inauguration of the eyres Henry II had signalled his intention of limiting franchises. The most radical aspect of the Assize of Clarendon in 1166 was the overriding of franchisal rights. It ruled that not even the most privileged lords could claim any right which prevented the sheriffs entering upon their lands to take view of frankpledge and to arrest suspects indicted by the prescribed procedures of the juries of presentment; moreover it insisted that in the case of those arrested after indictment by juries of presentment 'let no man have court or justice or chattels save the lord king in his court in the presence of his justices.'[81] Some historians have construed these provisions as presaging a general attack upon franchises and liberties which would gather force as the eyres developed; but since franchisal powers survived, were updated and multiplied, we should have to assume that Henry II was obliged to beat an ignominious retreat. This seems unlikely, especially since the Assize was made 'with the assent of the archbishops, bishops, abbots, earls and barons of all England'. It seems more likely that the king's intention in 1166 was to insist on drastic measures to combat prevalent crime, which could subsequently be relaxed at his pleasure by renewals of old privileges, and at the same time to assert the primacy of royal government after the lax days of King Stephen. Henry II may have refused to acknowledge the powers of local government acquired by magnates in Stephen's reign but he was not disposed to challenge rights well-established in the time

---

81. Clauses 5, 8, 9, and 11, *EHD* ii. 408–9.

of his grandfather. Under Henry II and his successors franchisal powers could be updated and extended, confirmed by royal charters and defended in the royal courts in the same way as freeholds. The development of royal government meant that kings had more exemptions and privileges to grant; it was a convenient form of patronage, and indulgence to the magnates' desire to dignify their status and augment their income by franchisal rights was one of the ways by which the crown secured their co-operation and their assent to the expansion of royal government.

On the other hand, although Angevin government may be said to have embraced the liberties, it did so in ways which ruptured their immunities. One way was by qualifying clauses in charters. King John, for example, confirmed to the abbot of Sempringham 'his court and justice', but with the proviso 'saving in all things our justice'.[82] Even more significant are the compromises arranged with those magnates who held privileged enclaves over which they had complete jurisdiction: they were allowed their courts for the hearing of pleas of the crown but could exercise jurisdiction only when the king's justices came to sit with them. For example, it was recorded on the Memoranda Roll of the exchequer in 1242 that when the eyre went to Berkshire the abbot of Reading 'has his court, so that the justices in eyre in Berkshire enter the abbot's court and hold that court with the abbot's steward so that justice is exhibited to all.'[83] Special sessions of the eyre within liberties were similarly allowed to the hitherto impregnable 'special jurisdictions' of the great abbeys of St Albans, Bury St Edmunds, Ely and Peterborough, at the particularly favoured royal foundation of Battle Abbey, and in the northern liberties of Beverley, Ripon, Tynemouth and Redesdale.[84] The precise arrangements varied, no doubt according to the influence or bargaining powers of the grantees. To a few, the archbishop of York's liberty of Hexham, for instance, and on behalf of the inner sanctum of the *banleuca* of Bury St Edmunds and of Glastonbury, the privilege was allowed of hearing all pleas, but they could take crown pleas only when the king's justices handed to them a copy of the articles of the eyre. This applied even in the most extensive of liberties – the Liberty of St Cuthbert administered by the bishop of Durham. It was in effect a 'shire' in the hands of a subject for the bishop could appoint his own

---

[82]. *Rotuli Chartarum 1199–1216*, ed. T.D. Hardy (Record Commission, 1837), i. 18. For a similar restriction on the Templars see Hurnard, 'The Anglo-Norman franchises', p. 438.
[83]. Clanchy, introduction to *The Berkshire Eyre of 1248*, p. xxxi and n. 3.
[84]. For special sessions of the eyre see Hurnard, 'The Anglo-Norman franchises', pp. 434, 454–5, Cam, *Liberties*, p. 203, Scammell, 'The origins and limitations of the liberty of Durham', pp. 465–6, M.D. Lobel, 'The ecclesiastical banleuca in England', in *Oxford Essays in Medieval History presented to H.E. Salter* (Oxford, 1934), p. 130.

sheriff and justices, but in order to hear crown pleas he had to attend upon the king's justices when they came to Northumberland and receive a copy of the articles of the eyre. It mattered not that the bishopric of Durham was held by a succession of retired royal servants who were most intimate with the king; the immense wealth of the bishopric, derived both from its estates and its jurisdictional privileges, was their reward, but royal favour was not unlimited.

As Helen Cam has said: 'It was the universal spread of royal justice which opened a breach in the walls of a liberty and transformed its lord from a semi-independent magnate into a "minister of the king".'[85] Not only were liberty holders being circumscribed in the exercise of their privileges, the privileges themselves were being transmuted into duties. The franchise of 'return of writs' may be said to symbolize the outcome of Angevin policy: the franchise kept out the sheriff and his bailiffs, but the lord had to enforce the king's writs by his own bailiffs; the privilege could be overridden if he defaulted, and he could be penalized for irregularities. The roll of the eyre in Berkshire in 1249 gives some instances.

> The sheriff is commanded to take into the king's hand the liberty of [the lady] Margery de Rivers because she does not have bailiffs who answer before the justices concerning attachments pertaining to the crown.[86]

> Nicholas Spyrun was found drowned in a ditch below Standlynch. The first finder, Juliana wife of Nicholas, does not come because she has died. This happened within the liberty of William de Dunstanville. No attachment was made so let the liberty be taken into the king's hand.[87]

Even more remarkably, William Maudit who had the franchise of *infangthief* in his liberty of Warminster was penalized for not exercising it. Within the liberty two men stole 40 marks from the saddlebag of a horse belonging to a merchant of Bristol. The merchant complained to Maudit's bailiffs who apprehended the thieves with the money. They returned the 40 marks to the merchant and delivered the two thieves, Peter and Roger, to the king's gaol at Salisbury castle. The roll records:

> William Maudit is present and fully admits that Peter and Roger were taken and detained in his court with the 40 marks. He says that he has the liberty of imprisoning thieves and of condemning and convicting them in his court and of hanging them from his gallows. He fully admits that his bailiffs dismissed Peter and Roger from his court and sent them to the king's gaol at Salisbury without doing judgement on them. So it is held that the liberty be taken into the king's hand. . . .

[85] Cam, *Liberties*, p. 192, cf. p. 204.
[86] *Crown Pleas of the Wiltshire Eyre, 1249*, ed. C.A.F. Meekings (Devizes, 1961), no. 13.
[87] *Ibid.*, no. 187.

Afterwards William Maudit comes and makes fine of 20 marks for his liberty.[88]

By the middle of Henry III's reign an explicit legal theory had emerged which saw franchises as delegated royal authority which could be withdrawn for failure to discharge it properly.[89] Its implications were tellingly expressed in a letter from the king in 1237 to the holder of one of the most ancient, prestigious and extensive of the special jurisdictions – the abbot of Peterborough:

> Since we ordered all the bailiffs in our realm to see that watches were kept by night against disturbers of our peace and commanded that the holders of liberties should see that this was observed in their liberties, we marvel greatly that you in your liberty of Peterborough have allowed homicide and theft to be committed, and have taken no steps to see that our peace is kept. . . . We enjoin you therefore that, as you wish to retain your liberty, you take care to deal with malefactors and peace breakers, so that it may appear that you are a lover of peace, and that we may not have to lay our hands upon your liberty because you have failed.[90]

Although Henry III granted and confirmed franchises as his predecessors had done, his barons had reason to fear that their rights were under threat. The royal courts pertinaciously challenged every claim to exemption and privilege, and royal lawyers put restricted interpretations on clauses in charters which were couched in general rather than specific terms. The abbot of Beaulieu lost his right to a special session of the eyre in his manor of Faringdon, even though it had been allowed in 1227, because King John's generous charter did not state in so many words that he should have it.[91] In 1257 the bishops and abbots protested to the king about new-fangled subtleties and legal quibbling.[92] The king himself, however, gave colour to his magnates' fears. He harangued his sheriffs assembled at the exchequer in October 1250 telling them, among other things which he expected of them, that they should not make return of writs to anyone without warrant; and he had a new item added to the articles of the eyre, 'concerning those who do not allow the king's bailiff to enter their lands to make summonses or to distrain for debts'.[93] The justices in eyre in Berkshire reported that 'The jurors present that Simon de Montfort and his bailiffs do not allow the king's bailiffs to enter the

---

88. *Ibid.*, no. 323.
89. Sutherland, *Quo Warranto Proceedings*, pp. 1ff., Cam, *Law-Finders*, pp. 40–1.
90. *Close Rolls 1234–7*, p. 556.
91. Clanchy, introduction to the *The Berkshire Eyre of 1248*, p. xxx.
92. Paris, vi. 363–5, Cam, *Law-Finders*, p. 41.
93. Paris, v. 339, *Annales Monastici*, i. 338.

vill of Hungerford to make distraints for the king's debts as they used to in the time of his predecessors.'[94] In 1255 the king launched inquiries throughout the realm into royal rights, which included questions about 'those who have return of writs, whether they have it by royal concession or sheriffs' acquiescence', about 'those who hold view of frankpledge without royal warrant', and 'about those who claim liberties without a royal charter'.[95] The inquiries were followed by royal writs demanding to know by what warrant (*quo warranto*) liberty holders exercised the right they claimed.

Powicke has exonerated Henry III from the charge of mounting an attack upon the franchises, arguing that 'the keynote was not hostility but scrutiny', and that it was but one example of 'a widespread tendency to definition under the guidance of men skilled in law and administration.'[96] It may however be suspected that a prime motive in the *quo warranto* inquiries was to supplement the king's revenue by obliging the holders of defective charters to pay to have them rectified. Most of the boroughs hastened to have their charters fortified with an explicit statement of the right to return of writs.[97] Scrutiny was not new: the exchequer had been accustomed to question exemptions and privileges which deprived the king of revenue; but barons harassed by royal bureaucrats and pettifogging lawyers must have mourned the passing of the days when difficulties could be resolved by a private word with a justiciar of baronial rank. Resentment at Henry III's rigorous policy on the franchises ran high in the 1250s. Walter Clifford was so exasperated by the serving of a royal writ in his liberty in the March of Wales that he forced the bearer to swallow the writ, seal and all.[98]

The eyres, justice and the law

At the visitations of the shires in 1227 there were 25 articles of the eyre. By the 1250s the number had doubled; by the early 1270s it reached 70. The additional articles included inquiries into coining, into the lands and chattels of foreigners, into those who held lands by military service but had not taken up knighthood, and into the franchises; but the majority were concerned with the operation of government in the localities and administrative abuses.[99] The additional articles of course expanded the range of crown pleas; and at the same time the amount

---

[94.] *The Berkshire Eyre of 1248*, no. 756.

[95.] *Annales Monastici*, i. 337.

[96.] Powicke, *Henry III and the Lord Edward*, pp. 327–8.

[97.] Clanchy, 'The franchise of return of writs', p. 65.

[98.] Paris, v. 95, Davies, 'Kings, lords and liberties in the March of Wales', p. 60.

[99.] Cam, 'Studies in the Hundred Rolls', chapter I, Meekings, introduction to *The Wiltshire Eyre, 1249*, pp. 27–33.

of business under the heading of civil pleas was greatly increasing. In the first half of the thirteenth century the Bench at Westminster closed when a visitation began and cases pending before it were adjourned to be heard by the justices on circuit. On the eyre in Berkshire in 1248 the justices heard 372 civil cases which originated in Berkshire and a further 167 cases originating elsewhere which had been referred to them. The following year the practice of closing the Bench was ended to relieve the pressure on the eyres, but the justices on circuit still frequently could not complete the business before them in a shire and had to adjourn cases to the next shire which they were to visit. It was not until after Henry III's reign that, in 1285, the justices were forbidden to adjourn cases outside the shire in which disputed property lay, and not until 1294 that the practice of hearing 'foreign' pleas ended altogether. In the middle of the century a thousand people or more might have to attend before the justices at a shire visitation and many of them from outside the shire.[100]

In the later years of the twelfth century a visitation of all the shires took about two years; in the early thirteenth century it usually took about three years; by the later years of Henry III's reign it would more likely take four to five years. The intervals between successive visitations of a shire lengthened. When Hubert Walter organized the eyres the intention was to have a visitation every four years; in Henry III's reign it varied between four and 10 years. What had been intended to be swift, regular and frequent had become protracted, burdensome and erratic. In 1261 the Crown bowed to a demand that the minimum interval should be seven years.[101] It is not hard to see why the country opted for infrequency, for an eyre had become a serious financial onslaught. It has been estimated that the proceeds of a visitation of all the shires equalled the annual income of the crown from all regular sources of revenue, and that the later eyres of Henry III's reign were vastly more profitable than the earlier.[102]

In the lengthening intervals between eyres there had to be more frequent judicial visitations on limited commissions – not for 'all pleas' but for 'assizes' (the intentionally swift possessory actions) or for 'gaol delivery' (to adjudge those arrested and awaiting trial for criminal offences). In the thirteenth century the trial of those accused of serious crime took longer than previously because trial by ordeal was replaced by trial by jury.[103] The emergence of a form of jury which

---

100. Clanchy, introduction to *The Berkshire Eyre of 1248*, pp. cviii–cix, Crook, 'The later eyres', p. 243.
101. Cam, 'Studies in the Hundred Rolls', pp. 83–8, Crook, *Records of the General Eyre*.
102. Meekings, introduction to *The Wiltshire Eyre, 1249*, pp. 112–13.
103. On the trial jury see P & M, i. 603ff., T.F.T. Plucknett, *A Concise History of the Common Law* (5th ed., London, 1956), pp. 118–25.

gave a verdict of guilty or not guilty may with hindsight be seen as one of the more notable features of the administration of justice in Henry III's reign; yet it was not the consequence of legislation but evolved under the guidance of the justices as an expedient solution to an awkward problem. The Fourth Lateran Council convened by Pope Innocent III in 1215 prohibited the clergy from taking part in judicial ordeals, and since the purpose of the traditional practice was to invoke a sign from Heaven the prohibition deprived ordeals of effective sanction. When the news reached England the country was in the midst of a civil war and judicial visitations were suspended. When they resumed in 1219 the minority council gave a provisional instruction to the justices 'because it was in doubt and not definitely settled before the beginning of your eyre how those were to be tried who are accused of robbery, murder, arson, and similar crimes.' Notorious male-factors 'of whom suspicion is held that they are guilty' were to be kept in detention; less dangerous suspects who would hitherto have been put to ordeal were to be allowed 'to abjure the realm' (that is to say, to depart into permanent exile); and those accused of minor crimes but who were generally of good character were to be bound over to keep the peace. The instruction concluded: 'We have left to your discretion the observance of this order, so that you, who are conversant with the people concerned, the nature of the offence and the truth of things, may act in accordance with your own discretion and consciences.'[104] There is no record of any further instruction: the discretion of the justices found a solution to the problem. From the one source of information available to us, the eyre rolls, we can see the procedure that emerged: the juries of presentment declared what crimes had been committed and who was suspect; the justices asked the accused, if he were present, what he had to say for himself and then pressed the jurors to say whether they thought him guilty. It might seem to the pre-judice of the accused to ask those who had declared him suspect for a verdict, but juries of presentment were obliged to declare what crimes had been committed and who was suspect even if they felt doubt-ful – they could be amerced if they omitted or concealed anything which had been brought to their notice; but having done this duty they were free at the justices' urging to say what they really thought, and more often than not their verdict was not guilty. There is a case on record of a crafty landlord who tried to get rid of an unwelcome tenant by accusing him of felony, but avoided the hazard of a personal appeal by obliging the local jury of presentment to indict; pressed by the justices 'to speak precisely' (*precise dicere*) the jurors revealed the truth of the matter.[105] The verdict, however, was rarely left to the

[104.] *EHD* iii. 340–1.
[105.] *Select Pleas of the Crown*, ed. F.W. Maitland (Selden Society, 1888), no. 170.

presenting jurors alone: commonly the justices had them confer with the representatives of neighbouring vills who were in attendance at the eyre, and sometimes added in jurors from other districts. On the Berkshire eyre of 1248, for example, verdicts in 35 cases were given by the jury of presentment and the four neighbouring vills, in four cases by the representatives of the four next vills and the presenting jury from a neighbouring hundred, in one case by the presenting jury from the next hundred alone, and in one case by the jury from the next hundred and the representatives from six neighbouring vills.[106] There were no fixed rules: the royal justices acted as they thought best in each case.

It was not so radically new a development as might be supposed. Surviving eyre rolls from previous reigns recording cases brought by private accusations reveal that the justices were frequently suspicious of the motives of accusers and interrogated the local jury of presentment about the case before allowing it, or, more often, quashing it. Moreover, from King John's reign and probably earlier it had been possible for the person privately accused to counter the accusation by alleging that it had been brought 'out of hatred and spite' and to sue a writ from chancery (the writ *de odio et atia*) to have a jury test the allegation.[107] If the jury said the accusation had been brought maliciously it was tantamount to a verdict of not guilty. Trial by jury in criminal cases as it emerged in the thirteenth century was then, we may say, an outgrowth of the custom of the royal courts. In the absence of a formal law on the matter, however, there was some doubt as to whether the accused could be required to submit to trial by jury; it was more satisfactory if he opted, as the phrase was in the eyre rolls, 'to put himself upon the country for good or ill', and he was allowed to object to some of the jurors or to ask for a jury from another district. It was not until after Henry III's reign that there was a ruling on what was to be done with those who declined to 'put themselves upon the country': by the Statute of Westminster of 1275 (clause 12) they were to suffer harsh imprisonment 'as men who refuse to submit to the common law of the land'.[108]

A major contribution to the overloading of the judicial business of the eyres was the readiness of the justices to hear complaints of injuries – civil or criminal – brought orally by individuals. In the later years of Henry III's reign these 'plaints (*querelae*) became as numerous as actions brought by writ. In part the hearing of plaints was an extension of the king's duty of responding to the petitions

106. *The Berkshire Eyre of 1248*, index, p. 601, sub 'Jury (crown pleas): composition of trial jury'.
107. Hurnard, *The King's Pardon for Homicide*, Appendix 1.
108. *EHD* iii. 400.

of his people, but the increasing number was chiefly attributable to the development of the legal concept of 'trespass' (*transgressione* – a wrong doing) which carried royal jurisdiction well beyond the established pleas of the crown.[109] Hitherto personal accusations – 'appeals' – which always began in the shire court, were transferred to the royal court if the appellor alleged that the offence had been committed 'in breach of the king's peace and feloniously'. Felonies were those heinous crimes which were pleas of the crown, and in order to have a judgement before royal justices instead of the shire court appellors were tempted to inflate the seriousness of the offence, presenting a theft as robbery or a beating as a wounding. Appeals of felony were frequently quashed on the ground that no felony had been committed; but when trial by jury replaced ordeal as a means of testing accusations, the justices pressed the jurors who found the accused not guilty as charged to say whether a lesser offence had been committed and punished the perpetrators for a trespass against the king's peace.[110] This opened the door to appeals which were limited to a breach of the king's peace and did not include an accusation of felony. Offences frequently alleged were a wrongful use of force, unwarranted detention of goods and chattels, and wrongful arrest and imprisonment. Complaints of trespass proved to be a useful way of uncovering and punishing abuses by local officials; but the major consequence was to bring many trivial offences before the royal justices which could have been dealt with by lesser courts. The importance for people below the rank of substantial freeholders of the development of actions for trespass has been likened to that for the higher ranks of Henry II's introduction of writ processes for land.[111] There was, however, a danger that the combination of the two would drain the life-blood from other courts.

Henry III's reign was fertile in judicial innovations, particularly in devising procedural actions in civil cases. Glanville's treatise, written about 1178, gives 39 writs for starting actions, Bracton's treatise, written before 1260, gives 121. New forms of action were a consequence of the experience which royal justices gained of cases before them, and sometimes of applications to the king for special remedy. The king was conversant with the law administered in his courts and with the problems and awkward questions which arose from time to time. He had a court which travelled with him – the *curia regis coram*

---

109. For the development of trespass see Harding, introduction to *The Shropshire Eyre of 1256*, pp. xxxii–lviii, S.F.C. Milson, 'Trespass from Henry III to Edward III', *Law Quarterly Review* 74 (1958), 195–224.
110. For examples see *The Berkshire Eyre of 1248*, nos. 787, 818, 896,1031, 1034, all of which include the phrase 'so that the king's peace is to be maintained the truth is to be inquired of the country'.
111. Harding, introduction to *The Shropshire Eyre of 1256*, p. liv.

rege.[112] It was served by four or five senior justices. The king himself, together with members of his Council, sat with them when he chose to or when his presence was needed. It was more professional, more systematic and more constantly in session than the *curia regis* of earlier reigns. It continued to operate even when the king went abroad, though the pleas were then summoned not 'before the king' but before the Council or whoever had been appointed to deputize for him. It heard and determined a wide range of cases which could in some way or other be said to be of concern to the king. It heard cases in which the interests of the king or his tenant-in-chief were involved; it took over pleas which the justices in eyre or on the Bench hesitated for any reason to determine; it heard pleas of miscarriage of justice and corrected errors by other courts. It heard both civil and criminal cases, and sometimes delivered a gaol and tried felonies in districts which the king visited; in the 1250s it interested itself particularly in the new actions for trespass; but the bulk of its business was usually civil.

There was one category of criminal business reserved for the king and that was applications for pardon for homicide.[113] The eyre rolls record many cases of homicide. On the Shropshire eyre of 1256, for example, there were 183 cases of homicide out of a total of 428 crown pleas.[114] Homicides were frequent not only because it was a violent age but also because in the absence of adequate medical attention a minor injury, such as a knife wound which turned septic or even a broken limb, could prove fatal. Contemporary opinion distinguished categories of homicide: the culpable (such as deliberate killing), the justifiable (such as causing the death of a suspect who resisted arrest), and the excusable (such as killing in self-defence or by mischance). The law on homicide, however, made no distinctions, crudely consigning all those responsible for a death to the penalty of hanging if under arrest or to outlawry if they had fled – unless the king granted a pardon. Henry III took his duty seriously and often had inquiries conducted locally into the facts of a case. It was proper to guard against the excessive use of force by, for example, gaolers preventing the escape of prisoners or foresters arresting poachers, and to oblige them to seek a royal pardon and to have their actions scrutinized; but many homicides were so obviously excusable that pardons should not have been necessary. For example the eyre roll for Shropshire in 1256 records: 'Roger son of Alan the miller and Richard son of Wyllot, who were

---

112. On the court *coram rege* see G.O. Sayles, introduction to *Select Cases in the Court of King's Bench*, i (Selden Society, 1936), pp. xxiv–xl, and *The Court of King's Bench in Law and History* (Selden Society Lecture, 1959), C.A.F. Meekings, introduction to *Lists of Various Common Law Records, Lists and Indexes: Supplementary Series*, i (Public Record Office, 1970).
113. On this topic see Hurnard, *The King's Pardon for Homicide*.
114. *The Shropshire Eyre of 1256*, p. xvi.

kinsmen, were playing ball with each other and it happened that Richard got the ball and Roger, trying to take it from him, fell upon Richard's knife accidentally and died eight days later.' Richard fled in panic, as many did who caused a death, and the justices were obliged to outlaw him, though they added a note to the record: 'But speak with the king.'[115] In a particularly chilling case in 1249 Katherine Passeavant pushed open a door and knocked over a child who fell into a vessel of hot water and died soon after. This happened in the liberty of St Albans and Katherine was imprisoned in the abbot's gaol to await trial. She was aged four. Her father appealed to the king who granted a 'total pardon' and ordered the sheriff to have her released.[116] Such problems would not have arisen if there had been clearer rules on the age of criminal liability, or if the justices had been allowed to acquit on the recommendation of a jury, as they were later in the century.

It may be thought surprising that Henry III, who had unrivalled experience of the workings of the law on homicide in the cases which came before him for pardon, did not seek to have the law modified. It may be that he welcomed opportunities to exercise the royal prerogative of mercy. An alternative explanation is that it is symptomatic of a reluctance by Henry III to engage in law reform. This too is surprising for law making was the highest expression of royal authority; but changes in the law of the land required baronial assent and he could be rebuffed. He preferred when he could to exercise royal authority by edict or ordinance instead of legislation. For example the important revision in 1242 of the arrangements for policing took the form of instructions to the sheriffs 'as provided by our Council'.[117] Matthew Paris says that later, in 1253, the king wished to reinforce the hue and cry by introducing a law in use in Savoy which obliged a district which failed to apprehend robbers to compensate the victims, but dropped it when he realized that so large a change in the law required baronial assent.[118] There was an indistinct boundary line between what the king might properly ordain and what required legislation with assent. If Henry III was cautious about it in 1253, he rashly overstepped it in 1255 in a mandate to the sheriffs declaring that he was unwilling to suffer any longer the loss to the crown which resulted from the sale of land by barons, and providing that no one henceforth should purchase land held in chief of the crown 'without our assent and licence' and ordering sheriffs to arrest those who did and to seize the land.[119]

---

115. *Ibid.*, no. 728.
116. *Close Rolls 1247–51*, p. 189, Hurnard, p. viii.
117. *EHD* iii. 85–7; for other ordinances see P & M, i. 180 n. 4.
118. Paris, v. 369, cf. Statute of Winchester, clauses 1 and 2, *EHD* iii. 460.
119. *EHD* iii. 360.

Changes in legal procedure straddled the boundary line: Henry II had put the Assize of Clarendon to his barons but had regarded the devising of procedural writs as a matter for himself and his expert advisers; so too did Henry III, but the barons had come to realize that 'to invent new remedies was to make new laws' and protested against the many unaccustomed writs.[120] A major reason for the demand to have a chancellor accountable to themselves was to stop the issue of new writs without their approval.

The only attempt at major law reform before the barons took control in 1258 came in 1236, and significantly that was when Henry III was trying to placate his barons after the uproar over his assumption of personal rule. The changes then made in the law of the land came to stand in the later Statutes of the Realm between Magna Carta of 1225 and the Statute of Marlborough of 1267. At Merton in 1236 the king in council with his barons discussed and resolved upon problems which experience of the workings of the law had brought to light: the widow who could not get her dower, the man who won a possessory action but was denied possession, minors saddled with debts incurred by their fathers, the hindrance to bringing common pasture into cultivation to meet the needs of an expanding population.[121] This was legislation involving no major legal principles but of considerable practical value. That there was no further attempt at legislation of this kind for 23 years was a serious failure of government and a fundamental reproach to Henry III's kingship.

Crown and Community

The grant by the crown of charters conveying privileges to towns, including powers of self-government, has for long attracted the attention of historians, so much so that government in the boroughs has often been considered in isolation from that of the rest of the realm and made to appear to be of a special character. Two misleading impressions in particular have tended to gain currency: that communal solidarity was peculiar to the boroughs, and that self-government implied autonomy. But no serious exception has to be made for the towns when considering the history of the government of the realm as a whole. Towns did of course have special requirements which were recognized from Anglo-Saxon times in the existence of 'burgage tenure' and 'borough courts'. Burgesses paid rent for their tenures and were freed from labour services. The borough court dealt with the

120. P & M, i. 196–7, Paris, iv. 363–7, vi. 363, Annals of Burton in *Annales Monastici*, i. 448, B. Wilkinson, *Studies in the Constitutional History of the Thirteenth and Fourteenth Centuries* (Manchester, 1937), chapter VIII.
121. *EHD* iii. 351–4, Powicke, *Henry III and the Lord Edward*, pp. 148–51.

relations between dwellers in the town, the regulation of trade and the protection of merchants. Town dwellers were not, however, before the Norman conquest, free from the jurisdiction of lords, nor was the borough court any more detached from the superior jurisdiction of the shire than were the hundred courts. The trend in the twelfth century was for townsfolk to be loosed from manorial jurisdiction (save for those towns which were totally under the control of a lord other than the king), and for boroughs to become separated from the administration of the shire. A grant by the crown of the *firma burgi* gave the burgesses the right to collect the town's share of the rents and dues owed to the king from the shire and to account for it directly to the exchequer instead of through the sheriff. Usually this also meant that they could appoint their own officials to administer the town's affairs. Collective responsibility for financial obligations could be followed by the grant of freedom from other aspects of the sheriff's jurisdiction; but so far from implying autonomy, self-government obliged the town to answer directly to the crown for all those functions which it had taken over from the sheriff. Its officials, even if elected by the burgesses, were treated by the crown as royal officials; and, like the sheriff in respect of the shire community, had the dual function of defending royal interests and acting on behalf of the community. Like the sheriff, borough officials were frequently ordered to requisition supplies for the king's needs and to provide horses and wagons. In respect of the eyres the boroughs were treated like hundreds, appearing before the royal justices and presenting pleas of the crown by a jury of 12 burgesses. Only a few highly favoured boroughs had the privilege of a special session of the eyre within the town. In other respects boroughs were like baronial liberties: they might acquire rights to exclude the sheriffs' subordinates and have 'return of writs', but they had to discharge the king's business by their own officials, and were liable to have their franchises suspended or revoked if they were remiss. In practice boroughs were more likely than baronial liberties to be seized into the king's hand. Even London had its liberties frequently suspended and its administration taken over by officials appointed by the crown, though usually only for short periods.[122] The boroughs, indeed, so far from being a distinctive element in the government of England up to the thirteenth century, may be said to encapsulate in concentrated form many of its characteristic features. In particular they illustrate the pervasiveness of royal authority.

It was no mark of distinction that townsfolk could act collectively through chosen representatives in pursuing their interests; villagers could too. Vills could bring complaints before the king's justices

---

[122.] G.A. Williams, *Medieval London: From Commune to Capital* (London, 1963), pp. 204–9.

against neighbouring communities, and sue writs from chancery. A royal writ of 1255 to the steward of the archbishop of Canterbury reminded him that 'by the law and custom of the realm' vills and village communities could pursue pleas and complaints 'by three or four of their men' in both royal and other courts, and ordered him not to deny that right to representatives of the vill of Sibton acting 'on behalf of the community' in the court of the archbishop's liberty.[123]

Shires too, though they might be supposed to be more amorphous than boroughs and vills, could canalize their aspirations into collective action. From the later years of the twelfth century many shires sought charters granting concessions, which, since they had to be paid for, could only have been achieved by a high degree of solidarity among the leading men of the shire both in negotiating a mutually acceptable bargain and in raising the money. In 1190 the government of Richard I accepted a proffer of 200 marks from the men of Surrey to have forest law lifted from much of the county; they were followed in John's reign by the men of Devon, Cornwall, Essex, Shrophire and Staffordshire, and in the early years of Henry III's reign by the men of Huntingdon, Somerset, Dorset and Berkshire.[124] Several shires paid to have local men appointed as sheriffs, or to retain an acceptable sheriff. The men of Devon paid additionally to have their sheriff limited to one annual tourn. Eight shires are known to have negotiated arrangements which gave a measure of local control over local government; but the charters they purchased were usually for a particular appointment or for a fixed term and had to be renewed at further expense.[125]

Collective action on behalf of the shire community came naturally to men who met regularly at sessions of the shire court, who shouldered the tasks thrust on local men by Angevin government, and who had constant business with the sheriff and his bailiffs. They were drawn for the most part from the middling ranks of society, from the knights and other substantial freeholders who had a reputation to uphold and much to lose from falling foul of the king's officers. The development of royal government enhanced the rôle of such men in the business of the shire, both directly in the duties it required of them and indirectly in the changes it wrought in the functioning of local communities. The dominance of the shire by great magnates, which would have seemed normal under the Norman kings and had come near to being institutionalized under King Stephen, came to an end in Henry II's time. As shire courts became busier and meetings more frequent magnates had withdrawn from regular attendance leaving their

123. *Close Rolls 1254–56*, p. 173, Cam, *Law-Finders*, pp. 79–80.
124. J.C. Holt, *Magna Carta* (Cambridge, 1965), pp. 52–3, Maddicott, 'Magna Carta and the local community', pp. 37–9.
125. Holt, pp. 53–60, Maddicott, pp. 27–9.

interests to be safeguarded by stewards, who were usually óf the same social rank as knights and substantial freeholders. One consequence was to give greater cohesion to shire government as its business was left to those resident in the shire and whose interests were for the most part confined to it – unlike the magnates whose interests were far-flung. The collective experience of such men penetrated into every corner of the shire. Juries of presentment for every hundred were empanelled from knights resident in the hundred, augmented, if there were not enough knights, by freeholders 'of the better sort'.[126] They received and sifted information from the representatives of every vill in the hundred, and testified about it to every article of inquiry of the eyre before the king's justices. The emergence of the trial jury enhanced the responsibility of such men for the well-being of local communities. Thirteenth-century trial juries were typically composed of the relevant presenting jurors together with the representatives from neighbouring vills – a combination of gentry and villagers. There was as yet no process of trial by the examination of witnesses and the arguments of attorneys: trial juries reached verdicts in the light of local knowledge both of the crimes committed and of the persons held suspect. That they often acquitted suggests that they were inclined to proceed to extreme measures only against the most trouble-some or vicious of their neighbours.[127] Their verdicts were more social judgements than findings upon the facts. They were deciding who was to be disciplined by punishment, who ejected from the community by outlawry, and who allowed to be reconciled to the community by acquittal after a serious warning had been administered by public denunciation in the indictments.

The aspirations of such men to gain a measure of control over local government ran counter to Henry III's aspiration to centralize control and to superintend the welfare of all his subjects through sheriffs and justices of his choosing. From the time he assumed personal rule, Henry III stopped the sale of concessions to shires, and abrogated those previously made whenever he could.[128] The sharper atti-tude to powers of local government in liberties was a parallel process. The ancient custom of shires with non-standard systems of policing and pledging was brusquely overridden.[129] Exceptions and privileges hindered the deployment of a royal authority, which, so Henry III claimed, was the best guarantee of the welfare of his people. He exhorted his sheriffs to care for widows and orphans; he instructed

[126] *EHD* iii. 303, cf. *Fleta*, ed. H.G. Richardson and G.O. Sayles, ii (Selden Society, 1955), p. 45.
[127] For discrimination in cases of homicide see J.B. Given, *Society and Homicide in Thirteenth Century England* (Stanford, California, 1977), especially chapter 5.
[128] Maddicott, 'Magna Carta and the local community', pp. 40–1.
[129] *Ibid.*, p. 42.

them not to distrain peasants (*rustici*) for the debts of their landlords
while their lords had the wherewithal to discharge their obligations; he
ordered them to inquire 'diligently and righteously' into how the
magnates treated their men, to correct their transgressions when they
could, and when they could not to report them to the king; he bade his
sheriffs choose as bailiffs only those who would deal justly with the
people.[130] At the same time he sought to monitor the behaviour of
sheriffs and their subordinates by including inquiries into administrative abuses in the articles of the eyre.

There were two serious flaws in Henry III's conception of an all-
embracing, benevolent, centralized government under the direction of
a considerate, paternalistic monarch. The first was that the king was
requiring more than the established methods of government could be
expected to deliver: it is significant, for example, that the eyres slowed
down as the king pressed for more central control. The second major
flaw was that Henry III himself betrayed the ideals he professed. After
1237 the barons would not agree to taxes for what they regarded as the
king's spendthrift habits and pretentious foreign policy; Magna Carta
had closed off opportunities for exploiting the feudal lordship of the
crown; so Henry III's government resorted to exploiting the profitability of administering the shires. The popular reform of 1236 which
had made the sheriffs 'custodians' instead of 'farmers' of the shires,
accounting for revenues due to the crown and receiving allowances for
their expenses, was abandoned: sheriffs were again required to proffer
lump sum farms with escalating amounts of 'increment'.[131] Responding to the exchequer's demands by an oppressive exercise of shrieval
powers was unpalatable to the men of standing in the shire community
who had taken up office after the reform of 1236. They withdrew,
leaving the field to those who did not scruple to increase the farms
charged to bailiffs of the hundreds, to treat the tourn as a money-
making operation, and to resort to chicanery and exploitation. A
particular source of grievance was the breach of long-standing local
agreements about suit of court: sheriffs were demanding unaccustomed suits, unreasonably requiring attendance when it was not necessary, expecting the attendance of all those who had divided up an
inheritance owing suit instead of allowing them to take turns or to
nominate one to serve for all, and for no other reason than to levy
fines for non-attendance. As financial pressures bore down on local
officials the invisible but critical borderline between accustomed petty

---

130. Speech of Henry III in the exchequer, 7 October 1250, text printed in M.T. Clanchy, 'Did
Henry III have a policy?', *History* 53 (1968), 215–16, paraphrased in T. Madox, *The History and
Antiquities of the Exchequer* (London, 1711), p. 612.
131. D.A. Carpenter, 'The decline of the curial sheriff in England, 1194–1258', *EHR* 91 (1976),
16ff., Maddicott, 'Magna Carta and the local community', pp. 43–6.

corruption and unacceptable oppression was more often crossed, and administrative powers more frequently abused. The infrequent eyres were an inadequate safeguard against administrative abuses. A special eyre to inquire into the operations of government in the localities was commissioned in 1255, but it seemed more directed to levying fines for malpractice than to remedying the situation. It was not followed by the dismissal of sheriffs as Henry II's 'Inquest' of 1170 had been. The eyres themselves were not free of the charge of abuse of authority in support of the exchequer's quest for money. The profits of eyres increased markedly. The visitations of 1246-9 raised £22,000 at a time when the crown's ordinary annual revenue was about £24,000.[132] It had long been the custom that after the discovery of a dead body the neighbouring vills were represented at the coroner's inquest by the reeve and four men from each; but from 1246 the justices amerced all the villagers who were in tithing if they did not attend. They amerced the pledges of accused persons who pleaded benefit of clergy when they appeared before the eyre. They imposed *murdrum* fines in cases which were obviously of accidental death.[133] Among the objections raised to the king's request in 1256 for financial assistance for his intervention in Sicily was 'the impoverishment of the kingdom by eyres'.[134] A Lincolnshire chronicler believed the purpose of the Provisions of Oxford to be 'for the relief of the condition of England wretchedly depressed by justices, sheriffs and other bailiffs.'[135]

Respect for Henry III's government was further undermined by his inconsistency and partiality: his friends were seemingly exempt from the rules applied to everyone else. His foreign kinsmen, well endowed with estates in many parts of England, repudiated the sheriffs' authority with impunity, setting up private enclaves for themselves at the very time that the king was ordering his sheriffs to make no concessions to magnates in the execution of the king's business, and was pressing *quo warranto* inquiries into unlicensed franchises. In Gloucestershire, for example, William de Valence refused to allow the sheriff's officials to execute summonses or to pursue the king's business in his lands; he withdrew the suits which were owed from his manors to the courts of hundred and shire; he denied the sheriff customary hospitality and refused to allow him to hear the pleas which belonged to his office.[136] The steward of William de Valence is reported to have boasted to a victim, 'If I do you wrong, who is there

[132.] *Crown Pleas of the Wiltshire Eyre, 1249*, ed. C.A.F. Meekings (Devizes, 1961), pp. 112–13.
[133.] Maddicott, p. 47, *The Roll and Writ File of the Berkshire Eyre of 1248*, ed. M.T. Clanchy (Selden Society, 1973), no. 746.
[134.] Annals of Burton in *Annales Monastici*, i. 387.
[135.] *Chronicles of the Reigns of Edward I and Edward II*, ed. W. Stubbs (Rolls Series, 1882–3), i. cxiv.
[136.] *Calendar of Inquisitions Miscellaneous 1219–1307*, nos. 143, 164.

to do you right?'[137] Matthew Paris alleges that in 1256 the king instructed the chancery not to issue writs which could cause loss or damage to named friends of his.[138] Evidence which came to light after the expulsion of the 'aliens' lends support to the charge. A Kentishman claimed that he was owed money by Roger Leyburn but had not been able to have him distrained or to have a hearing in the king's court 'because of the favour in which Roger stood at the time with William de Valence.'[139] Fulk Payforer complained that he had been opposed by a man who 'had so many favourers and maintainers, namely William de Valence and others of the king's Council, that he had completely despaired of suing out any writ against him.'[140] The chronicler of St Benet of Hume writing of the hatred felt for the 'aliens' says that 'native-born men were as it were disinherited and the magnates of England grieved that no Englishman could get his right or obtain a writ against them.'[141] The king's half-brothers were among the most oppressive of landlords. In the inquiries of 1259 William de Colevill of Hampshire testified that he held from Aymer de Valence, bishop-elect of Winchester, 60 librates of land in the manor of Itchel for which he owed suit to the bishop's fortnightly court at Winchester. Aymer, however, had compelled him to do suit to his hundred court at Farnham in Surrey, distraining him to attend, amercing him heavily for his absence, and disregarding a royal writ which allowed William to appoint an attorney to attend for him. The courts at Winchester and Farnham had been set to meet on the same day and William had been relentlessly harried for his unavoidable defaults. Amercements of 45 marks a year had been imposed on him, his plough-beasts had been driven off, and money had been exorted from his tenants. He estimated his total losses at some £300 in six years. As J.R. Maddicott writes in commenting on this case, 'It was the grievances of the William de Colevills of county society which the barons both deferred to and exploited in 1258–9.'[142]

The conjunction in 1258 of the crisis over 'the Sicilian business' with widespread disaffection in the realm over the operations of government and resentment over the influence exercised by the 'aliens', left the king with no option but to beseech the assistance of his barons. He was politically as well as financially bankrupt. He agreed 'to reform the state of our realm by the counsel of our loyal subjects' in return for a promise that the barons 'would loyally use their influence with the

137. Paris, v. 738.
138. *Ibid.*, v. 594.
139. Maddicott, 'Magna Carta and the local community', p. 57.
140. *Ibid.*
141. *Chronica John de Oxenedes*, ed. H. Ellis (Rolls Series, 1859). pp. 224–5.
142. Maddicott, p. 58.

community of the realm so that a common aid should be granted us.'[143] The proviso ensured that responding to the grievances of the shires would have to be in the forefront of the reform of the state of the realm. Hence three immediate measures: the commissioning of a special eyre to investigate complaints, the nomination of four knights in each shire to report directly to the Council of Fifteen on complaints of 'excesses, trespasses, and acts of injustice' as a preliminary to the visitations of the commissioners, and the Ordinance of Sheriffs which put local officials on their best behaviour pending the inquiries, and prescribed rules for the conduct of their administration.[144]

When it came, however, to taking more positive action difficulties began, for the barons' Achilles heel was the administration of their own estates, courts and liberties. The greater barons had developed bureaucratic administrative structures akin to the king's and often with even less effective restraints on misconduct by their stewards and bailiffs. Similar stories came from hundreds administered by baro- nial bailiffs as from those in the king's hand of suits unreasonably demanded, of undue amercements, of punitive distraints and endemic corruption.[145] Richard de Clare, earl of Gloucester, a long-time king's friend but allied with the reformers in 1258, was a rackrenting, arbi- trary, oppressive landlord whose malpractices equalled those of any of the 'aliens'; but there were lords who might have been expected to set better standards who were also culpable. The highly privileged abbey of Bury St Edmunds had its own coroner who was notorious for taking bribes to let people off serving on inquests, who had men falsely accused and arrested, and then took money from them to be released, and exacted fees for performing what should have been his duties.[146]

A critical question in 1258–9 was the extent to which, if at all, baronial liberties were to be opened to scrutiny and laws made which would rein in their officials as much as the king's. That the out- come was searching scrutiny and reforms of general application has commonly been attributed to a powerful group of disinterested refor- mers among the barons; but although this was a remarkable factor, it should not be overlooked that the momentum for reform in local administration was sustained by competition between king and barons for support in the shires. The barons did not gain total control of the king's government in 1258 to rule England in their own interest: the Council of Fifteen in which, by the Provisions of Oxford, was vested

143. *Documents 1258–67*, no. 1.
144. *Ibid.*, nos. 6 and 8.
145. H.M. Cam, *The Hundred and the Hundred Rolls* (London, 1930), e.g., pp. 174, 207.
146. H.M. Cam, *Liberties and Communities* (London, 1963), pp. 194–5. For Richard de Clare see Maddicott, pp. 56–7, 58, 61.

executive authority, was constituted by an elaborate procedure and reflected a broad cross-section of baronial and royalist standpoints. The Council did not have unfettered authority: in important matters it had to seek the approval of the wider body of barons represented by a Committee of Twelve who were to meet with the Council three times a year. The barons were thus accepting responsibility for what was done, but it was done by the Council in the king's name, and what was done was the outcome of bargaining between competing and conflicting interests. Although the king's authority had, as it were, been put into commission, he was not without influence. When the barons had previously complained about the conduct of royal administration he had demanded to know why they did not apply the principles they required of him to their own officials; when required to confirm Magna Carta he had always emphasized that it was to be as firmly observed by prelates and magnates.[147] It was his principal line of counterattack to sustain royal authority after 1258. In March 1259 he addressed letters 'to all his faithful subjects' to be read out in every shire announcing that 'for the betterment and relief of the state of our realm' he had secured from the Council and from the Committee of Twelve a sealed document stating that:

> Since our lord the king wishes and desires that swift justice be observed and done to all in common throughout his realm, and also wishes that whatever wrongs have been committed by his officers and by others in former time should be redressed, we will, grant, and offer on our part, that all wrongs which we and our bailiffs have done to our subjects or to our neighbours shall be corrected by the king and by his justiciar, or by those whom he shall appoint for this purpose, without hindrance or opposition from us and ours. . . . And we will hinder no one by threats, nor by power, nor in any other manner from freely making complaint of us and of our men, and from prosecuting his complaint, nor will we remember it against him, nor attempt any reprisal against him by reason of his complaints and prosecutions. . . . Moreover that same oath which the king caused his sheriffs and his other officers to take, we will make our officers swear, both those of our demesnes and those of our liberties, in our full courts before the four knights elected in each county . . . on condition that our franchises and free customs shall in no wise be infringed, and that this cannot disinherit us and ours. And we will do this at every change of officials; that is to say, they shall swear that they will loyally serve the king in what pertains to him and to his liberties, and us in what pertains to our franchises and demesnes; and that they will do right in common to all people. . . .[148]

This is a very significant document. At the moment which could be

147. E.g., Maddicott, pp. 52–4.
148. *Documents 1258–67*, no. 10.

regarded as the nadir of the fortunes of Angevin monarchy it represents the triumph of Angevin royal policy. It would have been unthinkable in King Stephen's day. It acknowledged that the realm was a unity within which common standards had to be observed under the crown, and that baronial liberties were integral parts of it, not immunities which stood apart from the king's government.

Although the principle was not disputed the implications of applying a common standard to all were not readily accepted by all the barons. Their hesitations provoked a concerted demonstration by members of the knightly class who came to the king's court at Westminster in the retinues of the barons but who spoke for the interests of the men of the shires. According to the chronicler of Burton abbey they protested to Edward, the king's eldest son and heir, to the earl of Gloucester and others of the Council 'that the lord king had completely performed and fulfilled all and singular that the barons had ordained and constrained him to do; and that the barons themselves had done nothing of what they had promised for the good of the realm, but only for their own good and to the harm of the king everywhere, and that unless a remedy was found the agreement [at Oxford] would have to be revised.'[149] The barons could not let the initiative pass to the king, nor lose the support of those whose influence was decisive in the shires. In October 1259 they agreed to a schedule of reforms, described in the document as 'provisions made by the king and his Council' and usually entitled by historians the Provisions of Westminster. They dealt comprehensively with current grievances concerning the procedures of all courts, but significantly the first three clauses dealt with abuses of suit of court 'at the courts of magnates and of other lords of such courts'. The fourth clause dealt with attendance at the sheriff's tourn, requiring attendance from those with land in several hundreds only in the hundred where they had a residence. The few clauses which did not deal with court procedure were principally concerned to improve upon the protection which the Angevin common law had extended to heirs against malicious lords. Strikingly the Provisions upheld an overriding royal authority: lords who unreasonably distrained their tenants for suit of court were to be swiftly brought to answer before the king's court, 'and if they fail to appear the sheriff shall be ordered to distrain them by all that they hold in his bailiwick.' And clause 16 required that 'No one in future save the king shall hold in his court any plea of false judgement made in a court of one of his tenants, since such pleas specially belong to the royal crown and dignity.'[150] There was indeed in the legislative aspects of the

---

149. *Annales Monastici*, i. 471, *Select Charters*, p. 331, translated in B.Wilkinson, *The Constitutional History of Medieval England*, i (London, 1948), pp. 171-2.
150. *Documents 1258–67*, no. 11, *EHD* iii. 370-3.

Provisions of Westminster nothing that the king could find objection-
able; when the barons' wars were over and he was fully in control they
were re-enacted in the Statute of Marlborough of 1267.[151]

The attempt to deal with the relations between magnates and those
subject to their jurisdiction exacerbated differences of opinion among
the barons about what their involvement in the king's government was
intended to achieve. Opinion polarized between those who thought
the purpose was to ensure that an untrustworthy king had sound
counsel and should be restrained from foolish acts, and those who
thought that the realm would be better governed through a baronial
politburo. The differences about intentions were heightened by
clashes of personality, and by the serious difficulties of resolving the
Sicilian business, achieving peace with France, and coping with a
perilous situation in Wales. The Council of Fifteen had ceased to
function by the end of 1260 in the way envisaged by the Provisions of
Oxford, and its failure discredited the idea of government by committee. A breakdown of law and order in the country seemed to
confirm the view of conservatives that it was rash to tamper with the
traditional structure of authority. The power struggle that ensued
resolved itself eventually into the simple but bitterly contested question of who should rule, the king or Simon de Montfort, the leader of
the diehards. If Simon could have consolidated his rule after his
triumph in battle over the king at Lewes in May 1264 England might
have become like contemporary Japan with a figurehead sovereign
and the totality of power in the hands of a feudal shogun. But Simon
de Montfort was a foreigner and the tradition of Angevin government
ran against him. He was defeated and killed in August 1265 in a battle
at Evesham in which many of his former confederates fought with the
royalist forces.

In retrospect it may be seen that the barons' claim in 1258 to
speak for 'the community of the realm' was as hollow as the king's
claim, as father of his people, to know where their best interests lay.
Yet if Henry III, in his peculiar way, represented the line of descent
of Angevin autocratic monarchy, the notion of a 'community of the
realm', as it was conceived at the time, was the outcome of a century of
Angevin government. Superficially autocratic monarchy seemed to
have triumphed in the closing years of Henry III's reign. The Dictum
of Kenilworth of October 1266, which concluded the period of rebellion, declared that Henry 'shall have, fully receive, and freely exercise
his dominion, authority, and royal power without impediment or
contradiction of anyone, whereby the royal dignity may be offended
contrary to approved rights, laws and long established customs, and

151. *EHD* iii. 384–92

that full obedience and humble attention be given to the same lord king, to his lawful mandates and precepts by one and all.'[152] Yet Magna Carta echoed in those phrases, 'contrary to the *approved* rights, laws, and long-established customs' and 'to his *lawful* mandates'. Moreover it could not be forgotten that when obliged to make a choice local communities had sided with the opposition to the king. When in 1261 the king had bid for a resumption of power and replaced with his own nominees the sheriffs who had been appointed by the Council from the knightly class in each shire, at least 16 shires defied him and kept out his appointees for several months.[153] When in January 1265 Simon de Montfort sought to establish his rule two knights from each of the shire communities and two burgesses from several of the borough communities had answered his summons to a parliament at Westminster.[154]

Crown and community had yet to be harmonized. Henry III's reign had done more to highlight the problems than find solutions. The eyre had been the key instrument in extending royal government and enforcing royal authority, but it was breaking down under the burdens thrust upon it. The practical solution for its administrative functions was to separate and reformulate its parts into specialized commissions which combined king's justices and local men. But the eyre had another function: it carried the king's court to the country and heard the petitions of local communities; the effective alternative was to reverse the procedure and summon representatives of local communities to the king's court when he met with his barons in parliament. The characteristic feature of the English parliament as it took shape at the end of the thirteenth century and developed in the fourteenth century was that those who constituted the Commons represented not estates of the realm but communities of the realm.

[152.] *Documents 1258–67*, no. 44, clause 1, *EHD* iii. 381.
[153.] Treharne, *The Baronial Plan of Reform*, pp. 267–8.
[154.] Powicke, *Henry III and the Lord Edward*, pp. 487–8; for illuminating comments on consultation with representatives of the shires see *ibid.*, p. 427, and J.C. Holt, 'The prehistory of parliament' in *The English Parliament in the Middle Ages*, ed. R.G. Davies and J.H. Denton (Manchester, 1981), pp. 1–28.

Index

Index

Proper names occurring only once in the text are not indexed unless particularly important.